ARCHITECTURE'S ODD COUPLE

ARCHITECTURE'S ODD COUPLE

Frank Lloyd Wright and Philip Johnson

—

HUGH HOWARD

BLOOMSBURY PRESS

NEW YORK · LONDON · OXFORD · NEW DELHI · SYDNEY

Bloomsbury Press
An imprint of Bloomsbury Publishing Plc

1385 Broadway	50 Bedford Square
New York	London
NY 10018	WC1B 3DP
US	AUK

www.bloomsbury.com

BLOOMSBURY and the Diana logo are trademarks of Bloomsbury Publishing Plc

First published 2016

ISBN: HB: 978-1-62040-375-4
ePub: 978-1-62040-376-1

LIBRARY OF CONGRESS CATALOGING-IN-PUBLICATION DATA HAS BEEN APPLIED FOR.

2 4 6 8 10 9 7 5 3 1

Typeset by RefineCatch Limited, Bungay, Suffolk
Printed and bound in the U.S.A. by Berryville Graphics Inc., Berryville, Virginia

To find out more about our authors and books visit www.bloomsbury.com. Here you will find extracts, author interviews, details of forthcoming events and the option to sign up for our newsletters.

Bloomsbury books may be purchased for business or promotional use. For information on bulk purchases please contact Macmillan Corporate and Premium Sales Department at specialmarkets@macmillan.com.

For E. L. H.

Each knew that he was in major respects a mirror image of the other, a realization that made it only easier to like, and to distrust, each other.

—Franz Schulze,
Philip Johnson: Life and Work (1994)

CONTENTS

PROLOGUE
THE MASTER AND THE MAESTRO   *1*

PART I
A MEETING OF MINDS

CHAPTER 1
TWO CONVERSATIONS   *15*

CHAPTER 2
PLOTTING A COMEBACK   *29*

CHAPTER 3
EUROPEAN TRAVELS   *41*

PART II
THE MOMA MOMENT

CHAPTER 4
THE NEW MUSEUM   *55*

CHAPTER 5
AN INVITATION ISSUED   *69*

CHAPTER 6

WRIGHT VS. JOHNSON *81*

CHAPTER 7

THE SHOW MUST GO ON *87*

PART III

ACTING OUT THEIR ANTAGONISM

CHAPTER 8

THE BANKS OF BEAR RUN *105*

CHAPTER 9

POLITICS AND ART *141*

CHAPTER 10

WRIGHT'S MANHATTAN PROJECT *167*

CHAPTER 11

PHILIP COMES OUT CLASSICAL *193*

CHAPTER 12

THE WHISKEY BOTTLE AND THE TEAPOT *225*

EPILOGUE

A FRIENDLY WRANGLE *261*

Acknowledgments 281
Notes 285
Sources 309
Index 321

ARCHITECTURE'S ODD COUPLE

The Master and the Maestro

You can't have a culture without architecture.
—*Frank Lloyd Wright*

September 20, 1955 . . . New Haven, Connecticut . . . Union Station

A MAN WEARING a cape and porkpie hat stepped off the train. Scanning the platform, he saw not so much as a raised hand to acknowledge his arrival. No one approached to offer respectful words of greeting.

This was unexpected.

Frank Lloyd Wright's face had graced the cover of *Time* magazine. Cabdrivers in Manhattan knew him on sight and hung on his every word. It was generally accepted that Ayn Rand had based the central character of her bestselling novel *The Fountainhead* on Mr. Wright. NBC had recently broadcast his black-and-white visage into America's living rooms on the popular television show *Conversations with Elder Wise Men*. In an era when fame was meted out in small doses, his outspoken opinions and an innate gift for attracting the public eye made Wright the only architect with a name widely recognized at the American supper table.

Yet on this day in New Haven, despite having been booked as the headliner for the inaugural event in Yale's "Perspectives" series, the eighty-eight-year-old Wright made his way from trackside by himself.

No apprentice waited on him, as one would have done at Taliesin, his home in Spring Green, Wisconsin (constructed in 1911), or at Taliesin West (constructed in 1937), the winter quarters of his school-cum-architecture practice in Scottsdale, Arizona. At his latest place of residence, his second-floor suite at the Plaza Hotel (dubbed, inevitably, Taliesin East), his arrival would have caused one or two or five acolytes to rise, to lift his bag, to seek the Master's approval.

Just last year the great university a few blocks away had bestowed upon him the honorary degree of doctor of fine arts. But Wright seemed to be the forgotten man as he emerged from the bowels of the New Haven rail station. All 609 seats in Room 114 were booked for the nine P.M. event at Strathcona Hall, and the event's organizers, the *Yale Daily News* and Yale Broadcasting Company, expected a great clamor. They were delighted at what seemed likely to be a standing-room-only crowd.

Still, Wright remained alone as he entered the great waiting room. On another day, he would have paused to critique Union Station, a Beaux Arts exercise of the late Cass Gilbert. Called by some the "vestibule of the city," the space was brightly lit by the midday sunlight pouring in from the ten towering, semicircular windows that lined the thirty-five-foot-tall walls of polished white limestone. Wright could not approve, of course; he had spent decades decrying the application of Roman and Greek details to contemporary buildings. In the presence of a suitable audience, he might have waved his rubber-tipped cane, pointing out the dishonesty of using fenestration from the age of Diocletian two millennia too late. But it seemed that no one knew or cared what he had to say.

Seething with anger, Wright settled on a solution.

He moved deliberately toward the ticket windows. If no one could be bothered to greet him, he saw no need to stay. He would simply climb aboard the next southbound train and return to Manhattan.

In that moment of resolution, Mr. Wright also knew whom to blame. That would be Philip Johnson, the man he knew best here in New Haven. After all, a few months ago, at another of the Ivies—at Harvard, no less—the younger man had cruelly and publicly dismissed him "as the greatest architect of the nineteenth century."[1]

———

ON THIS PARTICULAR September day, the forty-nine-year-old Philip Cortelyou Johnson drove himself to New Haven, as he ordinarily did twice a week during term time.

A few years before, he had established his base of operations in nearby New Canaan, Connecticut, setting up shop on the second floor at 89 Main Street. He shared architectural offices with a small and varying staff that consisted of a draftsman or two and a part-time secretary. Though it overlooked the village's busy main intersection, Johnson's place of business was austere, characterized by its "absolute order." All clutter, from drawings to drafting pencils, was banished to the many cupboards and drawers.[2]

Johnson liked New Canaan, which *Holiday* magazine termed a "conservative, pretty, station-wagon town."[3] Its convenience to Manhattan, an hour's drive southwest, enabled him to continue his on-again, off-again curatorial labors under the aegis of his closest friend, Alfred Barr, at the Museum of Modern Art (MoMA). There, in 1932, Johnson's first curatorial effort, *Modern Architecture: International Exhibition*, had established his reputation. That show also led to his first—and rather problematic—exchange with Frank Lloyd Wright.

While his architectural practice now showed genuine signs of keeping the hyperactive Johnson fully occupied, for the preceding half decade New Canaan had offered him both a respite from Manhattan and access to yet another career, since New Haven and its famed university were an easy, easterly meander along the coastal road overlooking Long Island Sound.

At Yale, Johnson's work as a New York curator and New Canaan architect took a backseat to his role as pedagogue. He had found a not-quite-professorial place within the university structure, functioning as a critic-in-residence at the School of Architecture. As at MoMA, he took no pay from Yale. Independently wealthy, Johnson could afford a need-blind approach to such jobs, and he reveled in the accompanying sense of independence.

He delighted in talking about design and buildings; his joy in architecture was infectious. Johnson possessed a fast-firing critical mind, and though he respected the disciplines of the lecture hall and design studios in New Haven, his candor and humor also meant his aphoristic tongue could shock and even offend people. For the students, his sometimes impolitic remarks and sharp critical assessments only enhanced his standing. He could and did say what he liked, and as one of his brightest Yale pupils, Robert A. M. Stern, put it, "He talked circles around the other critics."[4]

Johnson liked nothing better than to schmooze and amuse, and the neutral territory of the Yale School of Architecture suited him. He had earned his architecture degree at Harvard, but he could hardly have allied himself with its Graduate School of Design. Johnson had conspicuously avoided architecture department chairman Walter Gropius as he earned his architecture degree during the war years. (Their disconnect was personal and professional; Johnson admitted to liking neither the man nor his work.) Johnson cultivated mentors and friends in Cambridge, but many of them, including Gropius's old Bauhaus colleague Marcel Breuer, had since established peacetime practices in New York. Several of those, including both Breuer and John M. Johansen, had built homes in New Canaan. Together with Johnson, their cohort had established a Modernist bastion in what had been a predominantly clapboard New England town. They built houses of steel and glass, unadorned and geometric.

Although Yale's program still remained in the shadow of Harvard's (thus far, it granted only baccalaureate degrees), Johnson recognized the emerging talent there would soon bring it to the forefront. The regular faculty included architect Louis Kahn and a young architectural historian named Vincent Scully. R. Buckminster Fuller was among the many significant architectural thinkers who arrived periodically to offer commentary. ("No one had the kids eating out of his hand like he did," Johnson observed.)⁵ But landing Wright to lead an evening forum was something of a coup.

Yale had treated Johnson well. Just the preceding January, an exhibition of his works had been installed at the Yale Art Gallery, featuring models, mural-size photographs, and stereopticon slides of his work. Mounted by a recent graduate from the Yale School of Architecture who worked as an associate in Johnson's office, the little show had been a happy inversion for Johnson, usually the curator rather than the curated. Central to the show had been his most notable and, to some, his most notorious design.

That nearby domicile, which he had built for himself back in New Canaan, had become the most talked-about home of the postwar era. The very idea of the Glass House, completed in 1949, shocked people, with its walls of quarter-inch-thick plate glass. The house consisted of a single room, its open plan punctuated only by the bathroom, enclosed by a brick cylinder that rose through the roof. The place attracted the curious, invited and not. Johnson relished the attention, even when the house, as it often did, became the object of jokes. The *New Yorker* made light of it in a cartoon, and a column in the *New York Sun* observed that to live there "would be like living in Macy's window."⁶ Johnson merely smiled his Cheshire-cat grin.

He welcomed New York friends to New Canaan for weekends, but also made the Glass House an informal part of the Yale architectural curriculum. On Sundays, he conducted an ongoing charrette about the future of architecture. Attendees included Yale faculty, such as Paul Rudolph, Louis Kahn, and George Howe; neighbors, such as Breuer and Johansen; and other prominent architectural friends, including Eero Saarinen, I. M. Pei, and Edward Larrabee Barnes. The eminent English architectural historian Nikolaus Pevsner came to visit and stayed to watch the sun set through the full frame of the Glass House's I-beam structure.

These men argued and critiqued one another's works. For the students, a visit to Johnson's New Canaan home was a field trip of a unique sort, one that exposed them to both the controversial Glass House and Johnson's impressive circle of architects, journalists and critics, and museum professionals.

Frank Lloyd Wright had visited the Glass House. Two Connecticut commissions, including one in New Canaan, had brought the Master of Taliesin to the neighborhood in the early 1950s. He could hardly permit himself to like Johnson's unusual domicile. Just as he dismissed Beaux Arts buildings such as Gilbert's New Haven train station, Wright offered harsh criticism of the steel-and-glass structures of the International Style. He had for years dismissed them as "flat-chested," but he never tired of finding new ways to express his disapproval.

On a recent visit, Wright arrived unannounced at the Glass House. Primed for a resumption of the conversational combat that tended to characterize his interactions with Johnson, he found the owner was not at home. But Wright wasn't going to let Johnson's absence prevent him from delivering his opening gambit. The maid would do.

On entering the Glass House, he took in the large, sparsely decorated interior and the unobstructed view of the lush landscape outside. He assumed the look of a man surprised by what he saw, as if he'd never come through the floor-to-ceiling glass door before.

The well-trained maid—even in graduate school, Johnson had employed household staff—waited for the gentleman's reaction. Wright obliged:

"I don't know whether I'm supposed to take off my hat or leave it on."

His words left the woman wondering what to say—without knowing the rules of engagement, she had suddenly found herself in a conversational cross fire. But Wright wasn't done.

"Am I indoors," he asked with an air of faux innocence, "or outdoors?"

After a moment, the bewildered maid recovered herself—she was, after all, charged with tending to New Canaan's most famous curiosity and had encountered bemused callers before. She asked her elderly guest who he was and what she could do for him.

"Oh," he said airily, "just another foolish client. I want Mr. Johnson to build me a house—a glass house."[7]

She duly reported the encounter to Johnson. And he was left to ruminate over the peculiar calculus of his friendship with Wright. When he recounted the story a few months later, he did so with delight, calling Wright's wit "wonderful." Little did Johnson know the hat-on, hat-off anecdote would become an indelible episode in the public history of his house.

He did know, however, that when it came to Mr. Wright, one could only wait and wonder what he would say next.

———

THE BELATED ARRIVAL of a greeting party of undergraduates prevented Wright from boarding a southbound train. Offering a flurry of apologies, they cajoled the evening's lead attraction. Though he remained dubious, Wright was, as usual, available to young people. He agreed to remain in New Haven.

The architects-to-be escorted their guest to the Hotel Taft. This was perhaps New Haven's most prestigious accommodation, but Wright complained of the hotel's poor design. Surprisingly spry for his years, he booted ottomans out of his path as he strode across the lobby. Finally, his hosts managed to settle him into a room on the hotel's sixth floor.

A short while later, when the appointed time came to depart for the evening's events, a young man called from the house phone in the lobby.

"Can't give the talk," Wright announced. "I'm going back on the seven-ten train."[8]

A worried voice pleaded that an audience awaited, both in the auditorium and over the airwaves.

After a pause, Wright inquired, "Will it be over television?"

"Not exactly," he was told. But the guest again relented and soon descended to the lobby and strode out of the elevator. As the college paper reported the following day, he "waved his stick, swirled his cape, and marched across the Green . . . kicking pigeons out of his way as he went." His escorts followed.

This was Wright in his element: He liked attention to be paid. He enjoyed stirring things up, doing and saying the unexpected. He always had. And Yale, as both familiar and foreign territory, was the perfect place to put on a little show. He never assumed he was among friends, but tonight he was to share the stage with Professor Vincent Scully, Yale's young and passionate scholar of American architecture—but a man who, just two years earlier, had taken Wright to task in print for his narrow view of the International Style. Another panelist would be Carroll L. V. Meeks, a member of the faculty inclined to classical architecture. Wright's family motto—"Truth against the world"—was always operative, but on this evening of all evenings, his feelings still bruised, he was surrounded by men he perceived to be the enemy. The other person scheduled to join him onstage was Philip Johnson.

Once in Hendrie Hall, home of WYBC, his guides tried to make Wright comfortable in the studio for his pre-lecture interview. He doffed his cape and hat—but then he spied Johnson arriving. Once the evening's proceedings got under way the younger man was to deliver an appreciation of Wright, but the honoree had something he wished to say now. Like the captain of a warship maneuvering into position, Wright steered toward Johnson then hove to at hailing distance.

Professor Scully, also present, would remember Wright's "loud, clear voice."[9] Johnson later wondered whether Wright was speaking to him or for the benefit of those around them, but Wright's manner of delivery—another in attendance remembered it as warm—seemed pitched for all to hear.[10] His words shocked Johnson like an iced highball tossed into his face.

"Philip!" Wright exclaimed in mock surprise. "I thought you were dead!"

Frenemies Frank Lloyd Wright and Philip Johnson at Yale University on September 20, 1955. (Austin Cooper, *Yale Daily News*)

A nonplussed Johnson sidled over, but Wright wasn't finished. "To think of it," he reminisced. "Little Phil, all grown up, an architect, and actually building his houses out in the rain."

To that, Johnson offered no response.

————

THE NIGHT BELONGED to Wright. Reportedly more than two thousand people were turned away at the door, and a rapt audience in the hall listened in "an atmosphere of profound tribute."[11]

When Wright described his architectural vision, he claimed, as he often did, that his designs fulfilled the "great and noble promise of the Declaration of Independence."

He offered his architectural philosophy. He was a great lay preacher, his faith based upon what he called "organic architecture," a philosophy of building he defined for the Yale audience as "something with a spiritual meaning, something integral, something in which the same relation exists between the part and the whole as between the whole and the part, something built *of* the thing and *on* it."

Nature must be the foundation of organic architecture, he explained, invoking by name Samuel Taylor Coleridge, Henry David Thoreau, and "the real poet and singer of America," Walt Whitman. "We're going to be great by recognition of the study and expression of nature as nature: the reality of a building consists not in the four walls but in the space to be lived in."

The old man seemed to grow younger as he talked. He critiqued modern architecture, the university, and the church. Having mesmerized his youthful listeners, he closed with an advisory: "There is only one moral to all this: Hell, let's be ourselves."

The audience responded with thunderous applause.

Philip Johnson closed the evening's presentation. He praised Wright as "America's greatest living architect." He called Wright's work inimitable and termed Taliesin West "a work of poetry." Those in attendance remembered the tribute as deeply moving (Johnson himself would describe it, without apparent irony, as a "eulogy"). But Wright, hearing the honeyed words as a mea culpa for Johnson's dismissal of Wright's work as outdated, decided he still wished to have the last word.

When Johnson was finished, Wright responded, "Attaboy, Phil," loudly enough for the audience to hear. "Now you're on the right track."

———

TO CITE THEIR names is to sum up architecture in the twentieth century. First came the Master, Frank Lloyd Wright (1867–1959), and his provincial manner, the Prairie Style, which influenced the world. Much later, with the turn of the millennium, the Maestro's serial sponsorship of such varied modes as International, Post-Modern, and Deconstructivist made Philip Johnson (1906–2005) architecture's chief talking head. The man wearing the black-framed glasses with the circular lenses had become the ubiquitous face of American architecture.

In ways that no one before had done, the two placed architecture at the center of culture.

In the years they shared—between their first acquaintance in 1931 and Wright's death in April 1959—the two men were the yin and the yang, in love and in hate, the positive and negative charges that gave architecture its compass. A shared characteristic stands forth as a singular asset: Although each man lived into his nineties, neither, it seems, ever stopped talking. Their words might be barbed, witty, self-aggrandizing, pandering, or visionary, but in a profession where wise utterances are hardly commonplace, their pronouncements were consistently provocative. Both could be imperious, inspiring, funny, trivial, and profound, but each had a personal charisma and directness that made him good copy. Often they talked to and about one another, and their shared legacy amounts to a mixed bag of architecture, self-promotion, iconoclastic wit, and uninhibited ego.

They shared a deep commitment to the cause of architecture, but the two could hardly have been more different, separated as they were by age, region (Wright regularly expressed his dislike for Johnson's adopted home, Manhattan), and sexual orientation (Wright admitted to disliking the "homosexuals who dominate the art world").[12] They shared a restless creativity; the body of work that each produced over many decades of professional practice was eclectic and changeable, but their oeuvres rarely overlapped. Perhaps most of all they were separated by a great chasm in taste, with Wright the unreformed Romantic, Johnson the Modernist with an enduring fondness for the classical.

In their three shared decades, however, they built the two most admired and discussed houses of the century, Wright's Fallingwater and the Glass House, both of which took on personalities in their own right. The two men competed for the soul of Manhattan when the ziggurat on Fifth Avenue, Wright's Guggenheim Museum (completed in 1959), assumed its place overlooking Central Park, and Johnson's (and Miës van der Rohe's) tower for the House of Seagram, completed the previous year, reached for the sky in Midtown. In triangulating twentieth-century urban architecture, those two buildings are key coordinates.

Wright is a giant; to be certain, Johnson is the lesser architect. Yet they were essential foils for each other, and clearly discernible shifts in the careers of both men resulted when their careers collided. Johnson admitted frankly that, as he neared fifty, Wright challenged the critic-curator Johnson to devote himself to the practice of architecture, telling him, "Philip, you've got to choose." When Wright set out to build his house in a waterfall, he told a young apprentice conspiratorially, "We are going to beat the Internationalists at their own game."[13] Like colliding atomic particles, Johnson and Wright altered each other's paths.

Their dynamic was such that Philip Johnson could say—though only after the Master of Taliesin was dead—that Wright "changed my life."[14] Wright, operating from his presumed position of superiority, got no closer than asking, quizzically, of the Glass House, "Is it Philip . . . and is it architecture?"[15] Yet, together, the two men transformed the art of building in their time.

PART I
A Meeting of Minds

CHAPTER 1

Two Conversations

The onus of designing a new style any time one designs a new building is hardly freedom; it is too heavy a load except for the greatest of Michelangelos or Wrights.
—*Philip Johnson*

I.

January 1927 . . . The Plaza Hotel . . . A Mind of "Emersonian Quality"[1]

ALTHOUGH THE WAVY-HAIRED men looked a bit like father and son, they laid eyes on each other for first time that wintry day. The architect had made the meeting happen because he knew very well he could use all the help he could get. He admitted to just fifty-seven, but Frank Lloyd Wright was fifty-nine and struggling to reverse his slide into obscurity.

"Your pen seems pointed in the right direction," Wright had written the previous August to his luncheon companion, Lewis Mumford. After finding a Mumford essay in H. L. Mencken's widely read magazine, *American Mercury*, Wright sensed the writer might be a kindred spirit. The younger man had written admiringly of Wright's mentor, Louis Sullivan, extolling his "experiments towards a fresh and living architecture."[2] Wright wrote to suggest that the two might someday "'walk and talk' together."[3]

Mumford had responded promptly. "Your letter was very welcome; for I have been on the point of writing you more than once; and this gives me my opportunity."[4] Even though Wright professed a general dislike for

Frank Lloyd Wright looking surprisingly youthful at age fifty-nine. (Library of
Congress/Prints and Photographs)

cities and for New York in particular, with its rising skyscrapers and smog,
upon settling into the Plaza, his favorite Manhattan accommodation (the
presence of Central Park across the street helped a little), he had issued the
luncheon invitation. He asked Mumford to join him at the nineteen-story
château-style hotel overlooking Fifty-Ninth Street and Fifth Avenue.

A well-trimmed mustache lined Lewis Mumford's upper lip; his
hair remained thick and dark at age thirty-one. He carried himself with
confidence, his intense gaze hinting at the rigor of his intellect and the
firmness of his principles. Mumford's growing list of published writings
marked him as a formidable cultural critic, one who ranged over
the considerable territory that, in a borrowing from Van Wyck Brooks, he
called the "usable past." Though Mumford often wrote of literature
(he held Emerson in high esteem and labored on a biography of Herman

Melville), his thoughts on American architecture had begun to attract attention, as they would for the next half century.

The two men at the table found they shared an admiration for what Mumford called the "rooted dignity that the most gigantic metropolises do not often possess" (Wright instinctively distrusted the urban; Mumford thought it dehumanizing). Like Wright, Mumford looked askance at the widespread application of classical details, such as the Roman columns, pediments, and domes that had become usual at the turn of the century. Mumford dismissed the practice as the "Imperial Façade." When the "classic style . . . came face to face with our own day," he had written in his monograph on American architecture, *Sticks and Stones* (1924), "it had but little to say, and it said that badly, as anyone who will patiently examine [its] superimposed orders . . . will discover for himself."[5]

Lewis Mumford, photographed in 1940. (Eric Schaal/Pix Inc./The LIFE Picture Collection/Getty Images)

Mumford had written the words, but Wright spied in them the spirit of his own organic architecture, which, in 1914, he had defined as "an architecture that *develops* from within outward in harmony with the condition of its being as distinguished from one that is *applied* from without."[6]

As he neared his seventh decade, Wright wore his leonine mane of gray hair brushed back to reveal a widow's peak. As Mumford watched and listened, Wright, per usual, assumed for himself the role of Old Testament prophet, ready to dispense wisdom. As Mumford put it, "One could not be in the presence of Wright for even half an hour without feeling the inner confidence bred by his genius."[7]

His built designs had earned Wright the status of American architecture's éminence grise; however, despite wide admiration at home and abroad for his work, his personal life seemed an unending series of misadventures. Almost as soon as they sat down, Wright candidly recounted some of the terrible tribulations.

Mumford already knew much of the story since the nation's newspapers covered Wright's escapades in salacious detail. He had established himself in the closing decade of the nineteenth century and the first of the twentieth as America's most admired architect. He had altered the character of the streetscapes in Oak Park, his adopted home outside Chicago, where some two dozen examples of his Prairie Style houses stood. Then, suddenly, he had departed unannounced, abandoning his wife, Kitty, and their six children, in 1909. He had come to regard his suburban life as a "closed road," and he felt compelled, he later explained rather ponderously, "to test faith in Freedom."[8] He fled to Europe with Mamah Cheney, the wife of one of his Oak Park clients. Wright had hoped to work quietly on a book devoted to his architecture, but within days, news of the lovers' registration as Mr. and Mrs. Wright in a Berlin hotel hit the front page of the *Chicago Tribune*.

On returning to the United States a year later, the disgraced Wright had quietly commenced building a home, supposedly for his mother, in

Spring Green, Wisconsin. The site was the valley where he had summered as a child on farms tilled by his mother's brothers, men named Lloyd Jones. Though neither had yet obtained a divorce, Wright again aroused moral outrage by moving Mrs. Cheney into the new home, dubbed Taliesin (Talley-ESS-in). Then, as if in the spirit of divine retribution, a demented manservant set fire to the home in August 1914. Mrs. Cheney, her two young children, and four others, all trying to escape the inferno, were murdered by the hatchet-wielding manservant.

Wright, at work on a project in Chicago, returned to bury Mamah in an unmarked grave. "Why mark the spot," he explained, "where desolation ended and began?"⁹

After their lunch in 1927, neither Wright nor Mumford made note of what the other ate, but Mumford did record in his autobiography the substance of their conversation at the Plaza. "Before long he was also unrolling the story of the second marriage, with the older woman who had rescued him from his desolation, indeed, restored him to life after the grim holocaust at Taliesin."¹⁰

Miriam Noel had sought Wright out in the months after the Taliesin fire, offering companionship and solace. For a decade, they shared a domestic life. His international reputation grew when his Wasmuth portfolio, the German publishing project that contained one hundred lithographs of his work, gained wide admiration in Europe. Wright traveled often between 1916 and 1922 to oversee construction of his design for the Imperial Hotel in Tokyo. He designed Mayan-style homes in Southern California, incorporating cast concrete blocks in a technique of his own invention.

After first wife, Kitty, finally agreed to a divorce, Wright and Noel married, but relations between the newly legal husband and wife quickly deteriorated. Noel left after less than a year of legal union, in May 1924; by then Wright understood that her increasingly bizarre behavior was, in part, a consequence of her addiction to morphine. But Noel proved unready to quit Wright's life altogether. She sought vengeance after

Wright met and fell in love with the much younger Olgivanna Ivanovna Lazovich von Hinzenberg, whom he installed at Taliesin in early 1925. Olgivanna arrived with her eight-year-old daughter, Svetlana, from her first marriage. That December, Olgivanna delivered another daughter, Wright's seventh and last child, whom they named Iovanna Lazovich Lloyd Wright.

At the Plaza that noontime, Mumford got an earful. Noel had continued to pursue Wright. He would be arrested for violating the Mann Act, since he had transported Olgivanna across state lines (the 1910 legislation forbade the interstate transportation of unmarried women for any "immoral purpose"). Wright would also be evicted from Taliesin by creditors. As the two men talked, Wright admitted he needed money; that was why he had come to town. He told Mumford as they ate that he "walk[ed] the New York streets, hat in hand."[11] He brought with him Japanese prints he hoped to sell. Purchased in the Far East on his trips to Tokyo, his collection of Orientalia had proven a ready source of profits in the past, with the Metropolitan Museum of Art among his best customers.

Mumford marveled at the man before him. Wright's flouting of social conventions never seemed to burden him and, to Mumford's eye, neither did his financial worries. "None of the tragedies of his life," Mumford observed, ". . . corroded his spirit or sapped his energies: his face was unseamed, his air assured, indeed jaunty."[12]

Yet to those who knew them in those days, Lewis Mumford and Frank Lloyd Wright looked to be riding opposite vectors, the former in ascent, the other displaying all the signs of a falling star growing dim. Wright had admitted to Mumford in his first letter his unease at "reading my 'obituaries.'"[13] Critics abroad might praise him, but few commissions came his way—and that worried him. He wanted to retire the notion that his creative days were over; as he would soon write to Fiske Kimball, director of the Philadelphia Museum of Art and author of the newly published survey *American Architecture*, "[I] think, with Mark Twain, the reports of my death greatly exaggerated."[14]

Mumford found Wright's company bracing, his direct approach disarming. "Wright and I were never more friendly and at ease than we were at that first exploratory luncheon," he remembered later, years after Wright's death. But even as they talked, Mumford recognized the other man's motives. The architect wanted new doors opened before him. He needed help from younger men, not dismissal or reassurance about how great he once had been. He wanted to do new work. And Mumford understood that Wright wished to enlist him as an apostle, one who would help him preach the cause of architecture according to Mr. Wright.

When they parted, their lunch had produced no grand bargain, and Mumford would later recall, "Wright could not understand my unwillingness to abandon my vocation as a writer to have the honor of serving his genius."[15] Still, a valuable acquaintanceship had been established, and an on-again, off-again correspondence followed over many years. But other handshakes, other introductions and conversations, would also ensue.

One of the alliances Mumford would foster for Wright would be with a young Philip Johnson, not yet out of Harvard. Then it would be Wright and Johnson, with Mumford observing near at hand, who would become inextricably linked in the evolution of mid-twentieth-century American architecture.

II.

June 16, 1929 . . . Wellesley, Massachusetts . . . Enter Alfred Barr

LIFELONG BONDS CAN be the consequence of a moment. An accidental spark illuminates overlapping passions, and an abiding friendship is launched. Precisely that occurred on graduation day at Wellesley College in June 1929.

Theodate Johnson stood among the new alumnae. Passionate about music, she harbored ambitions of pursing a singing career, and the tall, handsome woman ("a brunette with blazing eyes," composer Virgil Thomson soon observed), would go on to a modest solo career, performing in an operatic mode in London and New York in the years to come.[16] But the enduring relationship struck that afternoon linked Theodate's only brother and Wellesley's newly celebrated professor of art. The alliance would endure for fifty-two years, ending only with Philip Johnson's eulogy for his great friend Alfred H. Barr Jr.

Barr was nothing less than an academic avatar. As a Harvard graduate student pursuing his Ph.D. in 1926, he accepted an offer tendered by Wellesley to teach a two-semester course in Italian painting. He chose the job over other junior professorships at Oberlin and Smith because the Boston-area school agreed to allow him to develop a seminar in modern painting. Few colleges of the day granted degrees in art history (Wellesley claimed to have been the first, just a few years before). None offered a semester course in Post-Impressionist art. "I took the license to teach as I liked," Barr later explained.[17]

In contrast, Philip Johnson, five years Barr's junior and a month short of his twenty-third birthday, remained a dilettante. Still in pursuit of his undergraduate degree in classics and philosophy, Johnson had already required two leaves of absence from Harvard to recover from black depressions (his Boston neurologist diagnosed cyclothymia, a now outdated term for mild bipolar disorder, which the doctor attributed to Johnson's homosexuality).[18] Having outgrown an adolescent stutter, Johnson impressed people with his intelligence, among them one of the preeminent philosophers of the day.

Professor Alfred North Whitehead befriended his witty and well-mannered student, even welcoming him to his dinner table. However, when Whitehead recommended that Johnson consider enrolling at the Harvard Law School to refresh his philosophical perspective, he recognized the suggestion as a thinly disguised hint that he ought to pursue another field. (Whitehead, who never flunked students, had given Johnson a B, which Johnson remembered without rancor, "meant the

The studious Mr. Barr, pictured in his museum in 1953. (Carl Mydans/The LIFE
Picture Collection/Getty Images)

same thing.")[19] Johnson took the hint, and having installed a grand piano
in his suite of college rooms, pondered a career as a concert pianist.
Sociable, evidently gifted but clearly unfocused, he remained very much
in search of his lodestar.

Young Professor Barr's educational path could hardly have been
more different. His reading of Henry Adams's *Mont-Saint-Michel and
Chartres* had opened his schoolboy mind to art history, an inclination that
took concrete form after he enrolled at Princeton at sixteen. The son and
grandson of Presbyterian ministers, he inherited something of their
nonconformist spirit. He heard no call to the church and its rituals but, as
he confided to a friend as an undergraduate, he chose to "open the shutter
of [my] soul to beauty."[20]

Having earned B.A. and M.A. degrees at ages twenty and twenty-one, he decided to study modern art. To his contemporaries, it seemed a quixotic quest. The general public after World War I had little taste for the new, and virtually no one in academia thought it a legitimate course of study. A small exhibition he curated at Harvard's Fogg Museum met mostly with critical guffaws, and of the artists represented, van Gogh and Cézanne were dismissed by the *Boston Herald* as "a crazy galoot" and "a poor painter with bad eyesight." The show earned Barr the opprobrium of another of the Boston newspapers, which high-handedly dubbed him "the very modern Mr. Barr of Cambridge and Wellesley."[21]

Mrs. Homer Johnson, herself a Wellesley graduate and president of the Alumnae Association, introduced her son to Alfred Barr. When Barr approached to offer his graduation-day congratulations to Johnson's beloved sister, a conversation ensued between the two men that soon excluded mother and daughter.

In minutes, Johnson found that Professor Barr occupied territory Johnson wished to explore. A casual interest in architecture had been heightened when Johnson, upon visiting Athens the previous summer, had been moved to tears at seeing the Parthenon. More recently, the young classical scholar's engagement with the ancient had given way to a growing fascination with the new. An article Johnson had encountered in the magazine the *Arts* by another twentysomething Harvard man, Henry-Russell Hitchcock, had rocked him: "I was so excited by it I almost trembled."[22]

The article focused on the architectural work of J. J. P. Oud. Describing him as Dutch architecture's *chef d'école*, Hitchcock saw in Oud's new work the influence of cubism and of the controversial Mr. Wright. Demonstrating a precocious willingness to describe what he perceived to be historic trends, Hitchcock identified the year 1922 as "of great importance for contemporary architecture," since, as Hitchcock pointed out, not only Oud but also the Swiss-born architect Le Corbusier and Walter Gropius of Germany produced radically new works that year.

While their buildings differed in many particulars, the three Europeans shared a revolutionary notion, one that galvanized Hitchcock and his reader, the impressionable Philip Johnson. "Architecture should be devoid of elements introduced for the sake of ornament alone," Hitchcock had written. "To the engineering solution of a building problem nothing should be added."[23] The notion of eliminating such elements as the Parthenon's columns and cornice was, for Johnson, an epiphany, one he recognized for its startling clarity, rightness, and freshness, its suitability to his time.

In contrast to Johnson's status as a fresh convert to the cause of Modernism, Alfred Barr had already assumed the mantle "evangelist," as he himself described his new role.[24] His Wellesley course on twentieth-century art, "Tradition and Revolt in Modern Painting," first given in 1927, took what he described as "a broad approach to contemporary art." The catalog description for Art 305 promised the class not only would examine "Contemporary Painting in relation to the past" but would do so in relation "to aesthetic theory and to modern civilization."[25]

When it came to the syllabus, the professor's tastes extended beyond painting to the graphic arts, theater, music, commercial and decorative arts, and literature. Barr divided the class into groups he called "faculties." Each subset of students was to look at a branch of contemporary design (such as furniture, ballet, automobiles, or the cinema), then report back to the class as a whole. Another assignment required each student to spend a dollar at a nearby five-and-ten store to purchase well-designed modern objects, which they would then present to their classmates as "constructive theatre."[26] As a group, the class also went to plays and listened to recordings of Debussy, Richard Strauss, and American jazz.

Barr's expansive primer on the modern also featured architecture. He invited Henry-Russell Hitchcock, then working on his master's degree at Harvard, to talk to his class. Hitchcock had never lectured prior to delivering his first discourse to the students of Art 305, but, as Barr explained simply, "I felt that Russell knew things."[27] Hitchcock put particular emphasis on the work of the writer, painter, and architect

Charles-Édouard Jeanneret-Gris; working as Le Corbusier, his fondness for horizontal ribbons of windows soon appeared in others' designs. Corbusier's turn of phrase, "a house is a machine for living," had generated much discussion, both in Mr. Barr's classroom and in the larger world of the artistic intelligentsia.[28]

Barr and his young women had ridden the Boston & Albany line from the suburbs into the Massachusetts capital, stopping along the way to admire rail stations designed by the first American architect to have a worldwide reputation, Henry Hobson Richardson (1838–1886). Built in Richardson's characteristic style, often of stone and brick, these structures managed to be Romanesque in spirit but were little ornamented. As Hitchcock soon wrote, H. H. Richardson "seemed to have created single-handed an American architecture."[29]

The final stop of Mr. Barr's Boston field trip had been neither a museum nor an architectural monument. Instead, the young women of Wellesley toured a just-completed manufacturing plant, the NECCO factory in Cambridge. The building, Barr wrote, was characterized by "the utmost economy in decorative motives and by the frank acknowledgement of utilitarian necessity both in plan and elevation."[30] The purity of its intention and functionality, explained Barr, gave the factory a new beauty.

Interest in what Barr had to say extended beyond that of the young women enrolled in the class. Other professors sat in. The shy Mr. Barr gained a reputation for deep thoughts; once, in delivering a lecture, he fell suddenly silent. He had been reading aloud lines from a Lenin speech; only after a lengthy silence did he look up at his students, smile apologetically, and say, "I'm sorry. I got interested."[31] Frank Crowninshield, editor of the widely read *Vanity Fair*, got wind of Barr, too, and published a version of the modern art questionnaire Barr had devised for his incoming students. Listing fifty people and movements, the feature inquired of its readers, "What is the significance of each of the following in relation to modern artistic expression?"[32] The answers amounted to a who's who of what Barr regarded as "modern expression."

Nine artists made the list, including Henri Matisse, American John Marin, cubist Fernand Léger, and sculptor Aristide Maillol. Writers were amply represented, including James Joyce, Jean Cocteau, and the poet H.D., as were key critics (Roger Fry and Gilbert Seldes); along with the theater (Luigi Pirandello and Eugene O'Neill's play *The Hairy Ape*); film (the *Cabinet of Dr. Caligari*); and even shopwindows (Saks Fifth Avenue). Frank Lloyd Wright was also among the fifty, and Barr identified him as "among the first great American architects to become conscious of modern forms as an expression of modern structure." Also listed was that bespectacled Swiss, Le Corbusier, who did double duty on Barr's list as a painter and an architect.

On the late-spring afternoon of the Wellesley 1929 graduation ceremony, Barr and Johnson's conversation progressed in moments from pleasantries to a high-toned intellectual discussion. According to the recollections of those present, the two men talked for more than two hours. Theirs wasn't the most obvious pairing: Dapper as always, his strong chin deeply dimpled, the handsome Johnson looked ready to jump behind the wheel of his stylish Peerless motorcar. Barr, gawky with small, boyish features partly obscured by thick, rounded spectacles, looked owlish and wise. The soft-spoken intellectual with the receding chin was more likely to be found with his nose in a book or poised in wordless contemplation before a painting than motoring around the countryside.

In his *Vanity Fair* quiz, Barr described a collector of modern art as "emancipated." On that June day, he found a disciple who shared his sense that the advent of Modernism was a liberation, and for Johnson, his introduction to Barr that day would loom large for the rest of his life. His time with Barr became in his memory a conversion experience. In recollecting their conversation over the decades, Johnson invoked the biblical story of Saul, the first-century Jew who, once a persecutor of Christians, converted and preached the new faith, going on to found churches and write significant sections of the New Testament. Johnson remembered his encounter with Barr as a "Saul-Paul experience."

Johnson's newfound taste for the new gained Barr's attention. By nature an introvert, Barr saw in the expansive Johnson a shared fascination. As Johnson would do often over the next three quarters of a century with interviewers, clients, and others, he displayed his gift for committing himself absolutely to the conversation at hand, adopting, at least for purposes of discussion, the other's point of view. As his longtime friend the architecture critic Ada Louise Huxtable later observed, "He responds to everybody on that person's own terms."[33] While Johnson brought a minimum of classroom knowledge—he had enrolled in just three courses in the fine arts at Harvard and failed to complete two of them—that shortfall didn't seem to matter. Both men understood that, aside from Barr's new course at Wellesley, little that was new in art had a place in the curricula at most universities. The omission intrigued them, and even as they talked, Johnson recognized he could share Barr's mission.

Like strangers at a bus stop, one with and one without an umbrella, Johnson insinuated himself under Barr's. As if insulated from the elements by the surrounding buzz of other conversations, they suddenly seemed alone; everyone else ceased to matter. Johnson later offered a terse summary of their Wellesley tête-à-tête: "In 1929, I met Alfred Barr, which was the start of everything."[34]

CHAPTER 2

Plotting a Comeback

My obituaries are all of such nature as to make me want to arise and fight.
—Frank Lloyd Wright

I.

Spring Green, Wisconsin . . . A Visit from Aleck

O UT OF AN impulse he never explained, Frank Lloyd Wright
began in earnest to cultivate contacts in New York in the mid-1920s.
He distrusted the urban in general and New York City in particular—in
a moment of pique, he called the place he was then coming to know
a "damnable, damned and damning city."[1] But Wright also recognized that
the energy and booming prosperity of Manhattan might suit his needs.

Perhaps he also took the challenge posed by a new friend, a unique
New York character named Alexander Woollcott (1887–1943), the theater
man who ironically observed, "You haven't lived until you died in
New York."

Upon learning that Taliesin was just fifty miles from Madison,
Wisconsin, where he was to deliver one of his witty but withering lectures,
the Tweedledum figure of Woollcott had made an impromptu appearance
at Wright's property on April 20, 1925. Then on the staff of the *New York
World*, perhaps the liveliest newspaper of the day, Woollcott was admired
for the sharpness of his tongue (he described Los Angeles as "seven
suburbs in search of a city"), as a longtime theater critic, and for his role

at the center of the group of New York wits who lunched at a round table in the Rose Room of the Algonquin Hotel. He counted among his boon companions Harpo Marx, playwright George S. Kaufman, and Charlie Chaplin. Overnight Wright would become a friend of "Aleck," as the writer fashioned himself. The two men would exchange visits and maintain a busy correspondence until Woollcott's early death almost twenty years later.

Flabby of frame, heavily jowled, and burdened with thick-lensed spectacles, Woollcott brought a more sympathetic perspective to his first visit to Spring Green than some journalists had. As he confided to Wright, he had spent much of his youth residing in an eighty-five-room house in

Aleck Woollcott, in costume and in character, ca. 1939. (Carl Van Vechten, Library of Congress/Prints and Photographs)

Phalanx, New Jersey. A mansion in scale only, the sprawling structure had been constructed in the 1840s to house a socialist community of 150 followers of French social reformer Charles Fourier. Most of the apostles departed after a fire destroyed the canning factory that had been the community's means of support, but the Bucklin family—including Aleck's mother, Frances Woollcott (née Bucklin)—remained in the onetime commune. During Aleck's childhood, Frances and her five children (Aleck was the youngest) found refuge at Phalanx, together with some fifty other relations. As one cousin observed caustically, the London-born Walter Woollcott, an unreliable husband and often-absentee father, seemed to reappear in his wife's life "chiefly for breeding purposes."[2]

Wright's own paternal circumstances hadn't been so very different. Though born in Wisconsin on June 8, 1867, Wright spent most of his first decade in Iowa, Rhode Island, and Massachusetts, as the immediate family followed William Carey Wright, a sometime lawyer, clergyman, teacher, and musician, from one posting to another. Younger sisters Mary Jane (usually called Jane) and Margaret Ellen (Maginel) had arrived by the time William Wright left the family in 1884 to return to his first wife. Anna Lloyd Jones Wright, estranged from her husband for good, resettled her children back in the bosom of her family in the Helena Valley, across the Wisconsin River from the town of Spring Green.

When the first Lloyd Joneses arrived from Wales in 1845, the clan established a close-knit community in the farming village of Hillside. The devout and hardworking family held itself in such high regard that the neighbors took to referring to the place as the "Valley of the God-Almighty Joneses" (the adult Frank Lloyd Wright came by his hauteur honestly). At age eleven, Wright had begun spending his summers on the farm, working shoulder to shoulder with his burly and bearded uncles. He milked cows, harvested grain, and cared for the horses as he "learned to endure the routine of continuous labor."[3] Yet, as Wright remembered in the autobiography he began writing in 1926, his "dreams went undisturbed beneath or above the routine."[4] The recollections of a barefoot boy exploring woods and fields would later coalesce in the architect's mind as the inspiration for his philosophy of organic architecture, informed as it was by the beauty, fertility, and order of the natural world. His house at Taliesin was one manifestation.

In 1927, Wright asked Woollcott to read an early draft of the book that would be published as *An Autobiography* in 1932. Woollcott refused. "A primitive instinct of self-preservation," he explained, led him to make it a rule "never to look at anybody's manuscript except my own, at which I stare with a mixture of nausea and infatuation from dawn to dusk."[5] When visiting Taliesin, however, Woollcott drank in all that he saw.

On his first visit, Woollcott remained at the house for only two hours, noting that it grew "like a vine on that hill-crest" and "pick[ed] up its colors from the red cedars, white birches, and yellow-sand limestone around about."[6] He found there a community in the making as, from the start, Wright had envisioned Taliesin as more than a permanent domicile, with his generous quarters at the front, a studio wing with space for office, drafting, and model-making in the middle, and a cottage at the rear for apprentices and farm laborers. Beyond lay garages, barns, and other agricultural buildings. According to Wright, Taliesin "was to be a complete living unit, genuine in point and comfort and beauty, from pig to proprietor."[7]

Woollcott saw it in more poetic terms, writing that Taliesin was "different from all other houses in the world . . . It is the peculiar gift of Wright and his like in this world—to build freshly as though we had all just come out of Eden with no precedents to tyrannize over us."[8]

After the New Yorker's departure that afternoon, the Taliesin family sat down to dinner. On rising from the table, however, Wright noticed smoke against the twilight sky—and that it billowed from his bedroom windows.

Once again, the house was afire.

Wright helped fight the flames, standing "on the smoking roofs, feet burned, lungs seared, hair and eyebrows gone."[9] The blaze was extinguished only by the downpour of a violent thunderstorm. Caused by an electrical fault in the telephone wiring, the conflagration destroyed the living quarters and consumed uncounted Japanese artifacts collected on Wright's travels. The house, a repository for painted screens, block prints, and embroidered fabrics on pillows and tables, was a smoking ruin. Among the debris Wright found "partly calcined marble heads of the Tang-dynasty ... and gorgeous Ming pottery turned to the color of bronze by the intensity of the blaze."[10]

Wright, with few commissions to occupy him, knew immediately what he wished to do. "I went to work again to build better than before because I had learned from building the other two."[11] By the time Woollcott told the story in print a few years later, "a new Taliesin crown[ed] the self-same hill."[12]

II.
Circa 1890 and After . . . Growing Up Wright

AS REBUILT AFTER the 1925 fire, the house was the unmistakable descendant of its two former selves and of its designer's Prairie Style houses back in Oak Park. As no one before him had done, Wright had devised a building style that produced buildings that seemed to rise like native flora from the soils on which they were planted.

At age nineteen and with just two semesters of engineering training at the University of Wisconsin to his credit, Wright had joined the architectural practice of Joseph Lyman Silsbee in Chicago in early 1887. He had come to Silsbee's attention the previous year during construction of the Unity Chapel for the Lloyd Joneses at Hillside (a surviving perspective drawing from 1886 bears the signature "F.L. Wright, Del[ineator]"). Like his undergraduate studies, his stay in Silsbee's office was brief; after less than a year, Wright departed to work for Louis Sullivan, another Chicago architect.

Though only thirty-one himself when Wright joined his office staff, Sullivan was already an accomplished architect, trained at both the Massachusetts Institute of Technology and the École des Beaux-Arts in Paris. During his five-year stay at the firm Adler and Sullivan, Wright learned engineering from Dankmar Adler and mastered biomorphic detailing sitting in an anteroom to Sullivan's office. Wright drafted leaves and vines, priding himself on becoming "a good pencil in my master's hand."

Buildings were reaching higher, thanks to the safety elevator (an innovation of the Civil War era) and to beams and uprights of steel mass-produced by the Bessemer process. Internal steel skeletons ended the de facto limit for tall buildings, namely traditional, load-bearing masonry walls, which thickened in proportion to height, consuming valuable floor space while restricting window size. Sullivan's high-rises—he would come to be called the "father of the skyscraper"—melded plain geometric forms together with intricate applied decorations. His buildings were more than taller versions of what had come before, thanks to highly original handling of the structures' bases, shafts, immense arches, and the crowning caps. Sullivan's office buildings and theaters were also recognizable by the three-dimensional surface decoration, not a little of it based on Wright's drawings, which distinguished the friezes, cornices, and spandrels.

Yet it was Wright's working knowledge of Silsbee's favored mode, the Shingle Style, that would be most evident in the first home Wright designed for himself after his 1889 marriage. The house facing Forest Avenue would accommodate the architect, his wife Catherine, and eventually their six children, born between 1890 and 1903. It had plain shingle cladding, uncomplicated massing, minimal trim, and simple gable rooflines, all departures from the ornamented Victorian styles of the day.[13]

During his time at Adler and Sullivan, Wright took on residential commissions that Sullivan, uninterested in designing houses, happily handed to his head draftsmen. In designing homes, two of which were for

Sullivan himself, the young Wright proved adept at adopting whatever the requested mode was, as early works are Queen Anne, Tudor, and even Dutch Colonial in style, though with details that would soon be recognized as uniquely Wrightian. Good word of mouth meant more commissions, some of which he accepted independent of Adler and Sullivan (Wright termed these jobs "bootleg houses"). However, when *Lieber Meister* Sullivan learned, in 1893, of Wright's moonlighting, Wright's beloved master dismissed his friend and favored pupil from the firm.

Wright recognized his sudden departure from Adler and Sullivan as an opportunity. To look at the corpus of his designs during the closing years of the nineteenth century and the first of the new one is to find his imagination at play in the suburban flatland around Chicago. More than a hundred designs, the work of Wright and talented collaborators, such as Walter Burley Griffin, Marion Mahony, and others, emerged from the octagonal studio that, in 1898, Wright added to his Shingle Style home.

His new style suppressed rooflines, favoring low-profile hipped and even flat roofs. Wide, overhanging eaves shadowed the low masses of the Prairie Style houses, as they came to be known. The tones and texture of the brick matched the dense prairie soils and enhanced the earthbound character of the houses, while their interior spaces had open plans that facilitated the flow between previously segregated living spaces. Immense hearths anchored the houses to their sites. Wright stylized the decorative vocabulary he learned from Sullivan, designing art-glass windows based on plants and trees and other visual cues, abstracting nature into geometric patterns of clear and iridescent glass.

Unlike the better-educated Sullivan, Wright proudly drew his inspiration from what he saw rather than what he learned; as Henry-Russell Hitchcock later observed, "never having studied in the American architectural schools of the eighties, there was much he never had to unlearn."[14] Wright actually turned down the chance to study at the École des Beaux-Arts, an opportunity proffered by Chicago architect Daniel Burnham, in the 1890s. Wright paid less and less heed to the traditions of the built environment, with its panoply of Victorian styles. His horizontal houses hugged the densely matted soil, conveying a sense of shelter from the hot sun and strong winds that whistled across the broad prairie. He also helped rethink the office tower with his Larkin Administration Building in Buffalo (1903) and the house of worship with the Unity Temple in Oak Park (1904).

Taliesin was a Prairie House with a difference. Wright initially designed the home on his return from Europe after his controversial departure from Oak Park. Left behind to Catherine and the children was his previous home, the evolutionary structure that came to be known as the Home and Studio. There he had carefully separated family life from work; at Taliesin, he would try a new paradigm, based on the recognition that his life was architecture.

Having spent time in Fiesole, a hill town north of Florence, Wright found on his return to the familiar Lloyd Jones topography (he always put great stock in what he called "the fresh eye") that his ancestral landscape in Wisconsin reminded him of Tuscany. Unlike his work in Chicago's suburbs, where his clients desired Wright houses to distinguish them from their neighbors, he built himself a country house that stood alone.

In *An Autobiography*, Wright called Taliesin a "natural house." It stood at the brow of a ridge overlooking the rolling farmland around it. At Wright's direction, the sand-colored limestone of its walls, quarried on another nearby hill, was coursed in a manner that resembled the stratified layers in the sedimentary bed; he wanted the house to appear as if founded on a natural outcropping. It wasn't a traditional house based on classical or other familiar architectural precedents. For that matter, unlike his own Prairie Style houses, which asked to be looked at, Wright's Taliesin sat like the chimera of the druid bard-prophet for which it was named. "I built a home for myself in southern Wisconsin—a stone, wood, and plaster building . . . as much a part of my grandfather's ground as the rocks and trees and hill."[15] It was a prideful place, certainly, a confident stronghold that managed to embody the Lloyd Joneses' motto: "Truth against the world." Yet, as Aleck Woollcott understood, Taliesin also solicited "the participation of the countryside."[16]

III.

New York, New York . . . Wright's New Friend

CLEARLY MOVED BY Taliesin—he found the place "inexpressibly consoling"—Woollcott wondered at what he called the "disparity" in Wright's reputation. "Here was a native American being hailed overseas as the outstanding creative genius of our time in architecture—an artist whose drawings were pored over and studied by every student in Europe."[17]

Alexander Woollcott knew something about fame. Against the odds, the owlish fat man had made himself a celebrity, perhaps the best-known humorist and highest-paid magazine writer in the United States. After writing dispatches from the front during the Great War (Sergeant Woollcott's copy, as edited by Private Harold Ross, appeared in *Stars and Stripes*), Woollcott spent years writing theater reviews in New York, making literary and theatrical friends—and not a few enemies. Though Woollcott once described him as "looking like a dishonest Abe Lincoln," Ross, after founding the *New Yorker*, hired his old army comrade anyway to write for his magazine. Woollcott soon had his own column, titled Shouts & Murmurs, and he regularly profiled friends, including Noël Coward, Katharine Cornell, Ruth Draper, and Broadway's preeminent couple, Alfred Lunt and his wife, Lynn Fontanne.

In writing his sketch of Wright, which appeared in the July 19, 1930, issue of the *New Yorker*, Woollcott did his bit for relaunching the architect's career, seeking to foster a "renewal of interest" in the man he called "the Father of Modern Architecture." While Woollcott shared some of Wright's sartorial affectations (Woollcott was often seen about Manhattan in a flowing cape, opera hat, and cane), more important to Wright were Woollcott's words. The writer advised his many readers that the architect "had been all but canonized in Japan." From Woollcott's typewriter, that amounted to a tease. He knew a good story when he heard it, and he couldn't resist telling the one about Tokyo's Imperial Hotel:

"It was [Wright's] task to rear a beautiful and spacious palace that would modestly take its cue from all the folkways and traditions of Japan." A further challenge was to "discover and express the secret of withstanding an earthquake." As it happened, Wright succeeded. According to initial reports, the hotel collapsed in a great temblor on September 1, 1923, but ten days later word arrived in America that Wright's engineering prowess had prevailed (he had, in effect, designed the structure to float on its concrete base). Despite one hundred thousand dead and the collapse of three quarters of Tokyo's housing, the Imperial Hotel stood, repurposed as a refuge for survivors. Wright's Japanese client termed it a "monument to your genius."

The controversies that had shadowed Wright for twenty years—adultery and divorce, the threat of bankruptcy, the violent deaths and two great conflagrations at Taliesin—no doubt put off staid Midwesterners. But not Woollcott, who dismissed the "sleazy scandals" as the result of "witless and vindictive indictments and all the ugly hoodlumism which the yellow newspapers can invoke when once an outstanding and inevitably spectacular man gives them half a chance." In a moment of mischief, Woollcott added, "Wright gave them a chance and half."[18]

Among the few who habitually addressed the architect by his first name (rather than as Mr. Wright), Woollcott had been generous with his Midwestern friend, lending money to a 1928 scheme by which a shell corporation, called Wright, Inc., leveraged the architect out of a deep financial hole with the purchase of the title to Taliesin after a foreclosure by the Bank of Wisconsin. Wright would more than repay Woollcott for his goodwill and kind words years later when he sent him a set of Japanese prints by the master Hiroshige.[19] After receiving them, an uncharacteristically bewildered Woollcott—a friend, seeing the prints "kicking around in a desk folder," had told him they were priceless—wrote to Wright. He was in character, offering, in offhanded fashion, "I have decided that I can't thank you enough for the prints so I shan't even try."[20]

Wright delighted in Woollcott's company. Once fellow passengers on a Pullman car from New York bound for Chicago reported two men of middle years taking turns playing a suitcase-size melodeon; Wright and Woollcott regaled each other with humorous songs.[21] Despite Wright's upbringing in a teetotaler family for whom the consumption of alcohol was akin to a mortal sin, he found a taste for a dram or two when Woollcott brought him a bottle of Bushmills Irish whiskey ("Boys, you have your youth and I have this," he would later say to his Taliesin apprentices, brandishing the bottle).[22]

Most important, Woollcott was helpful in Wright's climb back to prominence. Even after the Black Tuesday crash in October 1929 had signaled the sudden termination of Wright's few remaining architectural projects, Woollcott told his readers of Wright's series of lectures at Princeton in 1930 and an exhibition of his work at New York's Architectural League. Partly at the goading of Woollcott, Wright turned his hand to writing to supplement his income; soon he bragged to Woollcott of reaching beyond the architectural press to *Liberty* magazine and the $2,500 he had earned.[23]

All of Wright's labors—at the drafting table, behind the podium, with pen in hand—sought to tell the world that his talent hadn't ossified. Woollcott's testimonial in the *New Yorker* closed with an endorsement, invoking that word *genius* again. "If the editor of this journal were so to ration me that I were suffered to apply the word 'genius' to only one living American, I would have to save it up for Frank Lloyd Wright."[24]

With the new decade, Woollcott wasn't Wright's only New York friend to pass the word. "The day of your power is just beginning," Lewis Mumford assured Wright in 1930. "I salute you at the beginning of a great career!"[25] But he didn't merely utter sweet nothings in the sixty-three-year-old Wright's ear: In his 1931 book, *The Brown Decades*, Mumford reminded his audience of Wright's importance: "With the development of Wright's architecture . . . modern architecture in America was born."[26] Mumford's scholarship allotted Wright an essential place in the pantheon of American architects, along with H. H. Richardson and Louis Sullivan, and Mumford's view remains fixed in architecture texts to the present day.

Some of these words also reached the reluctant ears of Philip Johnson. From Mumford, perhaps, they meant more than from another authority. Johnson would later say of Mumford, not wholly in jest, that if he hadn't encountered Mumford's writing early in life, he would have become a "shoe clerk."[27]

CHAPTER 3

European Travels

You see I am really doing what Barr told me to.
—Philip Johnson

I.

The Twenties . . . An American Abroad

PHILIP JOHNSON WAS no stranger to the European continent. During the winter of 1918–1919, the Johnson family had sailed for Europe, where Homer Johnson, a wealthy Cleveland attorney, served at the pleasure of Woodrow Wilson and Secretary of War Newton D. Baker. While the father investigated a reported pogrom of Jews in Warsaw during the war just ended, the twelve-year-old son visited the Cathédrale Notre-Dame de Chartres with his mother, Louise.

Philip regarded the experience of that day as the climax of their weeks in France, and the image of the towering Gothic structure proved a fixing point in his architectural imagination. He would make regular—and usually reverential—reference to Chartres over the ensuing eight decades of his life, saying, "I'd rather sleep in the nave of Chartres cathedral with the nearest john two blocks down the street."[1] Despite the absence of domestic comforts, he was transported by the cathedral's beauty.

In the summer of 1926, Johnson embarked on a solo trip to England, fitting himself out in London shops with gloves, hat, and cane. Remaining true to his classical studies, he visited the Elgin Marbles at the British

Museum. On a visit to Stonehenge, he found the place disappointing. But in the days after he turned twenty, on July 8, 1926, Johnson again warmed to cathedral architecture. "Someday," he wrote home, "I am going to make a Romanesque architecture pilgrimage to Europe and have the time of my life."[2]

The following year, with Philip on leave from Harvard to regain his mental equilibrium, the family again made a transatlantic journey. During the late winter months that year, the Johnsons made stops in Sicily, Italy, Greece, and Egypt. Sixty years later Philip would recollect another aspect of the trip for his authorized biographer. With a museum guard, in a shadowy recess at the Cairo Museum, he experienced his first "consummated" sexual encounter.

By the time he next ventured abroad in 1929, more had changed for Philip Johnson than his growing acceptance of his homosexuality. He was a semester short of completing the requirements for his bachelor's degree, which his newly adopted mentor, Alfred Barr, advised him he must finish. At twenty-three, he contemplated his adult future, but, unlike many at his stage of life, he possessed not merely the legal independence of adulthood but freedom from financial worries.

During Philip's freshman year at Harvard, Homer Johnson, though very much alive, had decided to parcel out some of his financial assets to his children. Johnson's two sisters received title to certain of their father's most reliable investments, his commercial real estate in downtown Cleveland. To a man of property such as Homer Johnson, his gift to Philip seemed more speculative, as it consisted only of shares of common stock of the Aluminum Company of America. A college friend had given the Alcoa securities to Homer years earlier for legal services rendered when the fledgling company had purchased the friend's patent for an electrolytic process that proved crucial in reducing aluminum from bauxite ore. With the rapid growth in demand for aluminum in the prosperous 1920s, the shares had gained value at a great rate, making Philip a wealthy man, richer than his father. Even during the tough years of the Great

Depression, Philip's holdings would keep him more than comfortable, as Alcoa remained the only aluminum smelter in the United States.

With roughly a million dollars backing him—in an era when such a sum was truly a fortune—the young traveler lived well. He booked passage in 1929 on the most sophisticated ocean liner of the day, the SS *Bremen*, which, on its virgin voyage the previous year, had claimed the coveted Blue Riband for the fastest Atlantic crossing (driven by four immense steam turbines, the ship's top speed approached forty miles per hour). Johnson chose to purchase a land yacht, too, and onlookers at the quay that July watched as a crane lifted a new automobile to the deck of the *Bremen*. The Ohio-made Packard touring car was an exemplar of his life-long penchant for well-designed prestige cars.

Johnson acknowledged that his mind tended to move in "discontinuous jumps," so it's hardly surprising that his European travels had an unpredict-able pattern.[3] He disembarked in August 1929 at Bremerhaven, drove to Heidelberg, and for several weeks traveled around the German countryside, fulfilling the promise he had made to himself three years earlier to examine Romanesque cathedrals. He felt at home in Germany, not least since he had learned the basics of the language from a much-loved governess in child-hood. He indulged his taste for art and literature. His letters were punctu-ated with references to modern English novelists and European painters, among them D. H. Lawrence, Paul Cézanne, P. G. Wodehouse ("light reading of course"), Wassily Kandinsky, Virginia Woolf (*Mrs. Dalloway* "is wonderful"), and Paul Klee. He grew a mustache. A spur-of-the-moment shopping trip to London netted him expensive, bespoke suits that he described in a letter to his favorite correspondent, his mother, in whom he regularly confided. The tailored suits were early evidence of another lifelong pattern, a taste for dressing well. After flying back to Germany—air travel wasn't a means of transport that many tourists ventured in those days—he went on to the Netherlands. There his quest became contemporary build-ings, and he soon reported, "[I] have been traveling, rather fast to be sure, but travelling all over Germany and Holland to find modern architecture."[4]

A sustained visit to Berlin followed. Johnson feasted on the city's famed cultural life, which included opera and theater, music and dance, galleries and cinema. After dark, the nightlife included a permissive cabaret scene, "the widest open of any place little innocent Philip has ever been," he told his mother.[5] In this milieu nontraditional sexuality was celebrated as nowhere else in 1920s Europe. "I think if it can be told from the platform of a Berlin cabaret, it can be written in a letter to one's mother," he wrote to his family back in the States.[6] Though he stopped short of an explicit acknowledgment in 1929, Johnson found in the capital the freedom to exercise the sexuality he had spent years suppressing. Much later in life, he exhibited no such reticence in admitting that he found ample male companionship among the *gastfreundlich* (guest-friendly) Berliners.[7]

His time abroad that late summer and fall—he would remain until November—amounted to a good deal more than a simple joyride. Johnson's academic transcript lacked any sort of art-history survey, so his travels at the wheel of his Packard amounted to a short course in architecture as he shifted his focus from the Gothic to the modern. He followed good guidance, namely, his notes from Barr. It wasn't all architecture, and he wrote home to describe his acquaintance with Noël Coward in London, reporting the stylish Englishman had advised him to shave the mustache he affected. Yet as he vacuumed up culture of all sorts, buildings most often won his attention.

In seeking to understand architecture, Johnson learned that no book or lecture can convey the experience of a building as a visit can—seeing it in context, entering its portals, gauging its scale. A firsthand viewing enables the walking of hallways or aisles, pondering the heights, the absorption of textures. Even a remarkable photograph captures, at best, only one moment, and thanks to the dance of natural light, every building has an unending changeability. Johnson came to distrust photographs because they "freeze" architecture; he insisted that buildings had to be experienced, arguing that an architect's works must be judged on what he would come to call the "processional element," the experience of approach, of moving in space, from entrance, room to room, to exit. During those European months in 1929, Johnson taught himself to look at architecture. The insights gained would shape his thinking for the rest of his life, leading him eventually to decree, "Architecture exists only in time."[8]

In a Mannheim art gallery Johnson crossed paths with a young American architecture student. Also a Harvard man, John McAndrew brought a solid knowledge of building and, according to Johnson, was just as passionate about modern architecture as he. The two men decided to travel together and were soon joined by a young Swede they encountered named Jan Ruhtenberg. Also possessed by a yen for architecture, Ruhtenberg, once a private student of the German architect Miës van der Rohe, whose name the young Americans kept hearing, would gain them access to sites they wished to visit. Not that special entrée was required: As a friend had advised, "In Germany you need no letters of introduction. Where modern art is shown people are interested in informing you as much as possible."[9]

Johnson's kit included a portable typewriter on which he, a speedy typist, wrote letters home. Many went to his mother, and others to Alfred Barr. The letters reflected a tension in the young man's life, chronicling both his separation from Louise Johnson and his growing familiarity with the gospel of Modernism. Although Alfred Barr never expressed it in so many words, he had dispatched Johnson on a mission to explore what he regarded as architecture's future, asking his new friend to report back on what he learned. Even then, it seems, Mr. Barr was conceiving a plan for his disciple.

II.

1927–29 . . . Destination: the Future

JOHNSON'S ARCHITECTURAL TOUR included points of interest that Alfred Barr himself had visited not so many months before.

On leave for the academic year 1927–28 from his Harvard studies and his teaching duties at Wellesley, Barr's stated goal had been "to study contemporary European culture . . . [since] the modern field has scarcely been touched by American scholars."[10] He grew "green with envy" on finding much richer public collections of modern art in Europe than in American museums.[11] He spent two of his eleven months abroad in Russia, where, among much else, he encountered the work of the Constructivists, whose multidisciplinary approach integrated industrial materials into architecture and art. When it came to prescribing a plan for Johnson, however, he drew in particular upon what he had seen in Holland and Dessau, Germany.

Barr's predilection for the modern was instinctive. In a grant application before departing on his trip, he had written, "I find the art of the world in which I live far more absorbing and vitally interesting than . . . even that of the trecento in Italy."[12] He recognized change was in the air, as not only European artists but architects reacted to a world transformed by a disastrous war and advancing technology. The aristocracy that had led the world into war was in decline, and postwar Europe was badly in need of new housing for a rapidly growing population. At his first stop on the continent, Barr had encountered architecture that he thought was both a vital response to those needs and, just as important to him, distinctly modern.

Following in Barr's footsteps in 1929, Johnson, predisposed by Barr's counsel and the writings of Henry-Russell Hitchcock, reacted as Barr had.

Unlike the contemporary work that Johnson and Barr knew at home, the new buildings on view seemed to consist of abstract forms, of planes, lines, and geometric volumes. Symmetry no longer dominated, and instead of moldings and other decorative motifs that engaged the eye and unified the disparate parts of a building, patterns and proportions bound the whole. Everything seemed plain and pure, sleek and functional. As Barr expressed it, he detected "no compromise with dead styles, no revamping of the Beaux Arts."[13] As for Johnson, he admitted to a newfound dislike for unfunctional decorations and a fresh taste for solid colors.[14]

The buildings were unlike American architecture of the time, most of which had pitched roofs and decorative overhanging cornices, the products of a long line of descent, from Greek temples to Roman civic buildings. Such buildings had been revived in the Renaissance, then synthesized anew in the late nineteenth century, in particular at the era's most notable architectural training ground, the École des Beaux-Arts in Paris. But in Holland, Barr and Johnson found that J. J. P. Oud and other Dutchmen had flattened the rooflines and stripped off ornamentation, eliminating the false fronts of pilasters or columns and arches and archi-traves. In place of what Mumford called imperial façades, the Americans saw an honest expression of structure. Instead of a pretense of nobility, there was transparency. The structure could be read though the building's skin like bones viewed on that recent invention, the X-ray machine.

Having seen Oud's work in the Netherlands in September 1929, Johnson promptly proclaimed Oud the greatest architect in the world.[15] Johnson was deeply impressed by a two-story streetscape called the Hook, which integrated flats and glass-front shops. Punching the keys of his typewriter in a passionate burst, Johnson characterized it as "the Parthenon of modern Europe."[16]

Inspired by what he saw, he also began to think seriously about more than mere looking, deciding he would like to write a book about architec-ture, one that would be illustrated but with a minimum of theory.[17] Within days, he added another aspiration: Working in the new Dutch palette of primary colors and contrasting grays, he began to imagine himself a designer as he developed renovation ideas for his parents' homes. In a few short weeks, Johnson the tourist had assumed the guises of critic and architect, costumes that were new to him, immediately congenial, and, in retrospect, prophetic.

Barr's visit to the Low Countries had exposed him to the work of new painters such as Piet Mondrian; in Mondrian's "absolute expression of the geometric style," Barr saw Oud's building. Barr had found museums with van Gogh canvases blended with works of Rembrandt and Vermeer. "In Dutch museums," he reported, "it is possible to discover what is going on nationally and . . . internationally. Neither is at present possible in American Museums."[18] Yet at a later stop on his tour, in Dessau, Germany, Barr had been exposed to a model for looking at the visual arts in an even more comprehensive way. He dispatched his disciple to experience the Bauhaus, too.

––––––

IN THE YEARS following World War I, the Bauhaus had emerged as Modernism's Vatican. Though founded in 1919 in Weimar, the Staatliches Bauhaus moved to the industrial town of Dessau in 1925. On their initial visits there, Barr (in 1927) and Johnson (in 1929) embraced a new, collective design philosophy.

Walter Gropius, founder and architect of the new Bauhaus school, had been the central figure, but his college of cardinals included painters (among them Wassily Kandinsky, Paul Klee, and Lyonel Feininger) and other instructors, not least Marcel Breuer, who was both the school's "craftsmaster" and the teacher of furniture making. Intended to be what the expatriate American Feininger termed a "Cathedral of Socialism," the Bauhaus sought to meld the virtues of handcrafted objects (which were necessarily limited in quantity) into improved machine-made goods that could be mass-produced. The masters at the Bauhaus wished to serve a broad swath of society, not just the wealthy, who could afford the labor-intensive goods made by craftsmen.

Bauhaus translated loosely as "house of building," and as the name suggested, its most essential product would be architecture. "Let us together," wrote Gropius, ". . . create the new building of the future, which will encompass architecture and sculpture and painting in one unity and which will rise eventually toward heaven, from the hands of a million craftsmen, as the crystal symbol of a coming new faith."[19] At the Bauhaus, artist-led workshops taught typography, painting, weaving, bookbinding, sculpture, and photography. Gropius himself taught cabinetmaking, believing that good design across a broad spectrum of goods would improve the quality of life of the worker. Gropius took a self-consciously sociological view of architecture. In particular, when it came to large-scale development, he believed that addressing society's needs was key to design.

The main Bauhaus building embodied the school's principles. Barr looked upon his own college, Princeton, as a place of "imitation Gothic," and he worried that American students of architecture were working at designing "Colonial gymnasiums and Romanesque skyscrapers." Although Bessemer-steel frames had meant the exterior walls of tall buildings no longer had to support the building—each floor was independent, permitting curtain walls, as they were called, to enclose the structure—the decorative vocabulary had changed little in the United States. Whatever Louis Sullivan's genius back at the turn of the century, Barr saw design in America had lagged behind technology, as most of the new tall buildings were still decorated with classical or Gothic details, some with Art Deco stylings. But such buildings looked like taller versions of what had come before.

In contrast, the Bauhaus was a revelation. It was a place, Barr observed, "where modern problems of design were approached realistically in a modern atmosphere."[20]

Arriving in Dessau in October 1929, Johnson's first sight of the Bauhaus complex evoked a sense of wonder that rivaled the most powerful of his earlier architectural experiences. "We are reveling in having arrived in our Mecca at last," he scrawled on a postcard home.[21]

He saw a new architectural grammar. The Gropius building—actually a trio of L-shaped structures reminiscent of three flexed muscular arms hinged at the same shoulder—hadn't been conceived in terms of bases, shafts, and capitals, the essential grammar of the classical. The workshop wing in particular seemed to float above its recessed basement. It was as if Gropius had levitated a great glass box.

One wing of the Dessau headquarters of the Bauhaus designed by Walter Gropius, as photographed in 1930. (General Photographic Agency/Getty Images)

Tall walls of glass and horizontal ribbons of windows enclosed the entire enterprise, which included studios, classrooms, offices, and dormitories for students. The external structure of horizontal steel supports extended from an internal structure. "It is a magnificent building," Johnson wrote to Alfred Barr. "I regard it as the most beautiful building we have ever seen, of the larger than house variety."[22]

In the same letter, Johnson tested out his new critical facility: "The Bauhaus has beauty of *plan*, and great strength of design. It has a majesty and simplicity which are unequaled." Though still mastering the language of architecture, he felt empowered to employ a growing aesthetic fluency on Barr, testing the taste of terminology such as *restraint* and *perfectly plain masses.*

With the trip nearing its November end, a letter arrived in Berlin from Louise Johnson, and in responding to it, Johnson announced a reorientation in his life. Mrs. Johnson wrote inquiring whether he knew of his professor friend's recent change in status. Philip did: After just two years as a professor of art, the twenty-seven-year-old Alfred H. Barr Jr. had decided to leave Wellesley and to accept the directorship of a new enterprise. Even as Johnson and his mother exchanged letters, that new venture, the Museum of Modern Art in New York, opened its doors on the afternoon of November 8, 1929. The stock market had just crashed, but Barr's stock had risen remarkably.

Johnson's reply to his mother's letter can be read as a declaration of first principles. The sometime classical scholar, pianist, and philosopher had adopted a new set of coordinates in mapping his life. He had known for months of Barr's appointment, he wrote his mother. If she thought it odd that her son had failed to disclose Barr's career change, particularly given his copious and confiding correspondence in the preceding weeks, she had only to read on. Philip confessed to his new ambition:

"I would rather be connected with that Museum and especially with Barr than anything I could think of."[23]

Perhaps nervous that Barr might suggest, as Professor Whitehead had done, that he didn't quite have the aptitude to pursue his new passion, Johnson, for four months, had kept his new desire to himself, as if here were a risk that confiding his dream might cause it to disintegrate. But this time the rich-boy dabbler had identified a field to which he could devote his life. As Alfred Barr had said on being offered the directorship of the new museum, "[Being] a participant in this great scheme has set my mind teeming with ideas and plans. This is something that I could give my life to—unstintedly."[24]

Johnson, too, began to imagine that the new museum could provide the stage on which he could strut his stuff. And his performance—whatever the exact form it took—would surely concern architecture.

PART II
The MoMA Moment

CHAPTER 4

The New Museum

The American, or at least the American of the Eastern coast, takes it for granted that his public museums should be indifferent to modern art.
—Alfred H. Barr

I.

May 1929 . . . 10 West Fifty-Fourth Street . . . Imagining a Museum

THREE WOMEN BIRTHED the Museum of Modern Art. Abigail Greene Aldrich Rockefeller would be the museum's godmother. An heiress in her own right, she was married to John D. Rockefeller Jr., the only son of America's richest man. Though his interests tended toward traditional art and architecture—his pet project in the same period would be the restoration of Colonial Williamsburg—her husband helped Abby Rockefeller underwrite her collecting inclinations.

At MoMA, Mrs. Rockefeller would be joined by her friend Mary Quinn Sullivan, a former art teacher married to a lawyer with a lucrative New York practice, and by Miss Lillie P. Bliss, daughter of a well-heeled textile broker and manufacturer. The women all collected art; by the late 1920s, they owned canvases by Degas, Renoir, Cézanne, Seurat, Matisse, Picasso, Toulouse-Lautrec, Redon, van Gogh, Modigliani, Braque, and others. Aware that American museums rarely exhibited the artists they favored, the three decided to establish a museum in New York, one that, simply stated, would "exhibit works of art of the modern school."[1]

Acknowledging that the era's societal norms required a man to preside over the board of trustees, they approached A. Conger Goodyear, former president of the Albright Art Gallery in Buffalo. Carrying himself like the military man he had been (Goodyear had served as a colonel during World War I), he arrived at Mrs. Rockefeller's ten-story brownstone at 10 West Fifty-Fourth Street in May 1929, quite unaware that he was attending what would be looked back upon as the first executive meeting of the nascent museum. At 102 feet in height, the Rockefeller residence was the tallest private home ever built in Manhattan.[2]

A businessman by day, with broad experience in running railroad and lumber companies, Goodyear had engineered the purchase of Picasso's *La Toilette* for the Albright Gallery. Unhappy with his advanced tastes (the painting portrays an unabashedly nude woman admiring herself in a mirror), his Buffalo friends had promptly voted him off the gallery's board. In the eyes of the troika of New York women, however, that amounted to duty worthy of the Croix de Guerre. At their first lunch, they quickly approved of his manner and of the dignified gray garb he had bought for the occasion (which was thereafter referred to by his Buffalo friends as his "Rockefeller suit").

Halfway through the meal, the hostess inquired of her friends Mrs. Sullivan and Miss Bliss, "Shall we ask Mr. Goodyear the question we had in mind?" Invited to join their museum venture, he requested a week to mull the matter over, but he accepted the chairmanship the next day.[3]

Goodyear promptly added to the board several other modern art partisans, among them Frank Crowninshield, editor of *Vanity Fair*, and Professor Paul J. Sachs, director of the Fogg Museum. Sachs's Harvard seminar, "Museum Work and Museum Problems" (colloquially known in the field as "the museum course"), had already gained notoriety for the number of its students embarking on museum careers. Among Sachs's recent favorites were Alfred H. Barr and Henry-Russell Hitchcock, and Sachs immediately championed Barr to the museum's board. In keeping with the rapid pace with which the Museum of Modern of Art came into being, Barr cashed his first paycheck as director in early September.

Inspired in part by the multidepartmental mission of the Bauhaus, Barr's draft plan for the new museum laid out his notion that it would "expand beyond the narrow limits of painting and sculpture in order to include departments devoted to drawings, prints, and photography, typography, the arts of design in commerce and industry, architecture (a collection of *projects*, and *maquettes*), stage designing, furniture, and the decorative arts . . . [and] a library of films."[4] The wide-ranging approach he took to the arts at MoMA amounted to a variation of the subject headings of his pioneering Wellesley course.

By mid-September 1929, the Museum of Modern Art had a provisional charter, granted by the State of New York, and planning for an initial exhibition was well under way. A twelfth-floor space had been rented in the Heckscher Building, at the corner of Fifth and Fifty-Seventh Street. On Friday, November 8, at nine A.M., ninety-eight paintings by Cézanne, Gauguin, Seurat, van Gogh, and other Post-Impressionists went on view, drawing an astonishing forty-seven thousand people for the show's four-week run. Visitors rode an elevator to reach the museum's galleries, which had been freshly converted from nondescript office spaces. There were no guards, and the building's business occupants were inconvenienced by the volume of traffic ascending to the new museum.[5]

In just five months, three ladies, a gentleman from Buffalo, and Mr. Barr had made a museum.

II.

Winter 1930 . . . Midtown Manhattan . . . Pippo and Alfo

ON HIS RETURN to the United States, Johnson took rooms in Cambridge, planning to fulfill the requirements for his bachelor's degree during the spring semester. He needed to complete only one additional course and sit for senior exams, so his none-too-demanding academic schedule permitted frequent trips to Manhattan.

With his museum's four-person staff confined to two cramped offices, Alfred Barr often found refuge at street level in a Chinese restaurant; on his trips to New York, Johnson joined him there. Another diner who took part in many of their exchanges in the spring of 1930 was Margaret Scolari Fitzmaurice, Alfred Barr's fiancée. Her mix of Irish-Italian parentage and European upbringing suited the wide-ranging dialogue that was always seeking to discern artistic tides, especially in Europe. She taught Italian at Vassar and had met her future husband just months earlier in MoMA's galleries, in November 1929, when a mutual friend introduced Barr to "Daisy" Scolari.[6]

When the three got together, "the conversation was incredibly exciting and youthful. One idea would pile onto the next. Philip . . . was handsome, always cheerful, pulsating with new ideas and hopes . . . He was wildly impatient—he could not sit down."[7] Johnson's kinetic energy was such that, back in Cambridge, he had installed two lecterns in his room, one for his books, another for his typewriter, since he liked to study standing up.[8] Daisy observed the emergence of the mature Johnson and, forty years later, remembered, "His way of speaking, of thinking—that quickness and vibration—have not changed at all."[9]

The artistic bond between Johnson and Barr grew. In time, both would become superb proselytizers, men whose gifts for words enabled them to win others to their points of view. But in the early months of their friendship, they found their unspoken intuitions overlapped. They could look at a painting together and communicate their feelings on a preverbal level ("with grunts," according to Johnson). When in different cities, their correspondence also reflected their closeness. Barr had a fondness for pet names and adopted the salutation *Dear Pippo*. As for Johnson, his letters opened with *Dear Alfo* and often closed with *Love, Pippo* or *Pippesco*.

On paper and in person, their conversations usually concerned art and architecture, but Barr's confidences meant everything to Johnson. "Alfred Barr had faith in my ability to criticize and evaluate this dream in architecture that interested him, and felt I was good enough to do that. He represented not only a friend but a guru and a direction in my life."[10]

Another man who sometimes joined the Barr party eating lo mein on Fifty-Sixth Street was Henry-Russell Hitchcock, whose red beard suited his warmhearted way. He could take a little ribbing in the right spirit—and did when Barr, in an unusual wry moment, kidded him, observing that Hitchcock's name had "suffered post-baptismal hyphenation."

Known to his friends as Russell, Hitchcock's New England bloodlines ran back to the *Mayflower*. He grew up in Plymouth, Massachusetts, in a house chockablock with heirlooms (his physician father regularly added to the family collection, accepting early American objects in lieu of fees). Hitchcock as a small child was recalled as being fond of building blocks, and at "a tender though indeterminate age" he "began to draw house plans."[11]

Though Hitchcock spent his first college days in pursuit of a degree in architecture, his attention shifted with exposure to Harvard's pedagogical emphasis on connoisseurship.[12] He discovered that he liked nothing better than to subject an object to a close, physical examination, seeking to understand its origin and authenticity. Rather than studying paintings or sculpture, however, Hitchcock applied his scrutiny to his first love, buildings. Unlike some architectural historians, he established a lifelong rule: He insisted that, to write about a building, it had to be seen. He was known to design and even build structures on occasion, including a pergola he constructed of classicized cedar poles for a family in Plymouth and, later, a gallery wing for a historic Greek Revival house in Farmington, Connecticut, owned by a benefactor of MoMA.[13] But by 1930, Hitchcock was a credentialed professor and a writer with two books to his credit, including a monograph on Frank Lloyd Wright. Written and published in French, it was the first book on Wright in the language.

In April 1930, Barr appointed Philip Johnson to MoMA's Junior Advisory Committee, a post that he gained in part for joining what was, for practical purposes, an ongoing group-think at which Alfo, Daisy, Russell, and others shaped the new and exciting museum. Out of those conversations came the plan for another architectural peregrination in Europe.

III.

Summer 1930 . . . Racing Around Europe . . . An Exhibition Conceived

JOHNSON ONCE AGAIN brought along his own means of transport. As a graduation present to himself, he purchased a new Cord L-29, a racy, low-slung, front-wheel-drive automobile introduced that year. Into the boot of his convertible car he loaded a bulky German-made view camera to record what he saw.

Once in Europe, Johnson met up with both Hitchcock and Barr, and the colloquy about new buildings continued. But Barr had other obligations on his trip. Daisy Scolari had become Mrs. Alfred Barr in a Paris ceremony shortly before Johnson's arrival, and the couple had more than conjugal pleasures on their minds. "We had not a minute of honeymoon," reported Mrs. Barr (who would later be best known as Marga, the pet name Alfred gave her). The newlyweds were on a quest to find pictures by Jean-Baptiste-Camille Corot and Honoré Daumier for a show Barr was curating. "We were always on the warpath," the bride explained.[14]

For Johnson, the summer unfolded like a specialty travel brochure: His was a constant diet of architecture and more architecture. Again, he reported regularly to Louise Johnson back in the States. In one revealing note that August, he wrote from Berlin, "It is a strange fact that not one night has gone by but that I have had some dream on architecture. So it has got into my blood."[15] He met Le Corbusier, whom he didn't like but described as a genius. He got on well with J. J. P. Oud and even contemplated commissioning him to design a residence for his parents.

All the while, a working relationship with Hitchcock took shape. "My relation to Russell . . . is somewhat that of an apprentice," Johnson acknowledged, "but I struggle hard, and with some success to keep my judgment independent. I find that if I contradict loudly and positively enough that he begins to think he is wrong with his ideas after all and then we come to some agreement."[16] Together the two men made a survey, visiting not only the Netherlands and Germany but France, Belgium, Sweden, and Switzerland. A shared vision of how they might employ their knowledge began to emerge.

Johnson's travels the summer before had inspired him to consider writing a book. As for Hitchcock, he had taken to heart the criticism of their mutual friend Barr when, on reviewing Hitchcock's 1929 volume *Modern Architecture*, Barr complained the illustrations were "parsimonious . . . the text is worthy of at least three times the number of illustrations."[17] By June 1930, Johnson's and Hitchcock's independently conceived bookish notions had dovetailed into a shared plan for a more elaborate book they would do together. Their travels gained a new sense of purpose.

At first, the partnership worked well. Hitchcock was gregarious and likable; he loved good food, wine, and elegant clothes. But his personal habits began to grate on Johnson, who found his traveling companion hard of hearing, his beard unkempt, and his habit of smacking his food disgusting. Still, Johnson condescended not at all to Hitchcock's erudition and intellect, concluding, that, next to Alfred Barr, Hitchcock was "the most intelligent person on the arts I have ever met."[18]

A compromise was reached when Philip chose to rent his own quarters on arriving in Berlin, and Russell soon headed home to prepare for the next academic year. But Johnson, not yet having tired of looking at buildings and without any immediate obligations back in the United States, traveled to Czechoslovakia. His unlikely traveling companion was

Miës van der Rohe, to whom Jan Ruhtenberg had helped Johnson gain access. Although Miës seemed more bemused than intrigued by Johnson and the stream of American visitors who had sought him out, he had yet to see the built version of a new house he had designed two years earlier, and the two set off together for Brno.

Early in his career, Miës spent some twenty years designing traditional houses, but, in the mid-twenties, he had made a radical shift to designing dwellings suited to what he called the "modern period."[19] He employed new building techniques in a rational and functional fashion, in ways that soon won Johnson's wholehearted admiration. Always inclined to elevate those he admired to the status of demigods—superlatives such as *greatest* and *best* fell from Johnson's lips easily and often—he soon recognized Miës as his architectonic Zeus. As Johnson would observe after their Czechoslovakian sojourn, "Miës is the greatest man I have met ... He is a pure architect not mixed up with too many theories."[20]

IV.

August 1930 ... Brno, Czechoslovakia ... The Best-Looking House in the World

IN BRNO, MIËS enabled Philip Johnson to see the future. His glimpse was partial since the day was rain-swept and the great sprawling structure unfinished. Yet, like a recurring dream, Johnson's first visit to Grete and Fritz Tugendhat's new home forever altered the way he thought people ought to live. In time, that would come to include himself.

The family home he knew from his Ohio youth was unmistakably classical in style, with square columns that marched across its templelike portico. Built in 1845, at the height of the Grecian revival, with an overhanging gable roof, tall chimney, and clapboard siding, the Johnsons' vernacular, mid-nineteenth-century farmhouse conveyed a protective sense of warmth and enclosure. In visiting Brno, an industrial town in central Czechoslovakia, in August 1930, Johnson encountered a house that established new and radically different principles.

The most obvious contrast was the fenestration. Rather than having windows that seemed to fill holes in a wall, the principal living spaces in the Tugendhat House were enclosed on three sides by immense sheets of glass that extended floor to ceiling. (Not surprisingly, a generation later, the Tugendhat House came to be called the first glass house.)[21]

The glass accomplished more than merely keeping the elements out; Miës's design welcomed the outside in—and not only visually. Two of the four main plate-glass windows on the southern exposure, both roughly ten feet high, sixteen feet wide, and three eighths of an inch thick, could be lowered into the basement, opening entire sections of the wall in the manner of a power window in an automobile. The glass meant life in the house would be an ongoing dialogue between the surroundings, which were parklike landscapes, and the clean and simple interior, one shorn of the Victorian "trinkets and lace" that Fritz Tugendhat remembered from his childhood home.[22] Tellingly, Miës's first furnishing plan for the house included just one piece of "furniture," a plaster cast of a female torso by the German artist Wilhelm Lehmbruck.

Grete's parents had given the couple a half-acre plot adjacent to their own large in-town mansion, promising to underwrite the construction costs of the new house in their rear garden.[23] In 1928, the Tugendhats commissioned the Berlin-based Miës to design the house, and he had arrived in Brno that September to inspect the sloping meadow, which rose steeply to an upper boundary line with frontage on Schwarzfeldgasse, a quiet residential street. Months later, on the afternoon of the last day of the year, the couple visited Miës's atelier in Berlin to inspect his proposed design.

Their marathon meeting lasted until after the bells tolled the arrival of 1929. "The way he talked about his architecture gave us the feeling that we were dealing with a true artist," Grete recalled.[24] The clients needed the hours to absorb the architect's unprecedented design as rendered on paper. When Johnson visited the building barely a year and half later, he recognized the Tugendhat House was different in another fundamental way from the wood-frame house back in Ohio where he had spent his summers. "At the time," as Grete Tugendhat explained, "there was no private house which had yet been built with steel construction, so no wonder we were very surprised."[25]

In their days together, Johnson and Miës would establish no immediate rapport. Miës was two decades Johnson's senior, and while no doubt flattered by the younger man's enthusiasm, they had to rely on Johnson's German (Miës spoke little English), and however compatible their architectural tastes would prove, their personal differences were many. Johnson found Miës polite but stiff; as for Miës, he found the passionate young American a bit puzzling. Time would be required for Johnson to overcome Miës's distant manner. (Johnson's explanation: "Later, I realized what he needed was schnapps.")[26]

The son of a stonemason, Maria Ludwig Michael Miës grew up in a lower-middle-class family. As a youth, he learned the craft of building, working first as a runner at construction sites. Long before he put lines on paper, he gained a hands-on understanding of bricks and mortar. "That's really building," he would reminisce. "Not paper architecture."[27] Unlike the privileged Johnson, Miës attended trade schools as a teen and apprenticed in a furniture design firm before becoming, at twenty-one, a draftsman in the office of Peter Behrens, a Berlin architect who would also help train Le Corbusier and Walter Gropius. After service in the engineering corps of the German army during World War I, he altered his name—adding his mother's maiden name and appropriating the Dutch *nobiliaire* "van der"—and moved away from his training in neoclassical design.

He adopted the clothes of the professional classes, but with the face of a bulldog and an ever-present cigar, the man Johnson came to know had an unmistakable physicality. An avid photographer, Fritz Tugendhat captured his two visitors standing at the base of his house's garden façade. Although little more than a silhouette, Miës's barrel-chested figure commands the viewer's attention.

Miës chose to site the house atop the ridge where, with its street façade facing north, it appeared to be a one-story structure, consisting of a horizontal row of boxes and terrace space, with a garage at one end but no apparent entrance. Construction had gone slowly, and by October 1929, the house had been little more than an immense jungle gym of horizontal I beams supported by cruciform posts of angle iron bolted together. On Johnson's visit in August 1930, with construction well advanced, the young American found the entrance façade amounted to a sleight of the architect's hand—but the opposite elevation truly took Johnson's imagination captive.

Employing the lay of the land on the downhill side, Miës had set the structure into the slope, permitting a tall and wide southern elevation that consisted of two main floors atop a pedestal-like basement. The building presented as geometry. A horizontal ribbon of sheet glass ran the entire length of the building, fronting the main rooms in the house on the middle level, which was sandwiched between unornamented white bands of the tall basement below and the generous attic above. The basement level housed support spaces, including a boiler room, coal storage, and an "engine room" that contained the window-lowering mechanism. The bedrooms were located in the uppermost level. But the most essential space, visible behind a fifty-five-foot-long glass wall, consisted of the dining and living room areas, along with an office, library, and an enclosed glass "winter garden," a greenhouse for year-round propagation (see Fig. V).

The Tugendhat House defied tradition. The exterior curtain walls bore no load. That was left to the grid of steel supports covered by chrome sheathing, polished to a mirror finish; effectively vertical structural posts, they were located at roughly sixteen-foot intervals on the building's interior. (On Miës's floor plan, the pattern resembles the dots on a domino, with none at the periphery.) This singular mode of construction also meant that no interior walls were required for structural support, leaving a blank canvas. Johnson grasped its significance: "The plan of the living floor is for the first time as completely open as Miës could wish."[28]

The largely uninterrupted interior space that the visitor from America encountered wasn't entirely unprecedented; it was inspired by the open plans of Frank Lloyd Wright's Prairie Style houses, widely known from his 1910 Wasmuth portfolio. But the steel skeleton permitted Miës new freedom to expand upon Wright's notion of the open plan, in which formerly distinct interior spaces flowed into one another. The absence of structural walls meant the architect could define the spaces in any manner he chose, and as Johnson soon observed, the plan Miës devised "has the quality of a good abstract drawing."[29]

Using just two freestanding partitions made of luxury materials— one was a two-dimensional floor-to-ceiling plane made of honey-yellow onyx, the other a U-shaped dividing wall of Macassar wood—Miës managed to create a sense of discrete areas within a rectangular area of about 2,500 square feet. Here Johnson encountered a quintessential example of a principle that Miës van der Rohe would memorably (and repeatedly) enunciate: *Less is more.* According to Miës, "I said it first to Philip Johnson."[30]

The closer Johnson looked, the more apparent it became that Miës had planned these spaces in the minutest detail. Rather than partitioning off areas with plaster walls, he merely suggested room divisions; rather than rooms, there were recognizable zones and virtually no doors. The piano, placed against a wall, defined the music "room." Together with the Macassar wall, a circular dining table, fixed to the floor, established its space, which was entirely open on one side to the glass exterior wall.

A square rug of natural wool defined the living room seating area, with its glass-topped coffee table and six precisely placed cantilevered chrome and cushioned chairs of Miës's design. This island was at once a part of and apart from its surroundings (tellingly, Johnson was known to call it a "raft").[31] The sheet of onyx, roughly the size of one of the plate-glass sheets, screened the library and study space to the rear. Though its spaces were stripped down to essential elements, the Tugendhat House didn't telegraph function; rather, the sense was of an unbroken flow. Every element in the house seemed a distilled version of itself. Floor surfaces of travertine and linoleum (then a luxury material) and floor-to-ceiling curtains of shantung silk all added gray scale to the composition.

Miës oriented the house so as to employ the views as scenic wallpaper, changeable as the cycle of the day and variable as the seasons, with the immediate landscape shadowed by a great willow tree and the old city visible through a screen of trees at the base of the hill. Simple forms, rich materials, precise proportions, exacting furniture arrangements—all added up to a deceptively simple look that Miës himself would describe as *beinahe nichts* ("almost nothing").

Though Philip Johnson could not have known it then, he would borrow liberally from the Tugendhat House in conception and execution some twenty years later, but he knew on the spot that what he saw was important. As he wrote enthusiastically to Hitchcock, "[It] is like the Parthenon." He quickly acknowledged its subtlety, too, and perhaps even the shock of the new. "One cannot see anything from pictures," he warned. "It is a three-dimensional thing which simply can't be seen in two.

"It is without question the best looking house in the world."[32]

CHAPTER 5

An Invitation Issued

At the beginning of one of our conversations here at the Museum, Mr. Wright announced, "I am a very difficult man." We agree, but we still believe him to be the greatest living architect.
—Alfred Barr

I.

1931 . . . 424 East Fifty-Second Street . . . Miës's American Friend

THE METAPHORICAL SNOWBALL that became an architectural avalanche can be said to have begun to roll on a wintry day in 1931. On January 17, Philip Johnson convened a luncheon in a setting that established the precise tone the host wanted for the small gathering.

On his return to New York the previous fall, Johnson checked into the Biltmore Hotel. During his week aboard ship crossing the Atlantic, he had grown more certain than ever that he would not be content with merely *seeing* the new designs he admired; he wished to *live* the new mode. Though his sense of intellectual independence grew day by day, he had yet to throw off the apron strings that bound him to Louise Johnson, and Daisy Barr remembered him regularly phoning his psychiatrist for consults. He would consult his mother before hiring Miës van der Rohe to renovate his first permanent residence in Manhattan, an apartment at 424 East Fifty-Second Street.

Miës's frequent codesigner (and mistress), Lilly Reich, arrived to help execute the commission, and Johnson's friend from his first German travels, Jan Ruhtenberg, also crossed the Atlantic to New York to install bookshelves and cabinetry designed specifically for the apartment.[1] In this newly completed space a subset of MoMA men met to discuss the germination of "an Architectural Show."[2]

Among those who knocked on Johnson's door that January noon hour were Alfred Barr and museum trustee Stephen Clark, a prominent collector and moneyed grandson of the founder of the Singer Sewing Machine Company. Together with secretary Alan Blackburn, the three central figures settled into chairs that bore the MR imprint. Johnson had opened his wallet while abroad, and though he failed in his attempt to purchase original drawings by Le Corbusier, he had returned home with furniture designed by Miës van der Rohe, including a chaise longue, along with a painting by Piet Mondrian. As in the Tugendhat House, a rectangular rug defined the perimeter of the seating area where the discussion took place, and over the men's shoulders, Johnson's baby grand piano

Philip Johnson's apartment, as designed by Miës and decorated with MR furniture
(MoMA/Licensed by SCALA/Art Resource, NY)

staked its claim to an adjacent part of the main room. Johnson's "show apartment," as he termed it, was the Tugendhat House writ in miniature.

Alfred Barr hadn't traveled far to make the meeting: Johnson's friend resided in the same building. As a minister's son turned museum director and a polyglot European expatriate, the Barrs possessed limited funds, so their downstairs digs were less impressive than Johnson's. Since the Barrs' starter apartment featured an entertainment space furnished with two well-used bridge tables and four folding chairs, they often took advantage of the comforts on offer at Johnson's, where service was provided by Johnson's German butler.[3] Daisy found it amusing when Rudolph would announce in his not-quite-vernacular English, "Dinner can be served."[4]

In the weeks before the January meeting, Barr and Johnson maintained their incessant talk of architecture, with Henry-Russell Hitchcock regularly joining the conversation, traveling to town from his teaching job at Wesleyan University in Middletown, Connecticut. Barr directed the discussion. Since he hadn't been satisfied with the rubric—*Modern Architecture*—with which Russell had titled his 1929 book, he encouraged Hitchcock to take a more polemical approach.[5]

Barr's reading of the last decade's architecture was pointed. Over that period, he believed, "a number of progressive architects have converged to form a genuinely new style which is rapidly spreading through the world." Barr perceived a great wave of change, one with large historic precedents. The new style, he would soon write, "is as fundamentally original as the Greek or Byzantine or Gothic."[6]

The young men's talk was smart and the evenings convivial, although the assembled intimates couldn't agree on everything. Hitchcock admitted that Miës's interiors "just aren't my dish of tea," while Johnson insisted confidently, "For me it was it."[7] Mrs. Barr had been the first to recognize what the talk really signified. "[They] spoke incessantly about what architecture should be," she remembered much later. "They wanted to turn the tide."[8]

The plan that precipitated the January 1931 lunch had an inevitable shape. Alfred Barr's museum would be the venue where the new architecture could be presented to the public, and Barr would act the dramaturge. Henry-Russell Hitchcock's writings brought the necessary intellectual rigor, so he was to codify the emerging European architecture, which thus far consisted of a finite number of buildings, most of which the three men had visited. "We have a tremendous advantage over everyone else in that we have seen much more than everybody, and that we have no national bias whatsoever," Johnson observed.[9] As the chief American cognoscenti of the new architecture, Barr, Hitchcock, and Johnson felt confident the time had come to present their new creed to the American public.

Philip Johnson's assignment was to stake their claim to the new territory. Beyond his friendship with Alfo, the twenty-four-year-old Johnson brought no real qualifications. He lacked an academic post like Hitchcock's and held a merely honorary role at the museum as a member of the Junior Advisory Committee. Still, in the eighteen months since he met Barr, Johnson had made himself a persuasive critic of contemporary design. Articles and essays bearing his byline devoted to modern European buildings had begun to appear in the *Arts* and other magazines. His flirtations with book writing, his drafting of a few plans and elevation drawings, and his hiring of Miës and Reich had whetted his appetite for the right role. As he admitted to Alfred Barr, "What I most want to do is to be influential."[10]

Johnson's potent mix of ambition, money, and newfound confidence led to a preliminary, three-page memorandum titled "The Proposed Architecture Exhibition of the Museum of Modern Art," which he had presented to MoMA's president, A. Conger Goodyear, in December.[11] Barr made no secret of his support for the plan to present the "most prominent architects in the world" in his galleries. The document named names, and the nine architects cited included the most essential members of Johnson's personal pantheon (Miës van der Rohe, Walter Gropius, and J. J. P. Oud), as well as the designer that Hitchcock admired most, Le

Corbusier. The museum's trustees, who would insist the Europeans be balanced by Americans, were relieved to see the list also included Frank Lloyd Wright. With this list of contributors, Goodyear had given the exhibition the green light.

When the January discussion convened in Johnson's apartment, even the chairs reinforced the sense of newness. The men settled into steel-and-leather seats that bore no resemblance to traditional upholstered furniture. Rectangular, tufted leather cushions rested on X-shaped chrome frames; these chairs, used in the Tugendhat House, would soon be widely recognized as a hallmark of MR, designed with unmistakable, stylized curvilinear frames.

This, the first meeting of the exhibition subcommittee, had business to do. Prospective donors were the first concern, and Johnson, whom Barr had designated as the exhibition's director, needed letters of introduction to seek money to pay for the show. The committee agreed that one essential missive would be addressed to the head of the Aluminum Company of America, and Johnson was to persuade his father to add his influence, by both joining the subcommittee and contributing generously to the underwriting.[12] Philip left the luncheon with the assignment of creating a prospectus for private circulation to win over potential contributors.

Published two months later as *Built to Live In*, Johnson's essay amounted to a brief for the new architecture. He invoked Joseph Paxton's Crystal Palace as the "first prophecy of the new style ... an amazing structure of iron and glass." In a dozen paragraphs, Johnson then traced the lineage of independent American architects such as H. H. Richardson and "above all Frank Lloyd Wright." He wrote of new buildings, in both North America and Europe, that employed curtain walls, flat roofs, and sheets of glass. "Heavy walls of stone or brick with small windows were formerly a necessity. Now steel posts carry the load, converting the outer wall into a mere curtain. This has made possible walls of glass framed with steel, light walls of metal or tile and, in some cases, no walls at all. Flat roofs have become practical." The argument was a summary of the hundreds of hours of talk among the three-man brain trust, and their conclusion that the disparate efforts of many architects in multiple countries amounted to what Johnson termed the New Style. Johnson's text was accompanied by photographs, including an image of the Bauhaus, a lake house of Le Corbusier, and Wright's memorable Prairie Style Robie House (1909) in Chicago.

The paradigm would not be "a Greek temple made into a bank, a Gothic church [that] became an office tower, or, worst of all, a 'modernistic' hodge-podge of half-hidden construction and fantastic detail" (the latter was a none-too-veiled critique of Art Deco buildings, such as the new Chrysler and Empire State buildings). Instead, Johnson argued, "The modern architect builds to reveal beauty of construction, plan and materials."[13]

Under Barr's supervision, Johnson and Hitchcock proposed to take an inchoate collection of observations about new buildings and, as if they were wildflowers gathered in the fields, arrange them in a single vessel. In practice, mounting such a display to represent the new manner would not be easy—but for reasons none of them anticipated.

II.

West Fifty-Seventh Street . . . Surprising the Staid

SERENDIPITY VISITED PHILIP Johnson along with the ides of March: He soon got to mastermind a whirlwind dress rehearsal for the forthcoming MoMA show.

In celebration of its fiftieth anniversary, New York's staid Architectural League, a membership organization for the city's architects, decided to up-size its annual exhibition of current work. Installed in the Grand Central Palace, a huge hall constructed over the rail lines that served Grand Central Station, the league's exhibition would personify the establishment. As one commentator put it, "Fifty years, and the Architectural

League has become a habit. How accustomed it all seems. Columns and gables, gables and columns, the pictures scattered higgledy-piggledy over the big walls . . . Then upstairs among the booths the man who want[s] to sell an overhead garage door."[14]

The league, bound to a variety of commercial interests, wasn't keen on stylistic shifts. But Johnson leaped at the chance to begin putting new design notions before the public. When he heard league organizers had rejected the work of several architects working in the New Style, he saw an opportunity to stir up a little controversy.

Borrowing the precedent of the French Impressionists, Johnson and Alfred Barr engineered their own, antithetical *salon des refusés*. Called *Rejected Architects*, it would feature young designers at work in the United States. Perhaps the best known of them was Alfred Clauss, who would be represented in *Rejected Architects* by a proposed country-house design for Pinehurst, North Carolina (the client had been Louise Johnson, following her son's recommendation). Through the good offices of Julien Levy, who himself was about to open an art gallery that would specialize in advanced European art, Johnson secured a storefront owned by Levy's father, a New York real estate magnate. The exhibition overlooked Carnegie Hall from the north at 171 West Fifty-Seventh Street.

The small show opened on April 21 for a run of just two weeks, but *Rejected Architects* offered Barr and Johnson a public forum for presenting their ideas. Though no writer was credited, the unmistakable tone of the MoMA men was apparent to knowing readers who skimmed the exhibition's accompanying handbill. The attributes of the New Style were listed: The architects featured in the show relied upon function rather than symmetry, with an emphasis on flexibility, lightness, and simplicity. "Ornament has no place," the pamphlet explained, "since hand-cut ornament is impracticable in an industrial age. The beauty of the style rests in the free composition of volumes and surfaces, the adjustment of such elements as doors and windows, and the perfection of machined surfaces."[15]

Johnson put his native instinct for publicity on display, too. To draw attention to the little exhibition, Johnson paid men wearing sandwich boards to walk the sidewalk in front of the Grand Central Palace, with its colossal Tuscan portico. Passersby were invited to go across town: "See really modern architecture, rejected by the league."

Rejected Architects attracted only modest attendance, but the New York press paid attention. According to the *Times*, "The big exhibition at the Palace would have benefited by the inclusion of the [*Rejected Architects*] designs."[16] The *Brooklyn Eagle* went further, deriding the league's devotion to "irrelevant sentimental sculpture and reliefs, these cornices and false façades."[17] Johnson was so pleased that he went public a few weeks later with a signed article in the magazine *Creative Art*.

As if planting his flag, he made an announcement. The show, he claimed, had given "the International Style what might be called its first formal introduction to this country."[18] The architecture he liked had a new name—the International Style, a coinage of Alfred Barr's—and Johnson gained new confidence in his ability to pull off an exhibition.

III.

Completing the Roster

THE LITTLE PAMPHLET *Built to Live In* helped persuade other museums around the country to install the larger proposed MoMA show in their galleries and to pay for the privilege (among the stops would be the cities of Philadelphia, Cleveland, Chicago, Hartford, Los Angeles, and Cambridge). With other moneys promised by MoMA and its supporters (including Homer Johnson, Abby Rockefeller, and Stephen Clark), Johnson could begin lining up the talent to contribute to the MoMA show.

He wanted to display designs of Ludwig Miës van der Rohe, of course, but Johnson also wanted Miës himself to install the exhibition.

Johnson had persuaded Homer and Louise Johnson to commission J. J. P. Oud to design a country house for them with an eye to displaying a model in the MoMA galleries. Since his original pitch had included a section devoted to industrial housing, Johnson needed a tour guide in that sphere, where his own knowledge was spotty. He had written to Lewis Mumford, who agreed to write an essay for the catalog.

As the *Rejected Architects* show had come together, Johnson had gone back to Mumford, asking him to write something else: namely, a letter of introduction. The architectural novice Johnson did not know Frank Lloyd Wright, despite having cast him as a Promethean figure, a man whose earlier innovations had inspired the Europeans. Johnson had promised the MoMA trustees he could deliver Wright, and knowing that Mumford was among the notably few contemporary writers who praised Wright in print, Johnson enlisted his aid. A willing Mumford soon entrusted to the U.S. mail a letter that traveled from his Long Island City home to the Master of Taliesin.

"The museum of Modern art is going to hold an Architectural Show & Philip Johnson, the young man who is organizing it, would like you to be adequately represented in it. He is . . . still very young," wrote Mumford, "but I think it would be worth while to give him your attention."[19]

Johnson followed Mumford's letter with his own, one dispatched, rather inauspiciously, on April Fools' Day. Johnson made his purpose clear, explaining that the committee had in mind that Wright's work be represented by a model.[20]

Wright's reply was prompt but coy. He explained that many drawings, 450 photographs, and half a dozen models of his work were committed elsewhere for a summer tour. "Six European Governments have invited the exhibition," he bragged, "and undertaken all expense of transport and showing in the principal cities of Europe."[21]

But Wright also issued an invitation—the first of many—for Johnson to come to Taliesin. "There may be something I can do," Wright wrote, "and I should like to meet whether or no—." That was Wright's way: He preferred to take the measure of people in person and, preferably, on his own terms and in his own place, where he could show off his work.

Even before receiving Wright's less than wholehearted response, Johnson and Hitchcock harbored strong reservations about Wright. Johnson had said explicitly to Mumford, "[Wright] has nothing to say today to the International Group."[22] Johnson's infatuation with the Europeans blinded him to the American, and like so many others, he thought Wright long past his prime. Johnson also disliked Wright's fondness for applied decoration, his Sullivan-esque friezes and art-glass windows.

Johnson, along with the New Style architects he most admired, subscribed to the doctrine enunciated by a grumpy Austrian Marxist architect named Adolf Loos in his 1908 essay, "Ornament und Verbrechen" (Ornament and Crime). As if Loos's title didn't make the point, the text did: "The evolution of culture is synonymous with the removal of ornament from utilitarian objects." In gaining his recent architectural education, Johnson took as received wisdom that ornament was old-fashioned, whether the decorations were classical details (triglyphs, ogee moldings, columns, and pilasters); the sort of Art Deco elaborations that adorned the just-completed Empire State Building; or Wright's most recent mode of so-called textile blocks, which he had employed in the several Los Angeles homes he designed in the early 1920s.

As for Wright, he instinctively distrusted Johnson and the new "New York boys." Partly that was his nature: His ego was such that he thought everyone's talent paled beside his own. He was also wary of anyone, whether critic, newspaperman, or architect, whom he suspected of being less than entirely enthusiastic about his work, and Henry-Russell Hitchcock fell into that category.

True, Hitchcock had in 1928 described Wright as "perhaps the greatest American [architect] of the first quarter of the twentieth century" in the pages of *Cahiers d'Arts*.[23] Having praised Wright's early career, however, Hitchcock had looked to bury him in the same brief essay (as well as in his

1929 book, *Modern Architecture: Romanticism and Reintegration*), demoting Wright to the role of "forerunner" and "old romantic."[24] Predictably, such generalizations raised Wright's ire, prompting him to label Hitchcock, in a letter to Mumford, a "fool."[25]

Upon learning of Johnson's interest, Wright had written back not only to Johnson but to Mumford: "Johnson is evidently a feature of the little group Hitchcock is pushing . . . [and it's] not a very talented group . . . They are seeking to start a narrow movement and inasmuch as they have no choice but to all work and think alike . . . they may succeed with other natural born emulators." Wright labeled them "hard-charging propagandists."[26]

Whatever his doubts about Johnson's and Hitchcock's motives, however, a painful new reminder of how some people regarded him had appeared in December, when an article in the widely popular *Vanity Fair* dismissed him anew. "[Wright] is the one architect who is better known than his buildings," announced John Cushman Fistere, a young critic destined to edit the *Ladies' Home Journal* in the years to come. Not satisfied with his clever turn of phrase, Fistere diminished Wright further, terming him "an aging individualist" and, compounding the insult, called Raymond Hood, a man whose work Wright disliked, the better architect.[27] In the face of such dismissals, Wright knew full well he could benefit from some favorable propaganda, whatever its source.

The old warrior also intuited, as he told Mumford, "Some interesting battles are ahead of us.—I look forward with pleasure."[28] Wright would never shy away from a scrap.

IV.
May 1931 . . . Taliesin . . . Wooing Wright

THOUGH HE TRAVELED to the Midwest in the spring of 1931, Johnson failed to fit a visit to Taliesin into his schedule. He made his excuses to Wright, explaining that he hadn't realized how far Spring Green was from Chicago. But Wright also understood the underlying message: He just wasn't Philip's highest priority. Though Johnson's high flattery was pleasant enough to hear ("[a] show without you would be like Hamlet without the Prince of Denmark"), it didn't fool Wright.[29]

Writing in May, Johnson framed a specific request, asking for an original design of a country house. Thinking a bit more flattery might not be out of place, Johnson added, "I cannot but feel that your tremendous contribution to modern house planning cannot be over emphasized."[30]

Two weeks later, a confident Philip Johnson sailed for Europe, leaving his secretary to dispatch requests for photographs, biographical information, and a list of built works from Wright and the other American architects. Curators Johnson and Hitchcock, together with Alfred Barr, were off to make pitches in person to the European participants. They thought the American end of things was in hand. Wright had written to say a model was in the works, though the exact nature of the model—*Was it to be a country house? New or old?*—remained unspecified.

Neither Wright nor Johnson knew then that the months to come would see sparks fly, as for the first time they assumed the roles of twentieth-century architecture's flint and steel.

CHAPTER 6

Wright vs. Johnson

I am anything but a calendar.
—*Frank Lloyd Wright*

1931–32 . . . Lining Up the Architects

M R. WRIGHT—JOHNSON addressed the man with his honorific as most everyone did—did things in his own time. Johnson's other contributors seemed to grasp the significance of deadlines, but Exhibition Director Philip Johnson had trouble extracting so much as a photograph from Frank Lloyd Wright.

Johnson's summer abroad had begun with a meeting in the Hague with J. J. P. Oud, whose featured design in the show would be a model of the proposed Homer and Louise Johnson home in Pinehurst, North Carolina, a vacation house (never to be built) with a plan that included a swimming pool and tennis court, along with a dramatic elevated sunroom with the footprint of a tennis racket. When Johnson moved on to Germany, he met with Walter Gropius, where they agreed that a model of the Bauhaus headquarters in Dessau suited the MoMA show. Meanwhile Hitchcock visited Le Corbusier to commission a model of his Villa Savoye, a just-completed house in Poissy-sur-Seine. Built on a square plan with its main living space on the second level, which was cantilevered over supporting piers, the Villa Savoye shared with the Tugendhat House a grid of steel supports that meant the outer walls were not load bearing. On the roof terrace, the cylindrical walls of a solarium resembled a great steamship stack. Le Corbusier's design, a stark geometric exercise, seemed to embody his notion of a "machine for living."

With models in the works by masters Corbu, Gropius, and Oud, Johnson could claim excellent progress on three key fronts.

The arrival of Johnson, Barr, and Hitchcock in Berlin would be remembered by Miës as an "invasion." The Americans hoped Miës could be persuaded to design a house specifically for the exhibition, but after their visit to his atelier, Miës proved reluctant, ignoring a series of promptings from Johnson. Eventually, Alfred Barr proposed a solution. "Why not have him do the Brno house," he wrote to Johnson, "since it is the largest and most luxurious private house in the style?"[1] All parties soon agreed to the choice of the Tugendhat House, inspiring Johnson to travel to Czechoslovakia for a repeat visit. By August 15, he cabled home, his sense of relief easily read between the lines: MODELS STARTED ENLARGE-MENTS ALMOST DONE . . . FEEL WORK IS ALMOST DONE.[2]

Four months later, in December 1931, Frank Lloyd Wright would put Johnson's jaunty confidence to the test.

———

DURING THE SUMMER, Wright's commitment to the show had taken physical form when two large crates, sent at his expense, arrived in New York, packed with drawings and photographs. Always keen to be the center of attention, Wright had soon been unhappy to learn that, aside from a model, only half a dozen poster-size photographs would represent his large body of work.

He refused to grasp that he was merely a contributor to a group show, despite having seen the prospectus *Built to Live In*, which included images of buildings by the Europeans Gropius, Miës, and Oud, along with the work of a number of architects working in the United States, some American-born and others émigrés. Perhaps Wright persuaded himself to contribute because he expected that his stature as the best-known among them would guarantee his work would overshadow the Europeans, who were little known to the American public. Whatever Wright's thinking, Johnson had reason to worry when, months later, as the trees lost their leaves, no freight carrier delivered a model from Taliesin.

Wright had gone off on a junket to Rio de Janeiro to judge a competition, but his secretary, Karl Jensen, wrote in November to assure Johnson that two models, one for a theater, another for a house, neared completion. When Wright was the only contributor who had failed to deliver his model by the official deadline of December 1, the exasperated Johnson wrote a firm letter. He expressed his preference for the house rather than the theater, adding, "The model absolutely *must* leave Taliesin *before* December 30th."[3]

It didn't, though the New Year brought another promise. This time Johnson learned that *three* models were being readied. One model was of the previously mentioned theater, the second a house identified (for the first time) as House on the Mesa, and the last a gas station.[4]

An anxious Johnson faced a catalog deadline for which he needed a photograph of the Wright project. The exhibition schedule looked impossibly tight, with the opening of the show barely two weeks away. But Johnson could do little but wait and worry. When no photograph arrived for the January 18 press date, he wired Wright, demanding that photographs and plans of the House on the Mesa be sent by express.

Wright's response—a fiery telegram—made matters unthinkably worse: "My way has been too long and too lonely to make a belated bow to my people as a modern architect." He explicitly disowned two other architects in the show, Raymond Hood and his former protégé Richard Neutra, dismissing them as "a self-advertising amateur and high-powered salesman." Then he dropped the bombshell: "No bitterness and sorry but kindly and finally drop me out of your promotion."[5]

A stunned Johnson realized that Wright was withdrawing from the show.

THE LETTER THAT followed—addressed "My Dear Philip" and signed "Sincerely yours, Frank Lloyd Wright"—rewards a close reading. Perhaps more than any other missive of the many that Wright and Johnson exchanged over the nearly three decades of their association, the communication of January 19, 1932, consisting of some 650 words, unilaterally set the terms of their acquaintanceship.

Wright began by admitting to being "an uncompromising egotist."[6]

Then—and later—Johnson could hardly disagree. Even with Johnson in a position of power (he was, after all, the exhibition director), Wright employed his one piece of leverage, his architectural work. He would be stepping aside, he said, letting "the procession go by with its band-wagon."

Next he disclaimed responsibility for the problem, placing blame on Johnson, whom he accused of not making clear the character of the exhibition at the start. We can only imagine Johnson's response, but surely—expletives deleted—he thought of the prospectus, shown to Wright at the start and from which the plan had deviated little. But Wright was refusing to see any missteps as his.

Moving on, the self-proclaimed visionary asserted himself: "I find myself a man without a country, architecturally speaking, at the present time. If I keep on working another five years, I shall be at home again, I feel sure."

Did Johnson scoff? Likely he did, given his belief that the sun was setting on Wright's career. However, Wright's unlikely prediction would prove true. By 1938, just six years later, Wright would be on the cover of *Time* magazine, together with a house he built in a Pennsylvania waterfall. In a way he had never before been, he would be "at home again," this time at the very top of not only the architectural world but as a genuine celebrity well beyond the usual boundaries for an architect.

Moving to the circumstances at hand, Wright's letter of January 19, 1932, got personal: "I see too much at stake for me to countenance a hand-picked group of men in various stages of eclecticism by riding around the country with them."

Hitchcock and Johnson himself were the subject of the next onslaught: "Propaganda is a vice in our country. High power salesmanship is a curse. I can at least mind my own business . . . and not compete or consort with what are to me disreputable examples of disreputable methods that will get our future architecture nothing but an 'international style.'"

That new style, he observed, was a mere "cut paper style at that," one destined to fade.

Wright's letter was a withering dismissal of Johnson and the very idea of the exhibition. Wright even added an assertion of his own rectitude, explaining that to "join your procession" would be to "belie my own principles both of architecture and conduct . . . I shall at least not have sold out!"

Johnson read Wright's rhetorical tour de force, with its a mix of subterfuge, disdain, exaggeration, and self-justification. Until that moment, Johnson had imagined he was on the verge of a transformative moment in his personal status and for that of architecture in the public realm; upon absorbing Wright's words, Johnson's sense must have been one of free fall. He was a week from taking charge of MoMA's freshly emptied galleries to install an exhibition that was to be unlike any other ever mounted. Now, it seemed, he would have to do it without Wright, and despite his charge from the trustees, the show would lack a "forerunner." A strong west wind from central Wisconsin looked to be on the verge of scattering Johnson's ambitions like a house of cards.

But Wright hadn't quite finished. He added as a closing paragraph what must be read as a disingenuous invitation: "Believe me, Philip, I am sorry. Give my best to Russell Hitchcock and I expect to see you both here at Taliesin early next summer—with your wives. If you haven't got them now you will have them by then?"

With a final homophobic taunt—it was no secret that Hitchcock shared Johnson's sexual orientation—Wright put the template in place for architecture's odd couple. Like a dog and a cat forced to share the same home, Wright and Johnson would thereafter circle each other, looking for ways to coexist.

CHAPTER 7

The Show Must Go On

Architecture is always a set of actual monuments, not a vague corpus of theory.
—Philip Johnson and Henry-Russell Hitchcock

I.

The Museum of Modern Art . . . Picking Up the Pieces

FORTUNATELY FOR A thunderstruck Philip Johnson, Lewis Mumford brokered a temporary peace. Having received a carbon copy of Wright's letter to Johnson, along with a covering note addressed to Mumford in which Wright railed at length against the inclusion of Neutra and Hood, Mumford telegrammed the architect on January 21:

> YOUR ABSENCE FROM MODERN MUSEUMS ARCHITECTURE SHOW WOULD BE CALAMITY[.] PLEASE RECONSIDER YOUR REFUSAL[.] I HAVE NO CONCERN WHATEVER ON BEHALF OF MUSEUM BUT AM INTERESTED IN YOUR OWN PLACE AND INFLUENCE STOP WE NEED YOU AND CANNOT DO WITHOUT YOU . . .
>
> AFFECTIONATELY
>
> LEWIS

The same day, Wright replied. He wired Mumford: ALL RIGHT LEWIS YOUR SINCERE FRIENDSHIP TRUSTED I WILL STAY IN THE NEWYORK SHOW.

Having telegrammed Johnson of his change of mind, Wright's "boys" crated and shipped the model.

When it arrived in New York a few days later, an ebullient Johnson acknowledged its arrival: MUCH EXCITEMENT OVER THE HOUSE ON THE MESA[.] A MOST MAGNIFICENT PROJECT[.] I HOPE YOU WILL BE ABLE TO BUILD IT.[1]

The previous exhibition at MoMA had closed the week before, so Johnson had a manic four days to complete the installation of *Modern Architecture: International Exhibition* in the museum's five galleries. With a staff of one (he donated his time and paid the salary of his secretary, a recent Wellesley graduate named Ernestine Fantl), Johnson played the roles of registrar, managing the flow of models and photographs; teamster, unpacking crates; and designer, laying out the show and hanging photographs (from Germany, Miës had declined Johnson's request to design the show). Johnson even drew floor plans to accompany the images.

Alfred Barr contributed, too, and the installation of the photographs in what Johnson described as "a frieze around the rooms" bore a resemblance to Barr's mode of installing paintings. Barr disliked the traditional "skying" of paintings, in which pictures were hung one above the other; instead, he hung all of them at eye level.[2] The show was installed by the evening of the private preview, but the strain on Johnson took a heavy toll. Having worked himself to exhaustion, Johnson was not among those dressed in white tie on February 9. On the verge of collapse, he checked himself into an East Side clinic where he recuperated for several nights.[3]

II.

Modern Architecture: International Exhibition . . . *The Installation*

PHILIP JOHNSON HAD taken on a difficult task. Architecture simply doesn't travel well; unlike symphonies, novels, and paintings—those are movable experiences—buildings, being site-specific, cannot be transmitted from one city or continent to another. Thus, Johnson's goal of capturing the experience of an entirely new manner of architecture within the walls of a museum was no small assignment.

Modern Architecture: International Exhibition would be the last show to open in the museum's first home, since the Museum of Modern Art was moving to larger quarters on Fifty-Third Street. But for the purposes of Philip Johnson, wearing his curator hat, the Heckscher Building, located on the southwest corner of Fifth Avenue and Fifty-Seventh Street, was no particular asset. Built in 1921 with French Renaissance detailing, it rose to a tower topped by a copper pyramidal roof with a rooster weather vane at its peak. Handsome though it was, the twenty-five-story office tower had nothing in common with the stripped-down, functional aesthetic Johnson wanted to communicate.

Halfway to the top, MoMA's quarters occupied roughly half of the twelfth floor. After the fledgling museum had gained the lease to some four thousand square feet of office space in 1929, Barr had overseen a renovation, including the removal of pilasters and other architectural detailing. Chamfered walling had been added to the corners of the four galleries to better display paintings. Beige monk's cloth lined the walls, making the space a tabula rasa for art and, between February 9 and March 23, 1932, for architecture.

Johnson had the galleries plus a smaller entrance room in which to make the case for the International Style. Museum visitors that February encountered in the first room a model of a housing project, the work of George Howe and William Lescaze, the designers of the Philadelphia Saving Fund Society Building (an accompanying picture hung nearby of the PSFS Building, the first skyscraper in the International Style). Gropius's Bauhaus model dominated the room, and a pair of flanking galleries featured the show's housing section and a variety of images of buildings from around the world that Johnson and Hitchcock had identified as being representative of the International Style.

The last and largest gallery, which measured roughly fifteen feet by forty, climaxed the show, containing as it did four grand villas, each with servants' quarters. These were Oud's Pinehurst House, Le Corbusier's Villa Savoye, the Tugendhat House of Ludwig Miës van der Rohe, and Wright's House on the Mesa. Here, as in the other galleries, the walls were hung with photographic images, their bottoms aligned at waist height.

In his foreword to the exhibition catalog, Alfred Barr summed up the principles of the International Style as he and his colleagues conceived them.[4] The modern architect, Barr explained, could no longer regard a building "as a structure of brick or masonry . . . resting heavily upon the earth." Instead, the architect must think "in terms of *volume*—of space enclosed by planes or surfaces—as opposed to *mass* and solidity."

The modern architect, Barr continued, should be guided by the principles of *regularity* and *flexibility*. Symmetry, Barr warned, though a notion essential to the Classical and Renaissance architect, had become an "arbitrary convention." He proposed its place be taken by the skilled use of vertical or horizontal repetition (for example, flat roofs or windows in ribbons or stacks) and by a utilitarian asymmetry that reflected the usage of the building. Finally, ornament, like symmetry, was no longer required, its place taken by "fineness of proportions" and "technical perfection."

In sum, Barr's prescription for the contemporary architect was to think in terms of *volume* not mass; to forget *ornament* and *symmetry*; and, instead, to let *regularity*, *flexibility*, *proportion*, and *perfection* guide his or her design. And if his words seemed dogmatic, Barr advised the museum visitor to take a close look at the models and photographs on display.

Johnson's installation had a carefully composed uniformity. The photographs, most of which were about three feet high, were generously spaced for individual viewing, and the models, on tabletops, rested a suitable distance from the walls to allow inspection from all sides. A respectable thirty-three thousand people ascended the elevator at the Heckscher Building to view *Modern Architecture* during its six-week run, but the head count broke no records. To its organizers' disappointment, the show seemed unlikely to initiate a great and immediate wave of change.

The critical reception was muted. One commentator in the *Nation* acknowledged and, after a fashion, endorsed the exhibition's emphasis on domestic architecture. "We can be sure that houses more or less like these are what the man about town will build . . . New forms appeal to the aristocrat of modern taste."[5] Lewis Mumford, now ensconced at the *New Yorker* as its architecture columnist, offered a testimonial (after admitting a minor association with the exhibition). The exhibition "should not be missed," Mumford wrote, since "the best buildings in New York at the moment are the models and photographs that Mr. Philip Johnson has arranged with such clarity and intelligence."[6] Predictably, Beaux Arts architects were less keen; as William Adams Delano asked at a symposium conducted at MoMA, "After centuries of struggle to evolve a culture worthy of his position in the animal kingdom, is this to be man's end? No better, no worse than the insects, ants and caterpillars."[7]

Johnson summed up the chatter in a letter to J. J. P. Oud that he dispatched shortly before the show was crated for shipment to its next venue, the Philadelphia Museum of Art. "I may safely say that there was not one really critical review of the Exhibition. For the most part the critics make excerpts from the catalogue, or if they are constitutionally opposed to modern architecture, they merely remark that the Exhibition displeases them."[8]

For New Yorkers in 1932, *Modern Architecture: International Exhibition* amounted to little more than a curiosity. The essential strangeness of flat-roofed houses of steel and glass—and the houses did get pride of place in the show, as well as most of the coverage—left some people feeling disoriented, even a bit worried. The *New York Sun* reported that the Tugendhat House, in particular, raised "the alarm of the older ladies" visiting the show. "The Czechoslovakian house . . . by Van der Rohe, has living rooms entirely exposed through transparent glass, and the ladies looking at it drew their wraps about them shiveringly, and everywhere was heard the old witticism about the privacy of the goldfish uttered in something that seemed like nervous glee."⁹ For a public accustomed to thinking of *home* as a solid box, as a personal expression of privacy and security, the prospect of living in a glass house seemed strange indeed.

————

EVER THE CLASS bad boy, Frank Lloyd Wright had executed Johnson's assignment in his own way. Though he designed his submission specifically for the *International Exhibition*, Wright resisted the label; rather than *international*, he believed, "the house itself . . . might truthfully be called *twentieth-century style*."¹⁰

His inspiration flowed first, as it always did, from the proposed site. His House on the Mesa was to be native to its setting, which was several flat, elevated acres with a panoramic vista of the Rocky Mountains. In the late 1920s, he had made a series of automobile trips to Arizona, where several of his projects were either in the works or in the planning stage. En route he observed terrain that appealed to him—again, he prided himself on his "fresh eye," and perhaps more than anything else, varied landscapes stimulated his imagination. When asked to submit a design to Johnson's MoMA show, Wright recalled his travels through portions of Colorado, which offered stunning contrasts to the Midwest.

A visit he had made to a site on a trip to Denver to deliver a lecture, in December 1930, came to mind. Wright and his wife, Olgivanna, had been welcomed by a wealthy businessman named George Cranmer to his twenty-two-room home, constructed on the highest point in the city's fashionable Hilltop neighborhood. To Wright's eye, the Renaissance-revival-style house looked better suited to the Apennines than a mesa in central Colorado, but its parklike setting, swimming pool, stables, and gardens were still in his mind when he received Johnson's invitation a few months later to contribute to the MoMA exhibition.

The model of the House on the Mesa that arrived belatedly in New York, in February 1932, retained the horizontal quality for which Wright was celebrated. But this house was not a Prairie Style home. Intending to reflect the "sweep of the mesa," he designed an expansive set of structures that stretched some 360 feet end to end. Wings extended from the main axis of the house to embrace the garden and two water features, as a swimming pool was elevated above a much larger sunken lake nearby. Wright designed a distinct structure for the garage and service quarters; a main block to contain the bedrooms; and a wing with billiard room, living room, and roof terrace. An open "sun-loggia" ran the length of the house, the backbone of the F-shaped plan.

Wright's structural design called for use of the concrete-block system he had developed in 1923 ("textile block construction," he called it), employing patterned cast blocks, stiffened with steel reinforcing bars. However, he hadn't been entirely deaf to the Internationalists' conversation, as this new design simplified the look, using more plain blocks and fewer patterned ones, a shift that was symptomatic of other adjustments that Wright incorporated into his design for exhibition at MoMA.

To the careful listener, Wright's lecture at the Denver Art Museum in 1930 hinted at new thinking. "Architecture of the future," he had told his audience, "will mean extensive use of glass, simplification of form, freedom of space, comfort, and utility,"[11] sentiments curiously akin to some of those Barr enumerated in the catalog for *Modern Architecture: International Exhibition*. To the careful observer, Wright's use of cantilevered concrete roof slabs in the design of the House on the Mesa might have been seen as resembling their use in a widely known design by Miës van der Rohe for a country house dating to 1923.

The fenestration was also revealing—though not of immense sheets of plate glass like those used in Miës's Tugendhat House, Wright had designed window walls. His glass walling on the house's upper level, rather like stair risers and treads, stepped up and out, with only the downward-facing horizontal panes opening to permit air flow while the fixed vertical glass would block the strong winds of the exposed site. Cantilevered concrete floated above, suspending the glass screen in space.

Wright accomplished what he had said he would: The House on the Mesa was a "boundless new expression in Architecture, as free, compared with post and lintel, as a winged bird compared to a tortoise, or an aeroplane compared with the truck."[12] Though not a certified International Style house—Wright hadn't eliminated all ornament in favor of sleek, smooth surfaces—the flat-roofed House on the Mesa showed Wright moving the MoMA way.

Even if Johnson and Hitchcock chose not to pay heed to Wright's subtly shifting thinking, the man from Taliesin was certainly listening to the larger international conversation. He had adapted some of the principles the MoMA men cherished, including industrial materials, glass walls, and smooth surfaces.

Wright had decided to come along for the ride: He understood that a house need not be defined by its footprint alone but also by the form it took on rising into space. He was no convert—he was no one's disciple, ever, not even Sullivan's, he insisted ("though pupil, I think I was never his disciple")[13]—but he was looking around thoughtfully, just as the Europeans had given his Wasmuth portfolio serious consideration (Miës: "The work of this great master presented [in circa 1910] an architectural world of unexpected force, clarity of language and disconcerting richness of form").[14] The Europeans had adopted his free-flowing floor plans; and Wright's House on the Mesa was closer to the work of the International Style of the Europeans than Johnson and Hitchcock could (or Wright would) acknowledge.

Certainly Johnson understood that Wright's entire career had been an assault on the traditional view of architecture as plain boxes; as Hitchcock wrote of Wright, he "was the first to conceive of architectural design in terms of planes existing freely in three dimensions rather than in terms of enclosed blocks."[15] With the House on the Mesa he showed signs of moving away from ornament, even a willingness to think in terms of volumes, making the house grow larger as it rose. But Johnson still saw Wright as the outsider, and according to Johnson, the House on the Mesa was "a striking example of Wright's individuality and his skill in adapting a house to its surroundings."[16] Hitchcock concluded it was merely "a striking aesthetic statement of romantic expansiveness."[17] In response, Wright bristled.

III.

Missives from Spring Green . . . Communicating with the Master

INEVITABLY, THE HARSHEST critique of the *International Exhibition* came from within. To the consternation of Johnson, Barr, and Hitchcock—though surely not to their surprise—the man from the Midwest, armed with verbal slings and arrows, clambered out of the Trojan horse they had invited into their midst and attacked.

Wright had good reason to lash out. Two publications accompanied the show. The first to appear was the catalog, published by MoMA and bearing the same name as the exhibition, *Modern Architecture: International Exhibition*. Soon to follow was the independent book that Johnson and Hitchcock had been at work on since the summer of 1930, released as *The International Style Since 1922*. Taken together, the two volumes constituted something of a manifesto, and as the exhibition did, made the case that, having seen architecture's future, the authors had identified it as the International Style.

Crucial to the underlying argument was the placement of Wright in the architectural past, and the *New York Times* and other papers picked up the message. Wright's fears had indeed been realized: Upon viewing him in the context of the Europeans, *Art News* found his work wanting: "After continued contemplation of the new modes, even the work of such moderns as Frank Lloyd Wright begins to look overloaded and fussy."[18]

In his carefully crafted foreword to the catalog, Alfred Barr had set up Wright's demotion. He described Wright as "a passionately independent genius whose career is a history of original discovery and contradiction . . .

[and] his work, complex and abundant, remains a challenge to the classic austerity of the style of his best younger contemporaries." In short, Barr said, Wright was "one of the style's most important sources."[19] As for Johnson and Hitchcock, they didn't even bother to find a place for Wright's work in *The International Style Since 1922*; he and his designs were omitted altogether.

Wright decided that he had been no more than a tool in the hands of the MoMA men, that his status in their exhibition was that of an antique and an outlier. He said as much to Philip Johnson: "I no longer count . . . because I am historical . . . [so] I insist that every trace of my name in connection with your promotion be removed from the show when the show at the Museum of Modern Art closes."[20] Since the exhibition was booked to travel to fourteen more American cities where Wright was expected to be a significant draw, Johnson once again felt himself on the brink of disaster.

A new scramble to placate Wright ensued and, again, he relented. This time Johnson arranged for publication of a Wright essay in the magazine *Shelter*, in which Johnson had recently invested. Even when Wright's article appeared (titled "Of Thee I Sing," it was an unbridled attack on European Modernism), he had further complaints. "[My article] appears with objectionable editorial comment under an objectionable pirated photograph of the damaged model of the 'House on the Mesa' taken from an objectionable angle that best serves your objectionable propaganda."[21] Furthermore, Wright was irked that an editor's note preceding "Of Thee I Sing" condescendingly described it as a "clarification."

Wright vented his anger again, offering his most picturesque outburst to date. He lambasted the entire MoMA team, including the other architects in the show, but placed the biggest blame squarely on Johnson. "In short, Philip my King, a strange undignified crowd you are, all pissing through the same quill or pissing on each other. I am heartily ashamed to be caught with my flap open in the circumstances."

Wright addressed the letter to Johnson, but Hitchcock drafted his reply first, penning it in the heat of the moment. He expressed his shock

man's tenacity, his flexibility, his ability to do a big, brave thing—and Johnson had passed. Not long after his third threatened withdrawal from the show, Wright extended an invitation. "Of course, you will be welcome at Taliesin at any time," he wrote to Johnson. "Any feeling I have in this whole matter is directly personal to no one."[25]

Johnson took Wright at his word, agreeing to visit in July. The timing meant that he arrived shortly after Wright's first viewing of the *International Exhibition.*

Wright's finances had precluded a trip to New York in February, and having missed the first edition of the *International Exhibition* at MoMA, he went instead to Chicago's Sears, Roebuck building in June (it would be one of the show's two nonmuseum stops, the other in Los Angeles, at luxury department store Bullocks Wilshire). Despite its evident popularity—Wright described having to elbow his way through a "jammed crowd"—the exhibition itself, predictably enough, failed to win him over. Attempting as usual to offer the last, best bon mot, he dismissed what he saw in Chicago as "the exhibit of Phil. Johnson's traveling 'Punch and Judy' for European modernism."[26]

Late in June, Johnson and Hitchcock traveled to Chicago to conduct research for another architectural show at MoMA (*Early Modern Architecture: Chicago 1870–1910*, which would open the following January, posed the argument that Chicago, not New York, was the birthplace of the skyscraper). Despite the ebb and flow of hard words during the preceding months, the two Easterners took a break from their research into the three architects that they had cast as their protagonists for the Chicago exhibition (H. H. Richardson, Louis Sullivan, and Wright). Heading northwest, they drove the two hundred miles to the verdant Helena Valley in Wisconsin to spend a long July weekend.

They sought the sprawling domicile that sat just shy of the hilltop. Johnson first spied Wright's characteristic "great sheltering roof," as he put it. Like the wings of an unimaginably large eagle, the low-pitched hips seemed to float at the horizon line on the ridge. As the visitors approached, however, another aspect of the house's character grew more apparent.

As if Frank Lloyd Wright's once-manorial house hadn't been sufficiently ravaged by two disastrous fires, the whims of its owner were once again being visited upon the place: Wherever he lived, Wright was never content to stop changing things. Taliesin most definitely remained a work in progress, and Johnson would recall Wright's home on this visit as a construction site with "no phone . . . two-by-fours under all the cantilevers, and plumbing [that] didn't work."[27]

Once inside, Johnson, to his surprise, warmed to what he saw. "The living room at Taliesin East felt very intimate," Johnson observed, despite its large size and miscellany of contents, which ranged from drafting tables and chairs to a great hearth. "The room just kept growing with the people," Johnson remembered, "and it was intimate the whole time."

Unexpectedly impressed by what he saw, Johnson asked Wright directly, "How in hell did you do this particular space?"

Wright offered no prescription. "He didn't have the foggiest notion," Johnson remembered. "It just came naturally, like Mozart's music to Mozart."

Wright offered only, "I do it the way a cow shits."[28]

The time at Taliesin helped foster a Wright-Johnson-Hitchcock rapprochement. Although its principal subject would be the emergence of the skyscraper, the Chicago show that opened at MoMA a few months later featured the Winslow House, an early design of Wright's that could be decoded as compressing the base-shaft-capital approach to the skyscraper that Sullivan favored. The Winslow House (1892–93) had been Wright's first independent building. Johnson and Hitchcock in their catalog would call Wright "a *disciple* of Sullivan," a characterization Wright again quickly rejected. The catalog's last entry read, "Leaving the field of commercial building, [Wright] created a new domestic style which was to affect the course of modern architecture profoundly."[29]

The cold shoulder Hitchcock had directed toward Wright had clearly begun to thaw; Mumford noticed it even before Hitchcock himself did, wryly observing to Wright that "the learned Hitchcock . . . has almost become a disciple of yours, much though you might prefer to see him remain on the hostile side of the fence."[30] Mumford's note may have prompted one from Wright a month later, asking Hitchcock obliquely, "We see too little of each other . . . ?"[31]

The three men made an odd trio as they looked out over Wright's acreage. Wright gave Johnson and Hitchcock the tour, and they admired the Hillside Home School (though Johnson also described it as a "total wreck").[32] The somewhat slovenly Hitchcock, who tended to bathe infrequently, his red beard unkempt, wore a pink shirt.[33] The host, Mr. Wright, was the distinguished dandy, wearing a bespoke hat made by a hatter on the Place Vendôme in Paris. And the youthful but confident Johnson dressed in "lavender trousers, white shoes and pale green shirt,"[34] the utterly charming impresario who had proposed the exhibition that had been their field of battle. He had persuaded the board of trustees to proceed, chosen the architects, and installed the show. He had bullied Hitchcock into completing the text of the catalog (Hitchcock's prose could grow convoluted, and Johnson had a lifelong gift for easy, aphoristic speech), and Johnson had edited the manuscript. All the while he had blithely treated Wright like a second-class citizen.

In Spring Green, however, their disagreements seemingly forgotten, Wright treated Johnson and Hitchcock as honored guests. Johnson reported Wright was "unfailingly polite, unfailingly generous," but Johnson thought he knew why.[35] Wright permitted himself to overlook a great deal in those as passionate as he. "What appealed to him about Russell and me," Johnson concluded, "was that we were really interested in the art of architecture."

For Johnson, the show had been a rite of passage. He had told Barr his ambition was to be influential; the *International Exhibition* was a fulfillment of that wish. Johnson wanted people to pay attention.

Architecture was his vehicle, he had realized, eighteen months before as he gorged himself on Modernist buildings. It was the first time, he admitted with delight, that he knew "enough about anything ... to be boring to people."[36] Apparently he liked the sensation because, when Barr gave him the chance, he had taken charge.

His inexperience had suited the circumstances: No procedures were in place, little museum infrastructure, and few expectations. The galleries even lacked guards. "It was just a couple of people getting round a table," Johnson recalled of the exhibition's making. "The 1932 show was done from my bedroom. I just talked to the printer and he came in and grabbed the stuff off my hands and that's the way the catalogue was done. I just traveled and saw the stuff and took it off the architects' tables.

"There was nothing to it."[37]

On the other side, the wrestling match with Johnson and Hitchcock had brought out the best in Wright. In the years that followed, he aimed for new creative heights with a renewed energy, and some of the credit for stimulating him must fall to Johnson. The older man took a philosophical view of his relations with his critics: As Wright had written to Philadelphia Museum of Art director Fiske Kimball several year earlier, another man he regarded as no more sympathetic to the Wright way than the MoMA men, "You are a friendly enemy. They make ultimately the best friends."[38]

On July 2, 1932, Alfred Barr named Johnson chairman of the museum's newly established Department of Architecture. Johnson, the perpetual-motion man, would make exhibitions his mission for more than two years, and a series of shows went up under his aegis, including *Machine Art*, a collection of contemporary machine-made objects that won him admiring reviews in the New York papers ("Our best showman," offered the *New York Sun*, "and probably the world's best").[39] He was regarded as a young man in a hurry—his co-workers recalled him as running, not walking, as he made his way around the museum, with a half dozen more shows to his credit before he suddenly resigned in December 1934, leaving Alfred Barr and art and architecture as abruptly as he had adopted them that afternoon in Wellesley, Massachusetts. He was restless to be influential in other arenas.

Even after Johnson's departure, his view of Wright remained in place at MoMA for a few years; it become standard terminology at the museum in the mid-thirties to reference Wright, together with Sullivan, as "Half-Modern." But Johnson also applied a clever aphorism of his own devising to the man with whom he had established an oddly symbiotic relationship. His words weren't complimentary (nor were they intended to be); Johnson would not utter them publicly for Wright to hear for another twenty years. But his friends in those days recalled hearing his summary judgment.

Wright was, quipped Johnson, "the greatest architect of the nineteenth century."

PART III

Acting Out Their Antagonism

The Banks of Bear Run

My prescription for a modern house: first pick a good site. Pick that one at the most difficult site—pick a site no one wants—but pick one that has features making for character: trees, individuality, a fault of some kind in the realtor mind.
—Frank Lloyd Wright, 1938

I.

1932 and After . . . Wright's Second Coming

A FRESH RECRUIT at MoMA played a key role in Frank Lloyd Wright's resurrection, which climaxed with surprising suddenness in January 1938. In that month, after years of growing irrelevance, Wright's six-year-old prophecy came true, and he ceased to be "a man without a country, architecturally speaking."

Wright was about to disprove once and for all the dismissals of Philip Johnson. He was about to win over Henry-Russell Hitchcock, as the historian gradually became, in effect, a disciple. And a show consisting of twenty photographs would amount to MoMA's belated endorsement of Wright.

John McAndrew, who mounted the display, was the same man who had been Philip Johnson's traveling companion during his 1929 European interlude. Almost a decade later, he would also take some of the images that would be featured in the little exhibition that portrayed one particular house, and that lent the museum's voice to the chorus that praised Wright as the most vibrant force in architecture.

The subject of the show (and much of the talk) would be the unprecedented structure that Wright suspended like an abbreviated bridge over a fast-falling stream in western Pennsylvania.

McAndrew had arrived late at MoMA. As Alfred Barr, Chairman Goodyear, and Mrs. Rockefeller worked to create the museum in August 1929, the New York–born McAndrew stood staring at a van Gogh canvas in a German museum. He was looking over the shoulder of another young American, and once the two strangers dispensed with their "very bad German," they agreed it wasn't a very good van Gogh. In contrast, reported Philip Johnson, the handsome black-haired McAndrew "looked much better than his clothes."[1]

The two young Harvard men found they shared many friends, and more important, a love of architecture. As with Johnson's introduction to Alfred Barr a few months before, their conversation was exhilarating, with Johnson reporting that the two often talked long into the night. A classmate of Hitchcock's in Cambridge, McAndrew was two years older than Johnson and had earned his bachelor's degree at age twenty. Having gone on to complete the three years required for a master's degree from the Graduate School of Architecture at Harvard, he had only his thesis to finish.

That summer the two men teamed up to tour Germany. Johnson's sleek Packard took them to cathedral cities (they visited Worms, Mainz, Darmstadt, and Lorsch in a single day), but for the most part, they followed Barr's Modernist itinerary. "Alfred had told him where to go and what to look at," McAndrew remembered.[2] He accompanied Johnson to Holland and the meeting with J. J. P. Oud. They visited a house fronted entirely by glass; at the time, it was a revelation for both men. They talked vaguely of collaborating on a book, a prospect that Johnson completed in 1932, though by then Johnson had settled on Hitchcock as his writing partner.

During their travels in 1929, the measured McAndrew had offered Johnson a valuable critical equilibrium—as Johnson told his mother,

"[McAndrew is] just as enthusiastic as I, but less prejudiced, less apt to be a fanatic."[3] With his trained architectural eye, Johnson's new friend also brought expertise and knowledge that Johnson simply didn't have. He guided Johnson as he experimented with architectural design, brainstorming a renovation for an existing Johnson family vacation home in North Carolina, executing sketches (McAndrew was a trained draftsman), and borrowing the Dutch palette of pure yellows and blues and reds.

On his return to the United States, McAndrew traveled a quite different path from Johnson, remaining on the periphery of the MoMA crowd. After further travels to Mexico, he found a job in the architectural office of society architect Aymar Embury II, who specialized in country houses and schools in the Beaux Arts mode. When work slowed in Embury's offices during the early years of the Depression, McAndrew signed on to teach where Daisy Barr and Hitchcock had, at Vassar College, offering courses in drafting and in the history of architecture. He also designed a Bauhaus-flavored Modernist library space for the college that was installed within an existing Gothic building, the first specialized art library for undergraduates in the country.[4]

Then he accepted an appointment to Philip Johnson's old job at MoMA. Effective September 1, 1937, he became MoMA's curator of architecture.[5]

John McAndrew soon proved a more malleable Modernist than Johnson, as his first coup as a museum curator involved Wright, his erstwhile friend's old nemesis. The contact came his way courtesy of a Vassar graduate, Aline Bernstein (years later, she added the surname Saarinen upon her marriage to Finnish American architect Eero Saarinen). In fall 1937, Bernstein helped McAndrew gain entrée to her Uncle Edgar's "strange week-end house," which was then nearing completion outside Pittsburgh.

Intrigued by what he had heard, McAndrew posted a letter to the Edgar Kaufmanns, who owned the Pittsburgh department store that bore their name. In response, McAndrew received by return mail a generous invitation from Liliane, wife of Edgar. Explaining that "Bear Run was not in Pittsburgh but out in the country," she invited him to spend a November weekend.[6]

What he saw there led him to assemble the exhibition. Although titled *A New House by Frank Lloyd Wright on Bear Run, Pennsylvania*, the show featured the house that, almost overnight, became world-renowned as Fallingwater. As McAndrew remembered, "I think I was the first person from the outside world to see it."[7]

———

NO GREAT FLURRY of commissions had flowed Wright's way after *Modern Architecture: International Exhibition* opened at MoMA in 1932. As he admitted to various confidants, his financial situation remained tenuous, at best. Wright told one friend, the Viennese-born designer Joseph Urban in New York, "We are desperate here, Joe."[8]

Not only was Wright's drawing board barer than ever, but his files overflowed with unbuilt blueprints. Two canceled projects in particular rankled. For a successful developer named Alexander Chandler, Wright and a staff of fifteen had, in 1928–29, completed working plans for an Arizona resort called San Marcos-in-the-Desert. Although cost estimates had been prepared, the stock market crash on October 29, 1929, ended any likelihood the luxurious hotel would be built.

Another commission, this one for three glass-enclosed apartment buildings in New York City, the St. Mark's Church-in-the-Bouwerie Towers, prompted Wright to devise a highly original structural scheme that mimed the structure of a tree, in which a trunklike central core extended from a subterranean base or "tap-root," its floor plates cantilevered like branches. The *New York Times* published an announcement of the "odd-type buildings" on October 19, 1929, but again, the ensuing financial hard times meant no structure rose on the triangular site in Manhattan's East Village. The failure of Wright's entry at MoMA, his House on the Mesa, to inspire new clients had been yet another disappointment.

Then, in mid-1932, the resourceful Wright launched a new and different venture. Having already established alternate sources of income as a lecturer, writer, and dealer in Japanese prints, the architect decided to reinvent himself as an educator. He and Olgivanna revived a scheme they had first contemplated in 1928 for what they then called the Hillside Home School of the Allied Arts. It had been inspired in part by her experience in the early twenties at the Institute for the Harmonious Development of Man, where G. I. Gurdjieff used dance to enable his followers to reach for a higher level of consciousness. As originally conceived, the Wrights' Hillside School was to feature an art-based curriculum, including painting, sculpture, pottery, glasswork, metalwork, dance, drama, history, and philosophy, with a particular emphasis on architecture.

The 1932 prospectus proffered a new name: the Taliesin Fellowship. For an annual fee of $675 per apprentice (raised the following year to $1,100), the Wrights hoped to attract seventy "workers in the arts" to join an educational experiment with architecture as its focus.[9] "It is knowledge of architecture in [a] broad, organic sense that is essentially not only the salvation of twentieth-century life but," claimed Wright, "... the very basis of our future as a civilization."[10] The Fellowship bore little resemblance to a traditional architecture school, issuing no credits or degrees. The venture was as much a creation of Olgivanna's as it was Wright's, and music, dance, theater, and even spiritualism would be part of the training. The Fellowship also aimed to be self-sufficient, requiring apprentices to work in the fields, barns, kitchen, and laundry.

A school building stood on the Taliesin property, one that Wright himself had designed in 1902 for a progressive school run by his maiden aunts Ellen (Nell) and Jane Lloyd Jones. Though known nationally for its educational philosophy, which sought to integrate the natural world with that of the classroom, the Hillside Home School had been closed by the aging aunts in 1915 after several family setbacks, among them Wright's own social disgrace in Oak Park and the drama surrounding the Taliesin murders. Many of the derelict building's art-glass windows had been broken and its roof leaked, but the school's sandstone walls and oak frame remained sound.

The first project for the new students would be to fix up the Hillside Home School, and with the apprentices' arrival in October 1932, the work began. The former gymnasium became a theater, the Hillside Playhouse, for putting on plays and watching Sunday-evening movies. The former physics lab and art studio would be expanded into a five-thousand-square-foot drafting room. Wright had built his aunts a building that seemed to rise out of the ground, paralleling the horizon, one of his earliest Prairie Style buildings; the new structure and the school it housed both honored that past and served to invigorate its master.

The Taliesin prospectus promised the presence of "six honor men" to help express "the architecture of life, or life as architecture." Wright invited friends to join the team, including Lewis Mumford and Alexander Woollcott. Both demurred. They knew from experience that Wright wanted not so much collaborators as converts, and he had made clear the Fellowship would be his personal fiefdom. Apprenticeship, Wright had written, is "much like it was in feudal times . . . an apprentice then was his master's slave; at Taliesin he is his master's comrade."

Wright often talked of democracy, but clearly he liked the feeling of being surrounded by courtiers. The thirty original apprentices included women as well as men, and all were handed a hammer or a trowel; the drafting pencils and T squares would come later. Physical work was also to be done at Taliesin's primary house, where dormitory spaces were being constructed to the rear of the sprawling Wright home.

Some apprentices remained a year or less, but most stayed for two to four years. A few would call Taliesin their home for much longer, working as draftsmen and, when Wright's practice grew busy again in the late thirties, as clerks-of-the-works on building sites. Yet even some of the short-term visitors would have a lasting impact. One such joined in the autumn of 1934; his name was Edgar Kaufmann jr. (he insisted on the lowercase *j* in abbreviating *junior*).

At age twenty-four, Edgar jr. harbored no architectural ambitions. Though a man of evident intelligence—alert, dark-eyed, his mind intuitive and quick to question—he had chosen not to follow his father to Yale (where the elder Edgar had briefly studied engineering), but spent the academic year 1927–28 in New York learning to draw and paint with a private tutor.[11] Next he enrolled at the Kunstgewerbeschule in Vienna to study industrial design. A three-year apprenticeship in Florence followed, as he worked with the Viennese portraitist, typographer, and designer Victor Hammer. After some months spent learning bookbinding in London, Kaufmann returned to the United States, anxious at being a Jew in Europe as Hitler consolidated power in Germany.[12]

Short, small-boned, and bespectacled, Kaufmann's plan for life remained uncertain. Ought he to pursue a career in art or design? While his father would have welcomed him into the family retailing business in Pittsburgh, Edgar jr. preferred being a "would-be painter" and seemed content living in Manhattan. Then an indirect introduction to Mr. Wright opened a different path.

"I felt disconnected from the thoughts and ways of America after long study in Europe," Kaufmann explained. "A friend recommended Frank Lloyd Wright's *An Autobiography*; reading it, I believed Wright saw what I was missing."[13]

An interview at the Taliesin Fellowship was arranged, and barely three weeks later, on October 15, 1934, Edgar jr. took up residence in Spring Green. He soon confided to his parents, "I continue to get more and more enthusiastic about Wright and Taliesin." His tenure in Wisconsin would last less than six months (the homosexual Kaufmann began to feel unwelcome and out of place), but the Master's impact on the young man was great. As Kaufmann wrote to a friend much later, "My experience as an apprentice at Taliesin under Mr. and Mrs. Wright was the most important event in my life."[14] A filial imprinting occurred, as the young Kaufmann found inspiration in Wright's organic ethos, his passion and vision. Edgar jr. was captivated by what he called "the power of Wright's genius."[15]

When Edgar jr.'s parents arrived to experience for themselves what so enraptured their son, their visit would also have long-term consequences. Much taken with Wright, they soon commissioned the house that would reset the trajectory of twentieth-century architecture.

II.

1934–38 . . . A New Patron

EDGAR JONAS KAUFMANN (1885–1955) was no architectural novice. For twenty years he had maintained a fruitful relationship with Pittsburgh society architect Benno Janssen, who, in 1913, designed a thirteen-story terra-cotta addition to "the Big Store," Kaufmann's flagship at the corner of Fifth and Smithfield. The Kaufmann home in Pittsburgh's prestigious Fox Chapel suburb, called La Tourelle, was a 1925 Janssen design, a steep-roofed Anglo-Norman mansion with eighteen fireplaces, set on twenty-three acres with attendant stables, kennels, and greenhouses. In 1928, Kaufmann tried on another style, hiring Joseph Urban to update his store's interior in the Art Deco manner. Although the commission was never executed, Kaufmann's appetite for architecture remained catholic, his mind open to fresh ideas.

Wright was on the lookout for a new patron. His most reliable client, Darwin Martin, had lost his fortune in the 1929 crash and was in poor health (he would die in December 1935). He had earlier commissioned Wright to build not only a series of family dwellings but also the widely admired Larkin Administration Building in Buffalo, New York (1904–6); it was an office space like no other with its central, six-story skylit hall (the effect of which was, according to Wright, "one great official family at work").[16] Over three decades, Martin had been a reliable source of not only commissions and referrals but much good counsel and even loans (totaling some $70,000, never repaid).

With his Taliesin Fellowship experiment nearing its second birthday,

Wright kept his apprentices busy by alternating days of construction work with drawing time in the studio. But the drafting consisted largely of copying plans of previous Wright buildings. Exactly one new design had risen since the Wall Street crash five years before, a modest house in Minneapolis for a college administrator named Malcolm Willey. When the Willey working drawings had left Taliesin in early 1934, Wright remarked to his head draftsmen that the apprentices in the drafting room would, at least for the moment, be getting "poetry instead of drama."[17]

By the time Edgar and Liliane Kaufmann left Pittsburgh bound for Taliesin in November 1934, Wright and "E.J.," as Wright addressed him, had been in correspondence for several months. The civic-minded Kaufmann, thinking Wright might be a resource in rethinking Pittsburgh's urban character, had written in August, "I would greatly appreciate hearing from you . . . [if] you ever visit Pittsburgh or New York City."[18] Wright had dodged that invitation, pleading the expense of travel in his impoverished state. "There has been no building to speak of these past years," he explained. "Could I do anything for you by correspondence?"[19] But due diligence soon revealed to Wright that his new correspondent wielded real influence in Pittsburgh and, unlike Wright, seemed not to have been hobbled in the least by the Great Depression. On the contrary, when a sometime Taliesin secretary visited Kaufmann, he reported back that the city had substantial federal monies to spend on municipal projects, and that Kaufmann himself wished to build a planetarium in a small park near the store, which he then planned to give the city.[20] When Wright learned a few days later that Kaufmann also wanted a design for his executive office, it was clear that E.J. might just be the sort of serial client and savvy businessman Wright's portfolio lacked. Wright sent him a book about his work and an invitation.

"Your son Edgar is a fine chap," he told Kaufmann, with the admiring Edgar jr. in residence in Spring Green. "I hope you and Mrs. Kaufmann can come here and visit us someday."[21] The auspices for a meeting were in place.

On November 18, Liliane and E.J. turned into the drive at Taliesin. From the start, Wright and E.J. liked each other; their rapport was evident even to the apprentices. Unlike his soft-spoken son, E.J. was outgoing, a sociable man comfortable in conversation. He conveyed the vigor of an outdoorsman, a man of athletic build with a fencing scar on his cheek.

At Wright's request, Kaufmann addressed the assembled Fellowship members, attired as usual for Sunday dinner in evening dress. His host's fulsome report of the talk, printed later in the little community's newsletter, *At Taliesin*, identified the Kaufmanns as the "merchant prince and princess of Pittsburgh." Wright flattered Kaufmann, explaining that he was to be credited with demonstrating that "the romance has not dropped out of merchandising just because Marco Polo is gone."[22] Seated at high table in Taliesin's dining room, Liliane immediately took to Olgivanna's "courageous character," while E.J. got a firsthand pitch from Wright for his nascent master plan for a new kind of city based on the automobile.[23] Impressed by what he saw and heard, Kaufmann promised then and there $1,000 to underwrite the creation of a model for Wright's new cityscape, called Broadacre City.

A professional relationship—and more, a friendship and a creative partnership, which would endure for twenty years—was established that evening between Wright and Kaufmann. Neither man was afraid of public controversy (Kaufmann's mistresses were well-known to have substantial lines of credit at his stores), and both saw themselves as shapers of society.

E. J. Kaufmann, a highly successful businessman, saw in Wright a spirit and originality he rarely encountered. Wright's Taliesin, a combination manse, castle, school, and domicile, was the world as he would have it. Yet Kaufmann's host was no provincial; his ideas about cities and culture were expansive. Wright, in turn, saw Kaufmann as a man of influence and curiosity, one who both listened and arrived with real architectural needs. The designs for a planetarium and a new office were on the table, as was the more speculative possibility of public works that the well-connected Kaufmann might, over time, steer Wright's way.

No surviving document pinpoints the moment when E.J. asked Wright to add a weekend house to the list of possible projects. Yet, when the Kaufmanns retired to their bedchamber that first evening at Taliesin, the windows of their room in Wright's natural house framed a vista of a moonlit pond. In reshaping his landscape, Wright had captured the waters of a spring-fed stream, flooding the low-lying acres at the foot of Taliesin's hill. Thus, in the quiet of the November night, the Kaufmanns' sleep was accompanied, as it would so often be in the years to come, by the soothing sound of water tumbling and splashing over a steep stone drop just out of sight below their quarters.

———

KAUFMANN ISSUED THE summons: "It is time for you to appear on the scene."[24] Prompted by a telegram from Wright, Kaufmann wrote on December 4, 1934, shortly after his return home from Wisconsin. Kaufmann's envelope contained a check, as requested, a $250 installment against the total he had agreed to contribute to the making of the Broadacre City model. He took the opportunity, once again, to urge Wright to come East.

Looking to cement relations with his new client, Wright ordered his secretary to coordinate his schedule with Kaufmann's, and precisely two weeks later, Wright stepped off the overnight train from Chicago at Pittsburgh's Penn Station. At midmorning on Tuesday, December 18, Kaufmann ushered his guest into a waiting car. Wednesday, he explained, they would take meetings in Pittsburgh, but today their destination was rural Fayette County and the large parcel of wooded property Kaufmann had owned for sixteen months. There, he and Liliane had decided, they wanted a weekend home.

A key feature of the rugged 1,598-acre parcel was the watercourse called Bear Run. Originating in hillside seeps on wooded Laurel Ridge, its waters emerged in silence, following the steep natural fall line in the little valley. As it meandered westward, a whispering stream grew to a babbling brook. Bound for the much larger Youghiogheny River, it gained in volume and velocity as it dropped over a thousand feet and traveled perhaps three miles from its swampy origins. Then, in a dramatic change in the topography, the streambed fell suddenly away. For an eternal instant, Bear Run became a sheer wall of foam and cascading droplets, its waters tumbling some forty feet over a series of stone outcroppings.

Edgar Kaufmann knew Bear Run well. In the years before World War I, he had leased the property as a "summer club" for his female employees, naming it Camp Kaufmann. After arriving at Bear Run Station on the Baltimore & Ohio Railroad, the young clerks from the store enjoyed a rambling clubhouse, dance pavilion, bowling alley, cottages, tennis courts, and the surrounding woods and waters for swimming, hiking, and other activities. In 1921, Kaufmann had ordered a "Readi-Cut" cabin from the Aladdin Company of Bay City, Michigan, for his family's use. Raised on a steep hill, the large but plain wood-frame structure had a fireplace but lacked electricity and indoor plumbing.

The place had become an occasional summer residence for Liliane, E.J., and their son, but Camp Kaufmann went out of vogue in the early Depression years, and after the store clerks stopped coming, E.J. personally took title, in 1933, to the entire site. By then Edgar jr. was abroad, but his parents began contemplating a year-round weekend house. Travel to and from the Bear Run property had been made easier by the paving of the nearby state road in 1930, though that also meant that the country lane, now more heavily trafficked, had become a source of disagreeable noise and exhaust fumes.

Kaufmann planted many pine trees and commissioned a survey of the property to record man-made features and natural ones. The land was hardly primeval forest—in the nineteenth century, the acres had been logged, mined, and quarried—but Kaufmann was inclined to conservation. He ordered the removal of many dead trees killed by the recent chestnut blight and the planting of Norway spruce saplings in their place.

that Wright "should descend to unanswerable vulgarity." Hitchcock attempted to respond to some of Wright's specific comments, but his hurt feelings repeatedly bled onto the page. "I must say that at last I am convinced that there is no future reason for attempting to remain on working terms with you," he wrote in the letter's opening lines. In its last ones, he added, "I regret now that we have ever begun to know you personally." In between, he joined the pissing match himself, offering, "I suppose you can comfort yourself with the consolation—a proud one it is—that Michelangelo was impossible to get on with—and posterity has forgiven him."[22]

After pondering the matter for a few additional days, Johnson chose a different tack. He held his fire, shrugging off Wright's insults, and assumed a more apologetic tone. He admitted to being "greatly upset" by Wright's letter, but added, "There have been many misunderstandings on both sides . . . [and] I myself am not clear as to what mistakes I may have made in interpreting your point of view."

Johnson played diplomat, expressing the wish that they meet in person to talk things over. He even proposed taking Wright up on his repeated invitations to come to Taliesin, admitting, in a placating tone, "I feel as strongly as ever that I have a great deal to learn, much more so after this experience of trying to make an exhibition."[23] Johnson's letter was evidence of one lesson he had learned: To snipe back at Wright would only provoke the man further. Johnson's curatorial role had placed him in the middle, with an implied responsibility to act the role of mediator; thus, his moderate tone.

That didn't mean he had shifted his thinking. What he didn't say to Wright was that his essential view of Wright as Prairie Style architect remained. Just the weekend before he had written to Oud in Rotterdam, telling the Dutchman, "Frank Lloyd Wright was included only from courtesy and in recognition of his past contributions."[24]

———

YET JOHNSON HAD demonstrated himself a worthy adversary. As if in compliance with some warrior code, Wright had tested the young

For Wright and Kaufmann, in December 1934, the drive to the town of Ohiopyle, seven miles south of the Kaufmanns' isolated watershed, required two hours, much of which was accompanied by falling snow. As they neared their destination, the precipitation turned to a light rain, but as if scripted for maximum cinematic value, the arrival of the two men at Bear Run coincided with a clearing sky and a rainbow that spanned the valley. As E.J. recalled the moment a few years later, "[Wright] had been relaxing. With the rainbow he became alive. Turning to me he said, 'Surely something will come out of this journey; after all the elements through which we have traveled, the end is crowned with a rainbow.'"[25]

Wright and Kaufmann explored the property together. The Hangover, as the Readi-Cut cabin was called because of its location at the brink of a steep precipice, required only a cursory look. But Wright took everything in. They followed the dirt access road that wound deep into the heart of the acreage, paralleling a crook in the glacial cut that was the streambed. The sky was visible through forest canopy—the hardwood trees, mostly oak, had lost their leaves for the winter—but the many rhododendrons and pine, spruce, and hemlock trees colored the landscape winter green.

As they moved away from the Hangover and the highway, the sound of running water grew louder. Walking along a dirt track called Shady Lane, the two men arrived at a clearing where the overhanging branches abruptly opened to reveal a small wooden bridge ahead of them. The narrow truss bridge could accommodate just a single vehicle, but the view was dramatic. Wright looked down upon raw geology, a natural stairway of immense, misaligned sandstone treads. The stone surfaces descended into a steep ravine, half-obscured by racing water and December ice.

In musing on a new vacation home at Bear Run, the Kaufmanns had decided to move away from the road and closer to the cataract. "A lot of the family's time," Edgar jr. later explained, "and of course their guests' time as a result too, was spent basking on the flat rock at the base of the falls, walking in under the falls, getting a massage, sliding down the potholes, and having fun. . . . The drama of the water's movement and the charm of the noise that it made, were something that everybody appreciated a great deal."[26]

Wright and E.J. talked on December 18 and after, but the otherwise well-documented Bear Run project offers no details about Kaufmann's charge to his new architect. E.J. may have spoken of the family's fondness for the waterfall, much as his son later did. But Wright had instantly been drawn to the drama of the site and by Kaufmann's connection to it. "You love this waterfall, don't you?" Wright reportedly asked Kaufmann that afternoon. "Why not live intimately with it, where you can see and hear it and feel it with you all of the time?"[27]

Wright's visit to Pittsburgh was brief. He stayed overnight at La Tourelle and the following day surveyed Kaufmann's office space. He shopped at the Big Store, too, but soon he was back on the train, bound for New York to finalize details for the exhibition of the as-yet-incomplete model of Broadacre City, due to go on display at Rockefeller Center on April 15. Then he returned to Taliesin, a rail ride on the 20th Century Limited spent with his friend Alexander Woollcott.

Shortly after Christmas, a note arrived in Pittsburgh to Kaufmann on Wright's stationery: "The visit to the waterfall in the woods stays with me." Wright added a tease and a promise: "A domicile has taken vague shape in the mind to the music of the stream." But almost nine months would pass before anyone but Wright had any intimation of what that vague shape could possibly be.

III.

1934–35 . . . An Architectural Epiphany

To BEGIN, WRIGHT needed a topographical map. He requested one while in Pennsylvania and, on January 10, 1935, wrote to Kaufmann, asking, "When do we get the contours of 'Bear Run'?" In

February, after yet another prompting from Wright, Kaufmann finally ordered a detailed survey of the lay of the land near the bridge. It recorded the site in unusual detail, incorporating not only the pitch and yaw of the landscape but the large trees by species. It also recorded the all-important ledges and boulders that defined Bear Run. The map wasn't completed until March 9, and by the time it arrived at Taliesin, Wright was otherwise occupied.

Wright's long-moribund architectural business had suddenly showed signs of new life. A December 1934 visit to Taliesin by Dallas retailer Stanley Marcus led to a commission for a Texas house along the long, low lines of the House on the Mesa. Kaufmann's planetarium for Pittsburgh required cogitation, too, as did the design for the executive office for the tenth floor of the Big Store. In a steady buzz of activity the Fellowship apprentices worked intently toward an immediate deadline—the twelve-foot-square model of Broadacre City had to be readied for its New York debut—but the house for Bear Run generated no noticeable hum.

In early April, Edgar jr. and several other apprentices caravanned east from Arizona, where Wright and the Fellowship had escaped the Wisconsin winter to temporary quarters at La Hacienda, a ranch complex that belonged to Wright's San-Marcos-in-the-Desert client, Alexander Chandler. With the Broadacre model completed, Kaufmann accompanied a second vehicle, a truck painted Cherokee red (Wright's favorite color), its side emblazoned with the Taliesin insignia, a stylized Greek key in a geometric square. Despite a blinding dust storm in Kansas, the cargo was safely delivered, and the four six-foot-by-six-foot sections of the Broadacre City model were assembled in time to greet a curious New York public. In the *New Yorker*, Lewis Mumford described Wright's urban vision as "both a generous dream and rational plan."[28] The *New York Times*, *Architectural Record*, and other publications looked favorably on Wright's notion of a planned community, in which childless couples occupied a minimum of an acre and bigger families were to be granted larger plots.

Wright's accompanying lectures were well received, too, but with the New York events behind him, he headed back to Wisconsin. There, on

April 27, 1935, he wrote to Kaufmann, assuring his client that he was "ready to go work on the waterfall cottage."

The two men exchanged notes on another shared matter, too. After assisting with the Broadacre installation at Rockefeller Center, Edgar jr. ended his tenure with the Fellowship. Wright had warned his father— "Junior is sagging a little. He feels his end here with us is near, for which I am deeply sorry."[29] By early May, the son joined the father's business, and E.J. confided in Wright, "He will be a great help to me in years to come."[30]

Meanwhile, Wright needed money again. Despite the new work and the Fellowship, his financial problems persisted. He and E.J. corresponded in May. Would E.J. float a loan with some of Wright's Japanese prints as collateral? No, Kaufmann wrote, suggesting that Wright "cast elsewhere to help you out at this particular time."[31] Wright soon complained about the expense of the Broadacre exhibition, which, by mid-June, was packed up and on its way to Pittsburgh, where it went on display at Kaufmann's store.

Wright continued to make promises about the weekend house, writing on June 15, "We are starting on the Home at 'Bear Run,' a specially difficult project . . . You will see some drawings from us soon."[32] Meanwhile Edgar jr., now on duty at the store, reported that more than a thousand Pittsburghers a day viewed the show, and that his parents were excited to see the plans for the new office and country house.

Wright made a return trip to Pittsburgh at the end of June. He visited Bear Run again, but in the weeks that followed, Kaufmann received no plans for the waterfall cottage. Correspondence continued between Spring Green and Pittsburgh, and Kaufmann sent a $250 retainer on the house plans in August. Still, an increasingly impatient client saw no evidence that Wright had yet been inspired by Bear Run to put pencil to paper.

———

WITH A LATE-SEPTEMBER phone call, E. J. Kaufmann finally got matters in motion.

Until that Sunday morning, the pace of creation for the house on Bear Run had no discernible tempo. Kaufmann, having completed his business at a meeting of retailers in Milwaukee, announced, *I'm on my way*. Rich, impulsive, and accustomed to having people obey his orders—his store employed some 2,500 people—Kaufmann assumed the renderings were well under way. Wright had intimated as much in his letters.

In the fallow decade that preceded the arrival of the Kaufmanns in his life, Wright had become a prolific writer, offering expansive opinions on society and architecture. In several published pieces, he explained his personal approach to design, offering a prescription to other architectural practitioners. Typical was an article published, in 1928, in the *Architectural Record*, in which he instructed, "Conceive the building in the imagination, not on paper but in the mind, thoroughly—before touching paper. Let it live there—gradually taking more definite form before committing it to the draughting board."[33]

Frank Lloyd Wright was a mind's-eye architect. He didn't advance his designs draft by draft in the pages of notebooks; it's no accident that no Wright sketchbooks survive. In the full confidence of a man with great ideas, he risked the loss of the occasional fleeting fancy, keeping no cache of jottings to which he might later refer. The big solution, Wright believed, must emerge first. The accretion of details could follow.

At heart a romantic, Wright trusted what poet Samuel Taylor Coleridge called the "secondary imagination." According to Coleridge, writing a century earlier, "It dissolves, diffuses, dissipates ... [the secondary imagination] struggles to idealize and to unify."[34] Coleridge claimed that the lines of his poem "Kubla Kahn" came to him in a dream; on waking several hours after taking two grains of opium, he took pen in hand and furiously transcribed the lines as if from memory. While Coleridge's composition may be the prototypical literary example of all-in-a-moment creativity, Wright's seeming epiphany on the morning of September 22, 1935, was about to become architecture's.

"Come along, E.J.," Wright said loudly into the receiver of the hand-crank phone. "We're ready for you."

Edgar Tafel and Bob Mosher, two apprentices working nearby in the Taliesin drafting room, looked at one other. As far as they knew, not so much as a thumbnail sketch existed, not to mention elevations, plans, or presentation drawings.

Wright and E.J. had long since exchanged letters about the budget, and though Wright rarely permitted money to decide anything, he nonetheless understood Kaufmann's parameters. He didn't know the clients intimately, but they had traded visits to one another's homes, and his acquaintance extended far enough to understand that E.J. and Liliane required separate bedroom spaces (a not uncommon convention at the time for the well-to-do). Edgar jr. had been part of the Taliesin family; Wright was known to call him Whippoorwill (which other apprentices regarded as a mocking reference to the younger man's homosexuality). Wright would give the former apprentice—who had, after all, helped make the commission possible—his own quite independent quarters on the top floor of the Bear Run design. Wright also understood the house was intended for weekend use. In short, he knew the needs of the client and, thus, the program for the house.

He had visited the site at least three times. He had seen the stream first in the cold of December, then later in the warmth of summer. Edgar jr. had accompanied him on a third visit, remembering that "Wright spent the day" and that "the mountains put on their best repertoire to him—sun, rain and hail alternated; the masses of native rhododendron were in bloom; the run was full and the falls, thundering."[35]

Wright had been alerted some weeks earlier that Kaufmann was to be in Wisconsin; further, he had been preparing for this moment for many months. Certainly the design had assumed a shape in his mind before that morning. No doubt it had been "germinating" (his word) as he waited for what he called the "hour or more of what might be called insight." As

Wright said of the design process, "It is fleeting, it is evanescent. It's up here where you have to be quick and take it."[36]

With Kaufmann's big, powerful car thundering toward Taliesin— Milwaukee was just 120 miles away—Wright needed to render his vision of the place in a way that others, most specifically E. J. Kaufmann, could experience it. This wouldn't be a Prairie House, and though it would share attributes with Taliesin, it could not be a lordly Midwestern manor overseeing an agricultural landscape. Though it would reflect the lessons Wright had learned at MoMA, compliments of Philip Johnson, the Kaufmanns' Bear Run cottage would be something utterly new and different.

————

OCCASIONALLY, A PIVOTAL historic date can be identified. The morning Frank Lloyd Wright designed Fallingwater was one such.[37]

Edgar Tafel recalled that Wright, after hanging up the phone, strode out of his office and took a seat at a drafting table. Bob Mosher remembered Wright asking for the topographical map of Bear Run. When Tafel had written to Edgar jr. a month earlier, saying that the house design was "to some extent on paper," his half-truth probably referred to the redrawn plat of the site. Executed by the apprentices, this enlarged and cropped version of the survey Kaufmann had sent in March had been upped in scale from one twentieth to one eighth of an inch per foot. The rise and fall of the land at the waterfall were indicated, along with a few of the largest boulders and nearby trees.

Wright was known to work privately, sometimes in the blue hours of the night, usually in his own quarters where he had a drafting table. He may have executed some preliminary sketches for the Kaufmann house unbeknownst to others at Taliesin, but the recollections of those in attendance that September Sunday are consistent: He had no previous drawings at hand as he bent over his drafting table, the sloping roof of Taliesin's studio overhead, and laid a fresh sheet on top of the plan. He immediately began to draw.

At the Taliesin Fellowship, the ritual was *learn-by-do*—and to do it in the presence of Wright. Taliesin pedagogy called for the young men and women to work at building and drafting under his tutelage, but at regular intervals the Master himself would model for his followers the Wright way. An attention seeker by nature, he liked nothing better than to sit in the midst of the busy Taliesin drafting room, his apprentices at hand, watching, listening, learning. That morning the word passed quickly that Wright was setting to work. "He's in the studio," one apprentice said to another. "He's sitting down."[38]

A photo taken December 1937 of Wright at Taliesin in Spring Green, Wisconsin. Among the apprentices around him are Wes Peters (supporting his head with his hand), *Bob Mosher* (foreground, far right), *and Edgar Tafel* (behind Mosher, right). (Hedrich Blessing Collection/Chicago History Museum/Getty Images)

Wright began drawing a plan, an orthographic projection of what the elements of the house would look like from directly above. With his half century of experience, Wright drew with consummate grace and ease, his left hand maneuvering the T square north and south on the board. Using a standard-issue thirty-sixty-ninety drafting triangle, he positioned it with the point of the smallest angle pointed west, meaning lines drawn along its hypotenuse would soon define the front and rear of the proposed Kaufmann dwelling. With a clockwise turn of the triangle, Wright could draw the east and west walls of the rectilinear house, again using the hypotenuse. That was basic drafting, the techniques known to the most junior of draftsmen.

The most essential moment was at hand, as were a growing number of apprentices. Tafel and Mosher had been joined by others, and more were drifting into the studio. "We were all standing around him," remembered one.[39]

Wright led with the unexpected: His first lines on the sheet made it evident that this was no mere house with a view. His masterstroke was his insight that, to serve the genius of the place, the Kaufmanns ought to live in and above the waterfall, not look at it from below. That conceit was the inverse of what everyone else expected.

In blue pencil, Wright traced the sinuous line of the northern bank of the stream, which ran at roughly a thirty-degree angle to northeast. It would determine the placement of the front of the house's foundation. Wright indicated in red pencil several asymmetrically placed boulders that, back from the waterline, stepped up to the rock outcropping that rose to the rear of the house site. Wright then sketched a set of four supporting piers, perpendicular to the stream, extending front to back on the plan. They would be freestanding walls of laid-up local stone on footings of poured concrete. These "bolsters" would rise like the trestles beneath a bridge (see Fig. IX).

His pencils moved with great rapidity. Wright talked as he worked, in an undertone that was both directed at his pupils and a preoccupied expression of his thoughts.

Working with hard H-grade and B-grade pencils that made light and dark black lines respectively, he added the house's next level. As he sketched the perimeter of the first floor, that, too, surprised the onlookers. Rather than sitting atop the foundation walls, the main interior living space opened to a spacious terrace that reached the other side of the streambed and thereby doubled the dimensions of the footprint. This new area, sketched lightly, was entirely cantilevered, suspended without evident support over Bear Run.

Wright called the gravity-defying area a "tray," echoing his description of the cantilevers at his Imperial Hotel in Tokyo. For him it was a mind picture: "The waiter's tray supported by his hand," Wright had written in *An Autobiography*, "is a cantilever slab in principle."[40]

In Castell red pencil, he added the second and third levels for bedrooms, together with more terraces suspended like outflung arms over Bear Run. "Liliane and E.J. will have tea on the balcony," Tafel remembered Wright saying. "They'll cross the bridge and walk into the woods."[41] More red lines delineated the arrangement of the kitchen and bathrooms at the rear core of the house, along with a few furnishings. Wright moved to a second drawing, since Kaufmann's journey from Milwaukee was unlikely to require much longer than two hours. Yet Wright also found the time to second-guess himself, erasing the line that represented the front parapet of the second-floor terrace; instead of a setback, it now extended six feet beyond the one below.

A *section* drawing came next, with Wright rendering the house as if guillotined top-to-bottom along the north-south axis. The drawing revealed details of the house's construction, its ceiling heights, and other vertical elements.

As he said he liked to do, Wright had surely *walked the spaces in his mind*, but now he was conjuring his building onto sheets of paper. His commentary described the hearth rising from the floor. He planned a spherical warming kettle suspended nearby. "Steam will permeate the atmosphere," he explained. "You'll hear the hiss."[42]

With Mosher keeping the pencils sharpened, Wright soon shifted to a third drawing, this one a front elevation, delineating the face of a building from the point of view of an observer looking straight on from a horizontal vantage. Like the other two, the drawing that emerged was workmanlike, with evident erasures and corrections. Immediately clear, however, was that the Kaufmann house would have no true front façade.

When word reached him that Kaufmann had arrived, Wright rose and went to greet his client in his most ingratiating manner, one aristocrat greeting another. "Come along, E.J.," he invited.

On seeing the drawings, Kaufmann expressed surprise at the placement of the house. His notion had been for a "lodge." At first, he objected, "I thought you would place the house near the waterfall, not over it."

Wright explained, "E.J., I want you to live with the waterfall, not just to look at it, but for it to become an integral part of your lives."[43]

As he showed Kaufmann the several renderings, Wright's commentary ranged from the poetic and philosophical to talk of materials and textures. Before long he took Kaufmann off to lunch in the Taliesin dining room; Tafel and Mosher remained behind and, based on Wright's initial drawings, executed two more elevations. On Wright's return he picked them up as if they were his own and continued to lay out for Kaufmann his vision of the Bear Run house.

Mr. Wright and his drawings proved persuasive. One apprentice remembers the departing Kaufmann saying, "Don't change a thing." On returning to Pittsburgh, the client went to the soon-to-be-building-site and took his turn at picturing the building that would hang over Bear Run, laying out for his son in words and gestures the location of the rooms and terraces, explaining to Edgar jr. as best he could the unprecedented design that Wright had imagined for them.

Perhaps the most remarkable aspect of Wright's bravura two-hour outpouring was that, despite its many imaginative leaps—the trays, a stairway that descended to the surface of the stream, concrete trellises that, like a climber's piton, would anchor the house to the ancient rock of the sandstone cliff behind it—those first renderings portrayed a building that changed little in the coming years as the three-dimensional Fallingwater rose above Bear Run. Equally important, Wright's morning burst of creativity amounts to the single most accessible explanation of what he meant by *organic architecture*. The house that leaped from his mind that morning would make the notion of local, native, and natural building instantly comprehensible to millions of people in the decades to come.

———

WRIGHT WENT GOETHE one better. Johann Wolfgang famously said, "Architecture is frozen music." At Bear Run, Frank Lloyd Wright unfroze the score.

He described it this way to the next generation of acolytes at the Fellowship: "I think nothing yet ever equaled the coordination, the sympathetic expression of the great principle of repose where forest and stream and rock and all the elements of structure are combined so quietly that really you listen not to any noise whatsoever although the music of the stream is there. But you listen to Fallingwater the way you listen to the quiet of the Country."[44] Wright had polished his rhetorical skills during his years of architectural downtime, during which he earned money from his writings and lectures. "I think you can hear the waterfall when you look at the design," he would tell a television audience in the early 1950s.[45]

The actual building of the house at Bear Run proved much more arduous than might be suggested by its conception. Delighted with Wright's design, E. J. Kaufmann wanted to proceed quickly with construction. The draftsmen at Taliesin duly produced preliminary plans, which were mailed to Pittsburgh on October 15. Wright arrived to revisit the site a few days later. Even before the working drawings arrived in January 1936, Kaufmann ordered a quarry on the property reopened. Liberated by dynamite from ledge outcroppings, great blocks of Pottsville sandstone were loaded onto horse-drawn sledges for the short trip to the building site. But the construction schedule that Kaufmann had hoped would produce a habitable "mountain lodge" by fall would take much longer. Not until the close of 1937 would the Kaufmanns inhabit Fallingwater.

Despite his engineering training, Wright's sense of structure tended to the intuitive, and in 1936, with the use of reinforced concrete in domestic buildings in its infancy, there was no handbook. That led to a series of wrangles when Kaufmann, nervous at the unprecedented design, consulted Pittsburgh engineering firms. The first, Morris Knowles, reviewed the plans. After offering a detailed assessment, they damned Wright's design with their closing sentence: "In our opinion there could be no feeling of complete safety and consequently we recommend that *the proposed site not be used for an important structure.*"[46] But as more drawings arrived from Taliesin, Kaufmann chose to set aside his concerns for the moment, accepting Wright's judgment and proceeding with the project.

Wright regarded "slide-rule engineers" with contempt; he trusted his own instincts.[47] During a June 6, 1936, visit to Bear Run, Wright answered a question asked by Bob Mosher, his clerk-of-the-works. With construction about to begin, Mosher asked, "Can you tell me how to locate the exact datum [level] of the first floor?"

Gesturing toward the site of the proposed house, Wright instructed his fair-haired apprentice to climb to the top of a tall boulder. Grasping at saplings rooted in the rock's fissures, Mosher did as instructed, struggling to scale the eighteen-foot-tall boulder—this was indeed a unique building site. On reaching the top, he turned to face Wright, who stood just upstream at the bridge that spanned Bear Run.

"All right, Bobby, you've answered your own question," Wright said with a sly smile. Its top the benchmark, the boulder would anchor the Kaufmanns' important structure. With that understood, Wright got into his Cord motorcar and headed home to Taliesin.

After construction was well under way, a series of cracks appeared in the poured-concrete terraces. Again Kaufmann sought a second opinion, this time from the Metzger-Richardson Company, which specialized in the fabrication of reinforced concrete. The firm's structural analysis concluded that the cantilevers had been stressed beyond capacity and that supporting piers or posts beneath the overhangs were required. Otherwise, they warned, the building would collapse.

When he learned Kaufmann had consulted Metzger-Richardson and, worse, that steel had been added without his knowledge to reinforce the first-floor tray, Wright was apoplectic. "To hell with the whole thing," he wrote to E.J. He telegraphed Mosher, ordering him to "drop work and come back immediately."[48] A few days later, however, after his temper had cooled, Wright looked to get things back on track. "Explanation seems to be in order," he wrote to Kaufmann. But, his letter made clear, he wasn't apologizing. "I am a master-builder where I have conceived or I am nothing." He as much as volunteered to quit, saying, "It has never been difficult for anyone to get rid of me."[49] But in response, Kaufmann telegraphed, asking that work resume. It did, though new disagreements surfaced in the coming months, as contractors, workers, client, and architect squabbled, negotiated, and sought solutions to unexpected problems.

The design involved numerous innovations, including the stair that descended from the living room though a hatch to the streambed; it would help keep the house cool and enhance the sense Fallingwater was rooted to its watery site. Virtually every element of the unique structure had to be fabricated. The fenestration included window walls (one spanned the entire south elevation of the living room) and a stack of seventeen paired casements to the rear that rose three stories, all of which opened at the corner. Wright sent the Du Pont Company of Wilmington, Delaware, an earthenware pot for a color match; he wanted the Duco paint for the window mullions, interior shelves, and other elements to be his favorite shade, Cherokee red.

More concrete cracks appeared (as they would for decades to come).[50] Kaufmann made his peace with trusting Wright over the engineers, but work proceeded slowly. A single mixer with a rotating drum and capacity of roughly two cubic feet of cement produced the concrete. One batch at a time, the thick, heavy mixture was tipped into a wheelbarrow then dumped or shoveled into the form being filled. Despite the use of steel and concrete for the house's horizontals, Fallingwater would be a hand-made house. Work slowed for the winter of 1936–37, during which the flagstone floors were laid.

When the time came to install the finished interior surfaces—mid-April 1937 saw the house closed in—the casework and furniture began to arrive, all made to order to Taliesin drawings. The wood was black walnut, harvested farther down the Appalachian chain, a hardwood that thrives in streambeds.

The house resembled no other; even in the protean imagination of Wright, Fallingwater had no clear precedents nor, in the decades to come, would Wright ever again build anything quite like it. In some small ways the design resembled other Wright houses, notably the late–Prairie Style Gale House, with its multiple cantilevers, and Wright's most personal building, Taliesin, which recorded his ongoing interaction with land-scape.[51] Yet Fallingwater went further, a house that was roughly half terrace (2,445 square feet outside, with an interior space of 2,885 square feet). Because of the cantilevers, the trays seemingly levitated over the stream, no center of gravity was apparent.

From no two angles did it look alike. It rose as if built by the ancients, stone by bonded stone; it gained breadth compliments of the new tech-nology of reinforced concrete. Wright had talked for years of "breaking the box," and at Fallingwater the cantilevered terraces burst out all over; from some angles, Fallingwater can be said to resemble a colossal dresser with open drawers extending at random from three sides. Wright didn't build a box; he built a backbone, with essentially no conventional walls at the front and sides but patterns of windows. To those willing to acknowledge it—Wright would never be among them—a debt was apparent to Miës's Tugendhat House, which Philip Johnson had fallen in love with and which shared a room at MoMA with Wright's House on the Mesa in 1932. Though not precisely an ancestor, Tugendhat was a corollary cousin.

To an unusual degree, a single Fallingwater drawing would come to represent Wright's Pennsylvania masterpiece as words never could. This one wasn't made in a rush like the more workmanlike drawings of September 22. Wright's favored draftsman, an apprentice named John Howe, who would remain at Taliesin as long as Wright lived, recalled a particular day during the execution of the final drawings for the Kaufmann house over the winter of 1935–36.

"I remember Mr. Wright as he worked with relish one morning," Howe wrote. "He was dressed in his bathrobe, seated at a table by the fire in his study-bedroom."[52]

He was working on perspectives. While such drawings are of little use to a builder (they are full of distortions), perspectives are invaluable in communicating to people unfamiliar with translating orthographic drawings (plans and elevations) into mental pictures. The perspective drawing simulates what the human eye sees. Some elements in the drawing appear closer, others farther away, meaning the two-dimensional flat sheet conveys a surprisingly good approximation of a three-dimensional structure.

Howe watched Wright drafting. "I had brought the layouts in from the studio and was standing by with a supply of colored pencils." With the measured drawings at hand for reference, Wright could render the science of building in artistic terms. He bisected the sheet with the horizontal line of the top of the waterfall and rendered the craggy mass of boulders below. The bold structure he limned above thus seemed to rest on the falls; Wright, with a wink to the Beaux Arts stylists he disliked, set his house into its rugged setting as a classical temple might rest atop a pedestal.

The house was portrayed at a three-quarter angle but from below, a Lilliputian's view. Once Wright had sketched the bold outlines of the house, he began adding trees and vines that further connected it to the site, as if Mother Nature had already begun to embrace the concrete planes and rigid geometry.

The colored drawing would be Fallingwater's first public calling card, as Wright permitted its publication in March 1937 in the *St. Louis Post-Dispatch*.[53] But the house's national coming-out party was still to come.

IV.

1937–38 . . . MoMA Revisits Mr. Wright

WHEN JOHN MCANDREW arrived at Liliane Kaufmann's invitation, in November 1937, the last of the scaffolding had been removed from the Bear Run house. Although rugs, lamps, and other objects were still being fabricated and bare bulbs hung from the ceiling, the Kaufmanns had moved into their weekend escape.

The interior of house felt as revolutionary to them as the exterior; it was quite unlike anything else they had known. The main living spaces, in a classic Wright open plan—the kitchen and dining area to the right on entry, the library and sitting space ahead—managed, even in the absence of partitions, to be somehow discrete yet shared. The room had a strongly horizontal character, its low ceiling flattening the visitor's field of vision, not unlike the way the bill on a cap does. The temptation to look up was foreclosed, the horizontal field of vision defined, and the eye drawn, inevitably, to the wall of glass ahead. The view at Fallingwater was of tree trunks, high off the ground. The character was that of an aerie, a tree house.

The Kaufmanns' affection for the place was immediate. Edgar jr. wrote to Wright in those early days of habitation, "Time is teaching all of us to like you in the house, and the house in us, more and more." His mother's note to Wright was less elliptical: "We have had the two happiest weekends of our lives in the house."[54]

A young photographer looking to make his reputation also took the train to Pennsylvania that November, working on commission to the

Architectural Forum. The magazine would devote its entire January 1938 issue to Wright. The editors had hoped to feature a much discussed Wright design for a new office building for the Johnson Wax Corporation in Racine, Wisconsin (business was indeed improving for Mr. Wright), but unexpected construction delays meant that the Johnson Wax Administration Building, with its "lily-pad" columns, remained far from finished. That meant the nearly completed Kaufmann house had new importance when twenty-five-year-old William "Bill" Hedrich arrived to record it on film.

The Chicago-based Hedrich had already seen drawings of the house at Taliesin, but they failed to prepare him for what he found. On arrival, he studied the house at length. "[I] looked at it," he remembered, "for I suppose a full day before I opened up a camera."[55] Experiencing firsthand the reality of what Wright had imagined, Hedrich saw a house that defied the usual approach; no squared-up elevation shot could record this place. It differed from every angle and, he discovered, with each hour of the day. Hedrich shot at dawn; in the slanting light of late afternoon; and at dusk. Then he settled on what he knew would be his money shot. He had to buy a pair of waterproof boots to get the image, since he would position himself not only downstream but actually *in* the stream.

"[The water] was not that deep," said Hedrich, "but it was very, very cold."[56]

He planned his shot with great care. Seeking to avoid the false drama of backlighting, he snapped his shutter in the middle of the day: "I wanted the light on the front of the structure."[57] He regretted that the surrounding trees were leafless, but Hedrich's light meter told him that the pale autumn light permitted a long exposure. That meant his film could register the water pouring over the rock outcropping as a gossamer screen.

As if channeling Wright's perspective shot, he composed an image that would galvanize the world; indeed, his downstream, three-quarter view became and remains the iconic shot. Wright would approve of the outcome, praising it to Hedrich as "very acrobatic, very acrobatic."[58]

Young Bill Hedrich's photograph of the Kaufmann house, taken in late 1937. (Hedrich Blessing Collection/Chicago History Museum/ Getty Images)

Eventually, the master would acquire an enormous print (roughly forty by sixty inches) for the Taliesin collection, but that came later, after modest-size versions of the image had gained wide visibility.[59]

———

WHEN JOHN MCANDREW returned to New York from his visit to the Kaufmanns' house, he hatched a plan. Preparations lagged for an exhibition of the work of Finnish architect Alvar Aalto, originally scheduled for January 1938, and, needing to fill the galleries, McAndrew pitched a "one-man one-house show" to his MoMA colleagues. It made sense for many reasons, not least that MoMA's close association with German architecture in the Johnson era needed a counterbalance, since Hitler's Germany had emerged a dangerous and demonic presence in Europe. An exhibition devoted to a modern American architect seemed one method of redress. McAndrew made a good case for the Bear Run house, and according to the minutes of a meeting held on November 19, 1937, "It was decided that the exhibition of [the Kaufmann house] . . . would be a good subject."[60]

After a false start via an intermediary, the thirty-three-year-old rookie curator finally reached Wright, asking permission to mount an exhibition. In his telegram in reply, Wright alluded to Philip Johnson's mistreatment of him in 1932 and challenged McAndrew: ALL RIGHT JOHN LET'S SEE WHAT YOU CAN DO.[61]

While McAndrew raced to put together his little exhibition, powerful cultural forces in New York came together.

Henry Luce, then emerging as the most influential person in American magazine publishing, put Wright's face on the cover of *Time*, using as the backdrop the architect's most theatrical perspective of the house that, just a few weeks before, he had begun calling Fallingwater. In the text, Wright was called "the greatest architect of the 20th century."[62] On the prized inside cover of another of his publications, *Life* magazine, Luce ran an advertisement promoting the Wright issue of *Architectural Forum*, which he also owned. It featured Bill Hedrich's perspective view and claimed the issue devoted to Wright was "the most important architectural document ever published in America."[63]

By happenstance, McAndrew's little show opened in the Time-Life Building, where MoMA rented temporary quarters in the basement (excavation for the museum's permanent home on Fifty-Third Street had just begun). On display were twenty photographs, including Hedrich's essential view, and a few floor plans and elevation drawings. An accompanying catalog, little more than a brochure, used an excerpt from the text Wright had written for the special issue of *Architectural Forum*.

In New York on business, Edgar jr. visited on the first day, writing to Wright, "The total effect is strong and good; and much of the public, warmed up by the publicity in periodicals, will give it some study."[64] During its five-week run, the show attracted 14,305 curious onlookers, who walked the "air-cooled" galleries of the underground concourse. Many times that number would see the traveling version, which subsequently made stops in ten cities.

Almost overnight, Fallingwater became a landmark on the American architectural timeline. It also elevated Wright's status. As McAndrew confidently put it, "Our Old Master has again become a part of our living tradition."[65]

———

WITH PHILIP JOHNSON no longer at the museum to set its architectural agenda, his successor, John McAndrew, had launched an exhibition that cast an enthusiastic light on Mr. Wright. The show also handed Lewis Mumford the opportunity to proclaim in the pages of the *New Yorker* that Wright was "at the top of his powers, undoubtedly the world's greatest living architect, a man who can dance circles around any of his contemporaries."[66] At age seventy, Wright was back, Mumford wrote, "the perpetual youngness and freshness of his mind . . . never better shown."[67]

Yet despite Johnson's self-imposed exile, he was—at least as far as Wright was concerned—a spectral presence over the proceedings. Though bathed in the success of Fallingwater, Wright still nursed the six-year-old grudge that dated to his perceived humiliation at the hands of Johnson and the others at MoMA.

In designing the Kaufmann house, Wright amazed everyone, including his client. But rather than sitting back and allowing the house and its boosters to do the public relations work for him, Wright, never one to miss an opportunity to proclaim his greatness and opine on architectural taste, used pages of the *Architectural Forum* to go on the offensive. In his essay, he proclaimed his complete independence. Just in case anyone was tempted to think he had been influenced by anyone else in recent years, he wanted to set the record straight.

"The ideas involved here," he asserted, "are in no wise changed from the early work."[68]

Certainly Wright's structural daring at Bear Run was his own, but by claiming the house owed no debt to any source but his own imagination, he protested too much.

For those enamored of the International Style—Philip Johnson among them—the design of Fallingwater amounted to a recapitulation of certain themes with which Miës and others had launched European Modernism. Say what one will about Fallingwater's relationship to its site, the structure itself is extraordinarily *inorganic*. Imagine it relocated away from Bear Run and it becomes a set of horizontal forms (Wright's trays) that, from three sides, though tied together vertically by glass, consist of thin planes of transparency and light.[69] To the susceptible imagination—Henry-Russell Hitchcock's, for one—the variously weighted lines and geometric forms of its floor plan can be conflated with a plan by Miës or even an abstract painting by Mondrian.

Certainly Wright referenced his own work, not least Taliesin's rustic stonework. Equally, he most certainly didn't build an homage to, but rather, a critique of the Modernist movement, employing materials—expanses of glass, reinforced-concrete slabs—as he never had before. There is little ornament, none on the exterior, yet the house is also at one with its site's vegetation, rocks, and even its shadows. Wright permitted nature to do much of the work at Fallingwater, but admitted or not, the house was born of both his reaction to imported influences and the site on which he built it.

The house's concrete horizontals echo the rock ledges, its verticals the surrounding trees, as if the house matches the rhythms of the place. But in an unguarded moment, Wright also admitted that he quite intentionally drew upon other sources, too.

Cornelia Brierly's association with Taliesin would last three quarters of a century, though in 1935, she was a new arrival in Spring Green. As a student at Carnegie Tech a year earlier, she thought the classical Beaux

Arts system "uncreative" and wrote to Wright inquiring about the Fellowship. His letter in response had consisted of five words—"Come when the spirit moves"—and he signed it with a flourish.[70]

Just weeks before his September morning of drafting magic, he stood, on July 3, 1935, at the foot of the Bear Run waterfall. With the twenty-two-year-old Brierly beside him, he looked up at the boulders that defined the stream's west bank. With his only audience the running waters of the stream and young Miss Brierly, he let drop one large clue to the building's character: "Well, Cornelia, we are going to beat the Internationalists at their own game."[71]

The consensus of architectural history is that he did just that. Not that those he saw as his opposition acknowledged it at the time. At least while Wright was alive, Philip Johnson always spoke grudgingly of Fallingwater, usually applying his irreverent wit. In one 1958 lecture, he called it a "pioneer work," but quickly labeled it a "seventeen-bucket house" (for the number of buckets required to collect the water from leaks in the roof).[72] On another occasion, after spending a weekend as a guest of Edgar jr. at Bear Run, Johnson made it known that he found the noise of the waterfall distracting. As the younger Kaufmann remembered, Johnson said that "it excited his bladder."[73]

Only later, much later, a full two decades after Wright's death, was Johnson willing to embrace Wright as something of a fellow traveler. In his eighth decade, as Johnson collected his miscellaneous writings for an Oxford University Press omnibus, he saw the Bear Run house in a new context. In the book's afterword, he admitted that he had come to regard the Kaufmann house as not merely a response to the Internationalists. In designing it, Johnson thought, Wright "paid the [International] Style the ultimate compliment. Fallingwater of 1936 was Wright's answer: he showed he could do flat roofs and horizontal ribbon windows better than anyone."[74]

CHAPTER 9

Politics and Art

That was my bad political period.
—*Philip Johnson*

I.

The Late Thirties . . . New London, Ohio . . . The Errant Ideologue

PHILIP JOHNSON WOULD occasionally take a seat at a drafting table. By 1934, he had laid out an apartment at New York's Beekman Place for his wealthy friend Edward Warburg, which got Johnson-as-designer his first press notice, in the pages of *House & Garden*. His work was meticulous, so much so that, as Warburg remembered, "It really was an exceptionally beautiful apartment [but] . . . I always had the feeling that when I came into the room, I spoiled the composition. . . . If a magazine was slightly askew on the black coffee table, the mood was off-balance."[1] Johnson did another apartment for his sister Theodate, and as he moved to larger spaces, two more for himself. The latter, both on Forty-Ninth Street, must have felt familiar to his friends, since Johnson furnished them with the same Miës-designed furniture he had displayed in his first Manhattan digs, including Tugendhat chairs and the tablelike, tufted-leather daybed.

He added a new and central element on moving to 230 East Forty-Ninth Street. Johnson chose as the decorative focus for his sitting room a painting titled *Bauhaus Stairway*. He hung the large canvas, roughly five feet by four, near the floor, eye level for those seated on his low-slung chairs. At Alfred Barr's request, Johnson had acquired Oskar Schlemmer's oil painting in spring 1933 in Stuttgart (later, in 1942, he would give it to MoMA, where it would hold an honored place on permanent display). But in the year Johnson acquired it, Adolf Hitler became chancellor. *Bauhaus Stairway*, the first work of Schlemmer's to be sold outside Germany, seemed an elegy to a fading dream.

In the painting, youthful students climb a stair lit by a grid of windows, but the bright, utopian character of the scene is undercut by the implied motion of the figures, most of whom have their backs to the viewer as they ascend. The Staatliches Bauhaus had just been shuttered by the Nazis, and the *Studenten*, along with the Bauhaus's artistic ideals, could be said to be headed for an uncertain future in a volatile Germany.

Johnson's early design efforts proved far from exhilarating. Ground would never be broken for a house he sketched for himself, and as he recalled for his biographer years later, "I just figured that I could never be a Mies or a Le Corbusier."[2] (Clearly Wright wasn't at the forefront of Johnson's thinking.) After five years intimately associated with architecture, Alfred Barr, and the Museum of Modern Art, he decided to pursue a new path, and in December 1934, he submitted his resignation as director of architecture.

Along with his friend Alan Blackburn, who had rapidly risen in the hierarchy of the museum but resigned the same day, Johnson set off on what may, in retrospect, be kindly described as a bizarre and naïve quest—in an entirely new direction altogether—to explore an ideology that had seen fit dismiss so much that Bauhaus had stood for.

Fascist politics held a strong allure for Philip Johnson. During his 1932 visit to Berlin, he had joined his friend Helen Read, arts critic of the *Brooklyn Eagle*, at a Nazi rally in nearby Potsdam. He was mesmerized by the disciplined choreography of colorful flags, phalanxes of troops, and martial music, all prelude to the persuasive exhortations of Adolf Hitler.

Man-about-town Philip Johnson, photographed by his friend Carl Van Vechten, in 1933. (Library of Congress/Prints and Photographs)

Johnson's European travels convinced him, as he confided in Marga Barr, that the *Nationale Erhebung* (National Resurgence) would be "the salvation of Germany."[3] He also thought that Miës might thrive even in the changing circumstances, despite "the most stupid attacks on modern art." Johnson liked order in society and in buildings.

While Miës had "always kept out of politics," as Johnson observed, he himself could not resist.[4] Though he regarded Germany as his second home, he and Alan Blackburn decided upon a shift from art to politics back in the U.S.A. With the Depression at its peak, the intellectually inclined Johnson, always alive to new ideas, had encountered some large ones in a book by another member of the Crimson connection. Lawrence Dennis had graduated from Harvard a dozen years before them, but

Johnson and Blackburn made his acquaintance in New York. They found much to admire in Dennis's polemic *Is Capitalism Doomed?* (1932).

The author drew upon stints in the Foreign Service and international finance to construct an argument that portrayed capitalism as teetering on the brink of failure. Johnson found Dennis's thinking aligned with what he saw in Germany. Dennis regarded fascism as a "living religion." He concluded, "The people must have a prophet, and prophets have never come out of the world of profits."[5] Johnson imagined himself in such terms.

Rather than sailing to Europe for his usual summer art and architecture tour, Johnson, along with Blackburn, embarked on a road trip in 1934 in Johnson's big Packard Twelve, seeking to examine life in Middle America. To get a reading of Roosevelt's New Deal in action, they stopped at regular intervals to talk with people on the street in towns and cities. What they observed, Blackburn told the *New York Times* on their return, was the "inefficiency of government" in helping millions of people suffering from the effects of the Great Depression.

The two returned home certain that neither art nor the New Deal would solve the nation's social and economic problems. This precipitated their resignations at MoMA, but, as Blackburn explained to the *Times* reporter, "We have no definite political program to offer. All we have is our convictions.

"You might say that our plan is something like the view you get through an unfocused telescope. We know that we see something, but its outlines are not yet clear."[6] The thinking was admittedly fuzzy, but the passion palpable.

A subsequent road trip took them to the South to learn the methods of Huey Long, a sitting U.S. senator and former Louisiana governor. Despite his autocratic ways, Long's populist message, "Every man a king," won him wide influence. He championed the rural poor, and his proposal Share Our Wealth called for radical income redistribution, taking money from the rich and privileged, promising to provide every family in the nation with an annual income of $5,000. Huey Long fully expected his broad popularity to sweep him into the White House in 1936—he even wrote a book titled *My First Days in the White House*—but he was assassinated in September 1935, just a month after announcing his candidacy.

After attending Long's funeral in Louisiana (Johnson and Blackburn hadn't managed to meet the man in life), they returned North, taking up residence in the Johnson family's rambling Victorian house in New London, Ohio. Homer Johnson had been born in the rural town, and although prosperity came to him in Cleveland, sixty miles away, he had expanded his holdings in Huron County to include fourteen tenant farms and a large house on North Main Street, as well as the large Greek Revival homestead north of town, known locally as Townsend Farms.

The younger Johnson had never truly been a member of the village community. Though he summered as a boy in New London and rode horses around the countryside as a member of the landed gentry, he hadn't been permitted to mix with the local children and had attended school back in Cleveland (delivered there in a chauffeured limousine) prior to heading East for boarding school and college.[7] On his return as an adult to reside in New London, he still didn't look the part of a native, dressing in the long overcoat and fedora he favored. But he involved himself in local politics. A regular at town council meetings, he asked questions that required the town counsel to examine long-established procedures, and his enthusiasm got him an appointment to the local park board.

He launched a grassroots effort to increase milk prices. He announced his candidacy for state representative, but after winning the Democratic primary, he withdrew before the November election. By then he and Blackburn had allied themselves with another national figure, the Detroit-based radio priest Father Charles Coughlin, who published the weekly newspaper *Social Justice* and dismissed Democratic president Roosevelt's "government of the bankers, by the bankers, and for the bankers."[8] Coughlin had an immense radio audience of some 30 million weekly listeners, and his apparent power and visibility appealed to Johnson;

together with Blackburn, the two transplanted New Yorkers offered their services. After a night spent with Coughlin at his home outside Detroit, they founded a local chapter of Coughlin's National Union of Social Justice back in Ohio. Johnson would also design a platform for an enormous National Union rally in Chicago in late 1936, one that bore no small resemblance to the Hitler rally Johnson had witnessed in Germany. On the stage Johnson crafted, the tiny figure of Coughlin was outlined against an immense backdrop, as his booming voice exhorted a crowd that approached one hundred thousand people.

The two Manhattanites brought more than political activism to sleepy New London, population 1,500. To the surprise of his neighbors, Johnson updated his father's sprawling two-story house on North Main Street. Carpenters arrived to remove two interior partitions to create an open plan for the first floor, which had consisted of numerous small rooms, a reflection of the several additions and renovations since the construction of the house in 1867. What truly astounded the townspeople, however, was Johnson's change to the exterior. On the south wall, the clapboard siding came off and the stud wall behind was dismantled. In its place, Johnston installed floor-to-ceiling glass that opened a view out of—and into—the main parlor.[9]

Johnson's visual imagination worked in Miësian terms, and his architectural surgery transplanted a Tugendhat element into a vernacular Victorian house, a place that had been memorable for its large porch. The new wall of glass altered its character.

The Ohio idyll ended for Blackburn when he married a daughter of New London and abruptly moved back to New York with his new bride. The party the two men had founded—the Young Nationalist Movement to Save America from Communism—dissolved, and Johnson's political activity in Ohio ebbed. Back in New York, he reengaged with Lawrence Dennis and others of his political inclinations.

Johnson also resumed his periodic visits to Europe, and one of those visits, in 1939, was no innocent interlude. He was in Berlin when Germany invaded Poland. Sensing that events could erupt at any time, Johnson got himself accredited as a foreign correspondent for Coughlin's right-wing *Social Justice*, and he filed stories from Danzig. Unmistakably pro-German and anti-British in tone, his writing was inflammatory enough that the FBI soon opened a file on him. One letter he wrote at the time suggests Johnson's state of mind as he described a Polish town near Warsaw shortly after the blitzkrieg rolled through: "The German green uniforms made the place look gay and happy. There were not many Jews to be seen. We saw Warsaw burn and Modlin being bombed. It was a stirring spectacle."[10]

Despite Johnson's sympathetic view of Hitler and the Germans, the entire episode might have been lost to history except that he shared a hotel room for one September night in an East Prussian town called Sopot. The other man, a young CBS reporter named William Shirer, kept a firsthand account of those days. Shirer apparently disliked Johnson on sight, dismissing him in his journal entry as "an American fascist." When Shirer's book *Berlin Diary* appeared two years later, it became an immediate bestseller and Johnson appeared in it pages. "He has been posing as anti-Nazi," Shirer had written in his diary, "and trying to pump me for my attitude."[11]

The trip to Poland proved an inglorious end to Johnson's political adventures. He gained neither fame nor power (his Ohio party appears to have had fewer than 150 members); in fact, the misadventure became infamous, an embarrassment that, even fifty years later, had a way of periodically resurfacing. Abby Rockefeller would forgive him: "Every young man," she reportedly said at a 1957 board meeting when Johnson's candidacy for the MoMA board was under discussion, "is entitled to one bad mistake."[12] But some have seen less naïveté and more malevolence in Johnson's words and actions.

The up-and-coming young journalist Joseph Alsop may have had it about right when he prophesied in the *New York Herald Tribune*, at the time Johnson resigned from the museum, that the ex-curator was embarking on a "Sur-Realist Political Venture."[13] Like millions of well-bred, well-educated upper-class Americans in the 1930s, Philip Johnson spoke disparagingly of Jews; clubby, cocktail-hour anti-Semitism was a commonplace in privileged Protestant culture, though Johnson went further than most, reporting disapprovingly of the preponderance of Jews abroad (JEWS DOMINATE POLISH SCENE ran one headline on a Johnson dispatch in *Social Justice*).[14] The avid amateur, having succeeded in the art world, regarded politics as just another sphere where he thought he might exercise influence. For five years he tried, employing his overflowing confidence, charm, intelligence, and abundant funds (he contributed the significant sum of $5,000 to Coughlin's coffers).

His refusal to recognize the underlying violence of the National Socialist Party was certainly surreal. Johnson's place at the top of the social hierarchy left him singularly ill equipped to understand the sociology of Europe after the Great War. He had known no hardships, so the concept of affordable housing, a preoccupation of Oud and the Bauhaus, had no personal reality. He was moved by beauty, not by people (Chartres and the Parthenon brought tears to his eyes; children in a soup line did not). In assembling the landmark 1932 MoMA exhibition, he embraced the style of what came to be called Modernism. For him, the key was the abstract purity of glass and steel as art, and he failed to share the vision of its European inventors (and of Lewis Mumford) that modern architecture could be a means of building economical buildings to better the lot of Europe's postwar population. Not coincidentally, Johnson's favorite among the International Style buildings was the immense mansion Miës designed for Fritz and Grete Tugendhat.

Johnson had to know that those who had gained power in Germany held homosexuals in the same low regard they did Jews, but he chose not to acknowledge that danger. He was extraordinarily fortunate that his German escapade left his reputation only slightly tattered. His dilettantish charm saved him from a more permanent taint, just as it would repeatedly win him unlikely friends.

No less a figure than Bertrand Russell, teaching in those years in the United States, found him an engaging dinner partner. The British philosopher wasn't for a moment taken in by Johnson's politics and told a mutual friend about the evening. With a wry chuckle, he remarked, "[Johnson] is a diabolist . . . but how much pleasanter it is to spend an evening with a gentleman you disagree with than with a cad you agree with."[15]

Many events in Johnson's life can be well documented, but few details survive of the story of his political floundering in Ohio. The files from his fascist detour are thin, notably lacking in the long and confiding letters that his mother, friends, and family had grown accustomed to receiving. The clattering of his portable typewriter, so often heard in European hotel rooms in the late twenties and early thirties, either ceased or, perhaps, the letters he wrote were later relegated to the dustbin when Johnson realized the depth of his European folly. The result is that, for the most part, we glimpse Johnson in the late thirties largely as a man at the edge of the frame, an incidental presence in the recollections of contemporaries. One singular report in Johnson's own words—the telling of his ill-conceived cheering for Hitler in Poland—survived not in his files but preserved in his FBI dossier.

A consequence of this seemingly expurgated version of events is that Johnson's misdeeds never quite rose to the threshold where he felt obliged to offer a true mea culpa for his fascism and anti-Semitic statements. Instead, when challenged much later about his thirties politics, he habitually deflected. "I cannot explain it or atone" was a terse and typical refusal to confront the past.[16]

In contrast, Johnson's reticence to revisit that shadowy time did not extend to the career change he made in 1940, thanks in no small part to Frank Lloyd Wright.

II.

1937–40 . . . Two European Émigrés

AMERICA'S ARCHITECTURAL CENTER of gravity shifted in the 1930s. Its classical constancy, long resilient despite the presence of Wright's changeable work, began to absorb new influences. Johnson and his friends at MoMA had helped encourage a new austerity, and the move from traditional decoration to high function would also gain from the arrival of Modernist reinforcements from Europe. By 1938, both Miës van der Rohe and Walter Gropius had joined the German diaspora and settled permanently in North America.

Philip Johnson unabashedly disdained Wright, but Miës van der Rohe maintained his esteem for the Master of Taliesin. His admiration dated to Miës's days as a young assistant working in the Berlin office of Peter Behrens. Then—the year had been 1910—the Wasmuth portfolio had struck him and co-workers Walter Gropius and Charles-Édouard Jeanneret-Gris (a decade later the latter would adopt the name Le Corbusier) with the power of revelation. On traveling to America for the first time in 1937, Miës made a point of visiting Spring Green.

Alfred Barr deserves indirect credit for the first, Depression-era encounter of Wright and Miës. At the request of MoMA trustee Helen Lansdowne Resor, Barr wrote to Miës during the winter of 1937. He knew Miës's architectural practice in Germany was at a standstill and that Mrs. Resor and her husband, Stanley, wanted a house on their ranch in Wyoming. The couple ran J. Walter Thompson, the world's largest advertising agency. He was its head; she, a vice president of the firm, had a reputation as one of the most imaginative copywriters of the era. To Helen Resor, Miës seemed like just the man to design them a fine home.

"The site is magnificent in its surroundings and the house itself would be fairly large," Barr advised Miës. "It would involve certain problems of planning which I think would interest you."[17] With the Resors' ample means, a major commission was in the offing, and in July Miës traveled to Paris to meet and talk with Helen Resor at the Hôtel Meurice.

"I liked him immensely," she reported to Barr. "I have great respect for him and feel sure that after he sees the ranch . . . he will do a fine thing."[18] With few options in Germany, Miës sailed for America a fortnight later, together with Mrs. Resor and her two children, and at her expense. A day after stepping ashore in New York, he boarded a cross-country train, headed for the Resors' Wyoming ranch.

His schedule permitted him just one day in Chicago, and he spent it looking at works by H. H. Richardson, Louis Sullivan, and Wright. On his journey back East, he had more time, since he was being wooed by representatives of the Armour Institute of Technology, an engineering and architecture school in Chicago, with whom he met several times that September to discuss the directorship of Armour's architecture program. After taking an auto tour of Oak Park, he dispatched a telegram, on September 8, to Wright: WOULD LIKE VERY MUCH TO DRIVE TO TALIESIN AND PAY MY RESPECTS IF CONVENIENT TO YOU.[19]

For his part, Wright regarded Mies as an individualist, rather than a Johnson-style propagandist tied to a school or a style. He knew the Tugendhat House from both the architectural literature and the model in the 1932 *International Exhibition*; he saw in the Brno house originality and echoes of his own work. More disposed to Mies than to either Walter Gropius or Le Corbusier (Wright had rebuffed earlier attempts by both to visit Taliesin), he invited Mies for lunch on Friday, September 10.

To the surprise of the apprentices, the two men settled into an easy camaraderie. Communication wasn't simple, but one of the young Chicago architects who accompanied Mies, Bertrand Goldberg, had studied at the Bauhaus and spoke German fluently. He acted as Mies's interpreter, although Mies frequently resorted to hand gestures as he saw firsthand the buildings that he knew from the printed page.

Knowing Mies's exacting standards, his translator carped in German about some of the architectural detailing on view at Taliesin, then, as always, a work in progress, built by self-trained apprentices. "Shut up," Mies bluntly instructed Goldberg in German. "Just be grateful it's here."[20]

When he stepped out onto a Taliesin terrace, the usually taciturn Mies was impressed. "Freedom," he said in German. "This is a kingdom!"[21] Wright could not help but be disarmed by Mies's admiring words.

The luncheon guest would remain overnight; one day became two, then three. On the fourth day, Wright summoned a car and driver and personally escorted Miës back to Chicago. They stopped at the construction site of the Johnson Wax Building in Racine, Wisconsin; at the Unity Temple in Oak Park; and went on to the Robie House on the South Side of Chicago. On parting, Wright presented Miës with a Japanese print, a landscape from the hand of Hiroshige.

When Miës returned to Chicago the following year to head the Armour Institute, he asked that Wright introduce him at a welcoming dinner. Wright obliged in his own way: "I give you Miës van der Rohe," he said to assembled trustees and faculty. "But for me there would have been no Miës . . . I admire him as an architect and respect and love him as a man. Armour Institute, *I* give you my *Miës* van der Rohe. You treat him well and love him as I do."[22]

Despite his new life in nearby Chicago, Miës never returned to Spring Green; the September interlude during which Miës paid his respects to the Master did not flower into an enduring friendship. Still, in the personal library of some three hundred volumes that Miës brought from Germany, Wright was a significant presence. Among the several Wright-related titles were the Wasmuth volumes and a translation of Lewis Mumford's *Sticks and Stones* (1924).

In 1940, Miës would write an admiring essay about Wright's "incomparable" talent.[23] For the most part, however, the two titans went about their business as if no particular connection had ever existed.

————

WALTER GROPIUS—DAPPER, solemn, and precise—also arrived in the United States in 1937. He accepted an appointment to a professorship at Harvard's Graduate School of Design, then, a year later, became chairman of the Department of Architecture. Once installed in Cambridge, he expressed surprise at what he called his students' "vast ignorance" about the work of Frank Lloyd Wright.

Gropius brought to his new school not only his Bauhaus philosophy but also an open-eyed appreciation of Wright. On an earlier visit to America, Gropius had recognized both the Robie House in Chicago and the Larkin Building in Buffalo as "close to [his] own thinking and feeling."[24]

Wright pointedly ducked Gropius when the latter proposed a visit to Taliesin in 1937, but finally, in January 1940, the men talked at length. In Boston to deliver a lecture, Wright accepted Gropius's invitation to visit him at home in Lincoln, Massachusetts. Forbidden by the Nazis to remove financial assets from Germany, the immigrant Gropius had landed with little more than his books, papers, and a few Bauhaus furnishings. Within a year, however, the generosity of a Boston benefactor permitted him to embark on construction of a new home for himself, his wife, Ise, and their teenage daughter.

In contemplating his house's design, Gropius surveyed vernacular architecture in the region, then incorporated into his plans such traditional New England materials as fieldstone and wood clapboards. Though he employed local builders, his house on a four-acre rise overlooking an orchard differed from the older farmhouses in the vicinity. Its asymmetrical entrance, flat roof, and ribbon windows were a departure. His suppliers were bemused at his use of large sheets of plate glass, chrome banisters, commercial light fixtures, and glass blocks.

Gropius and Wright had met briefly thirteen months before—a photographer caught them in cocktail conversation at a major Bauhaus exhibition at MoMA in 1938—but their several quiet hours talking together in Lincoln tempered Gropius's admiration of Wright. He observed that to talk with Wright was to be on the receiving end of Wright's opinions; he experienced firsthand what he called Wright's "haughty arrogance." He learned their pedagogical styles differed radically. Gropius noted that Wright invited worshipful imitation among his Taliesin fellows, while Gropius, at the Bauhaus and Harvard, fostered another approach. Gropius's stated goal was to "help the student to observe and understand physical and psychological facts and from there let him find his own way."[25] In the years

Mr. Wright meets Herr and Frau Gropius at the opening of the Bauhaus exhibition at the MoMA, December 8, 1938. (MoMA/Licensed by SCALA/Art Resource, NY)

that followed, Gropius would also grow to resent Wright's pointed criticism of International Style buildings, like his own house in Lincoln.

———

WALTER GROPIUS WASN'T the only one to feel ill-treated by Wright that year. At the time of his 1940 conversation with Gropius, Wright was already anticipating a major show scheduled for the fall at the MoMA. It was to be the biggest celebration yet of his work, and John McAndrew had spent two days at Taliesin the previous September making preliminary plans. The exhibition was to include the construction of a full-scale house in the sculpture garden behind the museum's new Fifty-Third Street home. The Wright house was to be a prototype that embodied his newest thinking about good but affordable domestic design. He called such homes Usonian, a name he coined to identify a subset of his building built after 1936. These single-story dwellings were typified by low ceilings, open plans, central fireplaces, neither basements nor attics, and modular construction.[26] Installing a Usonian house in New York appealed to him, as a broader public could experience a scaled-down Wright house (his Usonian houses typically enclosed about 1,500 square feet), which embodied his gift for integrating living spaces, with the dining room becoming part of the living room, the kitchen newly convenient to the main public areas.

A Festschrift was also in preparation, a collection of admiring essays about Wright and his work. The proposed essayists included Lewis Mumford, Henry-Russell Hitchcock, Philadelphia Museum of Art director Fiske Kimball, Finnish Modernist Alvar Aalto, and all three of the Kaufmanns, E.J., Liliane, and Edgar jr. McAndrew invited Alexander Woollcott to contribute, too. Though he initially agreed, Woollcott withdrew due to failing health, suggesting that the museum reprint his 1930 *New Yorker* essay, but McAndrew chose not to pursue it, since the piece had already been published in a Woollcott collection. (The opportunity was sadly missed, as Woollcott would have no chance to refresh his insights into his old friend Wright, dying in January 1943, after suffering a heart attack during a radio broadcast.)

In 1940, Wright rode a wave, since commissions rolled in at Taliesin as they never had before. His major project at Racine, Wisconsin, the S. C. Johnson & Son administration building, commissioned in 1936 and, after constructions delays, completed in 1939, thrilled visitors with its half acre of open space beneath a translucent Pyrex tube ceiling supported by a forest of mushroomlike columns. A tour de force, the Johnson Wax Building had been a boon to Wright's commercial practice akin to Fallingwater's impact on his domestic commissions (see Fig. XX).

In preparation for the forthcoming MoMA show, Wright had set his apprentices to work making new models. He commissioned fresh photography in anticipation of an opening in October 1940, but the elements, as they had in 1932, came together slowly. At Wright's insistence McAndrew flew out to Taliesin in mid-September. DROP EVERY- THING, Wright had demanded. WANT TO SHOW YOU GENERAL SCHEME FOR CATALOGUE AND SHOW AND HOUSE.[27]

Had he been at hand, Philip Johnson might have recognized Wright's tone as an ill omen. The plan soon began to unravel. Wright demanded more space (it wasn't available). He wished to retitle the show *In the Nature of Materials*, and he prepared his own cover design for the accompanying catalog. Then, upon reading the essays McAndrew had commissioned, Wright grew furious. If the essays in hand were published, he telegrammed, THERE IS GOING TO BE NO EXHIBITION.[28]

The negotiations that ensued resembled those of January 1932, with McAndrew writing a groveling letter to Wright ("May I beg you one last time to reconsider, and . . . not just because I am in hot water.")[29] The show was saved, but delayed until November. The Usonian house in the garden was eliminated from the plan, and Wright arrived to dictate the installation of the models and images. Having been shunted aside, McAndrew found himself writing letters of apology to the contributors to the catalog; Barr would not permit the essays to be rewritten to suit Wright's ego, so no accompanying publication went to press. To Wright's irritation, the museum also distanced itself from the installation, inserting the clause "arranged by the architect himself" into its invitation and signage.[30]

When the show finally opened, the critics were not persuaded by McAndrew's press release, which bore the headline GREATEST LIVING ARCHITECT COMES TO MUSEUM OF MODERN ART. The *New York Times* critic Geoffrey Banks wondered whether the claim was "dangerously exaggerated."[31] And *Parnassus* magazine described Wright's show (it had become his in every sense, not McAndrew's) as a "bewildering mélange of blue-prints, architectural renderings, scaled models, materials and photographs," for which, the writer observed, "surprisingly enough there is no catalogue."[32]

Had the catalog been published, the public would have encountered Miës's encomium, among others. His essay described Wright as a "master-builder drawing upon the veritable fountainhead of architecture." He concluded, "In his undiminishing power [Wright] resembles a giant tree in a wide landscape, which, year after year, ever attains a more noble crown."[33] But Wright wasn't ready to let Miës or anyone else define him. As long as he lived, he guarded that prerogative as closely as he could.

————

ALTHOUGH PHILIP JOHNSON had next to nothing to nothing to do with the exhibition that Wright called "the show to end all shows," he did reach into his own deep pockets for $500 to help underwrite the planned (but eventually stillborn) Usonian house. As a MoMA adviser and confidant of Alfred Barr's, Johnson kept abreast of Wright's antics and, feeling a sense of déjà vu, sympathized with McAndrew's frustrations.

Having moved from New London, Ohio, Johnson reestablished New York as his home base, rejoining his cadre of MoMA friends. At a personal crossroads, he looked to distance himself from politics, and his first instinct was to reengage with architecture. He resisted the urge to return to the day-to-day bureaucracy of museum life, with its demanding schedule of installing one season's exhibition even as the plan for the next one (and the one after that) competed for attention. Certainly he liked the impact his public voice had had, but he wasn't ready to settle for resuming his old roles of curator and critic. Or to do battle with the likes of Wright.

He felt the stirrings of a latent desire to design. Ten years before he had assured his parents, "I have no . . . intention of doing any building at this my youthful age. There are too many problems I should like to work out first. The strategic time is later, though if I had all the money in the world I would just build continuously, keep on experimenting."[34] By 1939, however, he had reached a new emotional low that led to a rethink, a return to an old inclination.

"Despair. Personal despair ... I realized I wasn't writing, I wasn't contributing anything to any cause, black, white, or indifferent. I realized that there was something terribly, terribly lacking. And I'd always liked designing, and I thought, if you like it, for Christsake, Johnson, what stops you from going to school?"[35]

Concluding it might just be his long-sought-after vocation, he decided to reinvent himself as an architect.

His qualifications for admission to architecture school had both strengths and weaknesses. On the plus side, his time at MoMA amounted to a valuable credential, and the accompanying notoriety did not hurt. His connections at Harvard ran deep from his undergraduate years; and he knew Gropius, now a department chair at the Graduate School of Design. Johnson's lack of undergraduate training in engineering or mathematics was worrisome, as was the culture of the GSD, where most of the other applicants were recent college graduates, typically ten or more years younger than thirty-four-year-old Johnson.

Another not-so-small matter was his lack of drawing abilities. He was acutely aware that his was not a deft hand at the drafting board. On arriving in Cambridge to talk of his possible architectural future, he met with another recent arrival at Harvard, Marcel Breuer, the Gropius protégé who was helping establish GSD's place at the cutting edge of world architecture. As Johnson remembered the moment, he confided in Breuer, who, surprisingly, didn't seem notably concerned about Johnson's drafting skills.

Breuer asked the applicant to flex his hands and fingers.

Johnson complied.

"They work all right," Breuer told the prospective student. "I don't see any problem." No further examination was required.

In the fall of 1940, as Wright and McAndrew wrestled over the installation on West Fifty-Third Street, Philip Johnson boarded a train for Boston, on his way to matriculate at Harvard's Graduate School of Design. He would later see the moment as "going out into the wilderness to seek my fortune."[36]

III.

1940–43 . . . Cambridge, Massachusetts . . . Back to School

JOHNSON RENTED A small house a few blocks from Harvard Square. The neat two-story structure at 995 Memorial Drive, with its view of the Charles River, suited him. The elder statesmen among his classmates, eager to make friends, he entertained lavishly. His means permitted him to hire an Irish maid and to set an elegant table, with fine china and silverware.

His style impressed his new acquaintances. One, a Midwesterner named Carter H. Manny Jr., wrote home to Michigan City, "This guy must be made of money. He spends it like a drunken sailor."[37] According to another fellow student, John Johansen, Johnson was savvy enough to leave his rich-boy ways at the classroom door. "He . . . didn't stand above or to the side of us in the studios."

Initially, however, Johnson's work left his new peers unimpressed. "We didn't see him as having much talent," Johansen remembered, "and didn't take him seriously as a designer."[38] One first-term assignment for a beach pavilion made clear that Johnson intended to iterate the Modernist notions he had previously championed at MoMA. His project bore an unmistakable resemblance to a Miës design, but his professors approved. One member of the jury—Walter Gropius himself, whose charge at the GSD had been to update the curriculum from its Beaux Arts traditions— singled out Johnson's design for praise.

Johnson found himself surrounded with a talented cohort of architects-in-the-making; in addition to Johansen, other GSD students of the era who gained later fame included Paul Rudolph, I. M. Pei, Edward Larrabee Barnes, and Ulrich Franzen. As his fellow students set about fulfilling the degree requirements in the expected way, Johnson, his confidence growing by the day, conceived a novel approach to earning his M. Arch.

By spring 1941, he was planning a house for himself, which he proposed as his senior project. He persuaded his professors that, rather than merely devising, designing, and drawing a senior project, as most of his fellow students would do, he would build his thesis and reside there.

Various currents competed for the attention of Johnson and his fellow students; one was Frank Lloyd Wright. Carter Manny in particular maintained an admiration for Wright, one partly born of family connection (his parents were friends of two of Wright's children). "[Philip] was always trying to wean me away from Frank Lloyd Wright," Manny recalled.[39] In the end, Johnson failed, as later in the war, Manny would become a Taliesin apprentice.

During the winter of 1941, Johnson began to develop a plan for a small house, one very much suited to his own needs. He found a convenient site, having often walked past an empty lot on Ash Street in Cambridge, the vector that led directly from his rented house on Memorial Drive to the Harvard campus. In May, Johnson took title to the eighty-foot-wide, sixty-foot-deep plot at No. 9, on the corner of Acacia Street.

Even in its early stages—by summer Manny sketched a version of his friend's proposed design in a letter home—Johnson's house promised to shock his neighbors in suburban Cambridge. Most of the nearby dwellings were wood-frame structures that dated to the mid-nineteenth century; their builders, working in the local vernacular of the Greek Revival, had applied corner boards and raised gable roofs that resembled pilasters and pediments, thereby identifying the otherwise plain buildings as the geometric descendants of classical temples. Just blocks away were aristocratic Georgian mansions lining "Tory Row," the old King's Highway, which predated the Revolution (one had housed George Washington during the siege of Boston and, later, been Henry Wadsworth Longfellow's home). The streetscapes on other blocks featured elaborate Victorian houses in Queen Anne, Second Empire, and Gothic modes, with turrets, mansard roofs, broad porches, or band-sawn bargeboards.

Cantabrigians had certainly encountered new architectural ideas before; indeed, in proximity to Johnson's proposed house stood a home that, when constructed in 1882–83, had been a certifiably innovative house, a landmark in the evolution of American architecture. Just one block north of Johnson's new property, at the corner of Brattle and Ash streets, stood the Mary Fiske Stoughton house, built for a wealthy widow. Alfred Barr, Henry-Russell Hitchcock, and Johnson himself had acknowledged its designer, Henry Hobson Richardson (1838–86), in *Modern Architecture: International Exhibition*; they saw Richardson as one of the carriers of "modern American architecture, the thread which passed from Richardson to [Louis] Sullivan, from Sullivan to Frank Lloyd Wright."[40]

An early example of the Shingle Style, the Stoughton House hinted at a new simplicity. It was a distant forerunner of the designs Johnson cogitated upon for his site a few doors south. Richardson had distilled the traditions of the houses nearby, incorporating a turret, bay windows, and intersecting gable roofs. But instead of calling attention to the eclectic elements, he cloaked his admixture of shapes in a skin of uniform shingles that conformed to the undulating shapes of the house. No scrollwork carpentry elements distracted the eye; the minimal trim was painted to match the deep olive green of the shingles. Even the porch was withheld, a hollow within the mass of the house. The windows, grouped in twos and threes with numerous small lights, added to the horizontal feel, making the house look lower. Though already twice added to, in 1900 and 1925, Richardson's Stoughton House was a fixture in Johnson's landscape, a house that used materials in as plain a manner as he himself would.

By the time Johnson obtained his building permit in September 1941, Richardson's design seemed no more than an incremental shift from the other houses in the neighborhood. Johnson's house, which was to be the first freestanding work of his design to be completed, was a more radical departure. As a local paper, the *Cambridge Chronicle-Sun*, would soon observe, it was a house "the like of which Cambridge has never seen before."[41]

———

PREDICTABLY, JOHNSON BORROWED the basic idea from Miës van der Rohe. In his last years in Berlin, the burly German had designed a series of houses within enclosed courtyards. Though only one was built, all of Miës's "court-houses," in Johnson's words, consisted of a "flow of space . . . confined within a single rectangle formed by the outside walls of court and house."[42]

Johnson decided the configuration suited the increasingly dense Cambridge streetscape, where small lots could mean nosy neighbors. The house he envisioned consisted of an elongated, "earth-hugging" box some sixty feet long and just twenty feet deep. Once he decided upon the basics, Johnson hired draftsmen in the office of G. Holmes Perkins, a local architect and Johnson's friend Manny's tutor at the GSD, to execute the working drawings. This established a lifelong pattern of collaboration: Like the restaurateur with a gift for conceiving a place and selling it to the public, Johnson became the front-of-house man with back-in-the-kitchen assistance. His hirelings also produced a model that earned him a spot in an advanced design class, taught by Marcel Breuer.

With the attack on Pearl Harbor that December and a sudden scarcity of some building materials, Johnson shifted from his original (and Miës's) specification of brick for the court-house. To assure construction in wartime, Johnson substituted stressed-skin plywood for the house and the enclosing fence. On-site construction got under way in mid-April 1942 when the wall and roof panels, prefabricated in New York, arrived to be bolted and glued together on-site.

The house sat well back from Ash Street, with a narrow driveway behind. But even before his neighbors could react to it, the low, flat-roof building disappeared behind a nine-foot-tall fence that enclosed the courtyard. The combined indoor-outdoor space of the house and courtyard nearly filled the site, leaving only the driveway to the west, a minimal setback on the abutter's side to the north, and a strip of trees and plantings adjacent to the sidewalk lining Acacia Street to the south. The fence that lined the main frontage on Ash Street stood at the very edge of the sidewalk, which meant that, to anyone walking by, Johnson's abode had the forbidding air of a fortress. No windows looked out upon the street, and together, the house and contained garden occupied roughly two thirds of the 4,800-square-foot lot.

Louise Johnson came to admire her son's work-in-progress in May, but at least one neighbor was less impressed than Johnson's mother. He filed a complaint asserting that the house was too close to the property

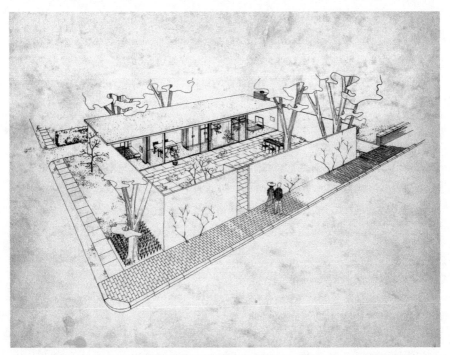

A ca. 1943 sketch of Philip Johnson's Thesis House, which nicely captures the stockadelike quality of its relationship to passersby on the street. (MoMA/Licensed by SCALA/Art Resource, NY)

lines and that the stockadelike fence exceeded the local code restriction by a full two feet. The courts declined to order Johnson to correct the violations, ruling that no one had been harmed. The elements of the simple house came together quickly, and Johnson took up residence in August 1942.

As a first work, the Ash Street house suggested both the transparency and the guardedness of its designer. The inhospitable fence at streetside implied a resident within who wanted to remain anonymous; however, once inside the keep of Johnson's castle, a visitor got the opposite message, as the front wall of the house, made entirely of glass, revealed a bedroom left, the dining space at center, and a living room right. The interior was open, with a minimum of partitions to the rear to enclose the two baths, utilities, and kitchen, and only a partial wall screened the bedroom. A bookcase helped define the dining area. The fireplace on the north wall was one of the few traditional elements. The house had almost no storage, with neither an attic nor a basement.

Johnson decorated the house with the Miës furniture from his New York apartment (including the chrome-and-leather slung chairs and the flat daybed with the bolster cushion), and he arranged them in a nearly identical rectilinear arrangement. Diaphanous curtains could be drawn across the glass to cut the glare. The floor was a uniform light carpet.

If Johnson wasn't quite ready to open himself to the world, he was utterly unabashed about revealing his admiration for Miës. Johnson's chosen vernacular, with its expanse of glass fronting a simple box, was fresh in the context of staid Cambridge; in its urban setting, its seethrough character seemed an unlikely choice. Even to his fellow students, the house was a surprise: According to Ulrich Franzen, "It was the first Miësian house that any of us had seen."[43]

In fact, the Ash Street house was a paradoxical trope. The enclosing fence discouraged entry, but once the outer boundary was breached, the usual barriers were nowhere to be seen; the garden was a part of the house. Paradoxically, the transparent wall looked out on the solid palisade wall that blinded the peering eyes of passersby (one trade magazine of the day criticized Johnson for his disregard for the "traditional American neighbourhood pattern").[44] That sense of privacy was, in part, illusory: there could be no closely held secrets since anyone on the second and third floors of the surrounding taller houses nearby could easily look down upon the happenings in Johnson's house and courtyard.

The place was strange enough that it took some getting used to. One guest did his imitation of a confused bird: The man walked directly into the glass wall. "He fell to the floor more or less unconscious," another guest remembered. "I remember Philip looking very annoyed and saying something like, 'Damn fool.'"[45]

Perhaps the fellow had partaken of the drink that flowed freely—at Ash Street, Johnson hosted an ongoing salon where he welcomed his guests saloon-style, with drinks served by a Filipino houseboy. His many guests included not only Harvard architecture students but old friends Alfred Barr, Henry-Russell Hitchcock, and George Howe.

Despite Johnson's pique, the guest who was confused by the glass demonstrated that the owner-designer had succeeded in accomplishing what he set out to do. Though it was (and is) unroofed, the exterior walled garden, as the disoriented guest demonstrated, isn't quite separable from the interior. The house and the walled garden are elements of the same space as adjacent rooms are in a normally partitioned home. The four immense sheets of plate glass that constitute the front wall separate the interior of the house from the garden *and*, simultaneously, integrate the garden into the house.

Architecture, at its most basic, concerns light, space, and shelter, and Johnson's apprentice house is a distillation of just those elements. The long, shallow house has the aspect of an open-front lean-to, its front a wall of light during the day. Thus, his so-called court-house isn't defined by the presence of a roof over the house or its absence over the courtyard. It's a building united with its garden, obvious yet subtle, a place that, like Johnson, asked not to be seen even as it called attention to itself.

When constructed in the early 1940s, the Ash Street house was a whispered promise of buildings and landscapes to come.

Johnson's litigious neighbor wasn't the only one who disliked the place. Neither Gropius nor Breuer approved. "People felt it didn't jibe with the street," Johnson recalled later, "and they were right—it didn't."[46] On the other hand, many of his architectural peers, never having seen a house of its kind before, liked what they saw. Ulrich Franzen thought it was "very simple and very beautiful," and John Johansen called it "stunning."[47]

Always an insightful observer, Marga Barr found 9 Ash Street a "special place." Once Johnson lent her his little house, where she and her daughter Victoria spent a spring break from their respective schools. They experienced the place as no cocktail-hour visitor could but as round-the-clock inhabitants. For her, the glass-faced house seemed "serene" and "logical." She also thought it amusing that, as the enclosing fence didn't quite reach the ground, the feet of passing pedestrians could be seen. (Johnson himself remembered neighborhood ladies trying to peer under.)

Mrs. Barr also understood it was very much Philip's place. "As we sat in the living room or in the yard we felt magically secluded in a conscipusly [*sic*] elitist ambience, a special place where every space, every piece of furniture had its own special preordained location. While Philip was absent he was yet the 'genius loci' and—as in all his other works large or small, it is impossible to alter his arrangements. Whoever does is a vandal."[48]

CHAPTER 10

Wright's Manhattan Project

The building is non-traditional, non-representational, non-historical abstract art in its own right; indeed, it not merely coincides with the contents, it supersedes them. You may go to this building to see Kandinsky or Jackson Pollock; you remain to see Frank Lloyd Wright.
—*Lewis Mumford*

I.

June 1943 . . . Spring Green, Wisconsin . . . Taliesin

FRANK LLOYD WRIGHT received an invitation to Johnson territory in mid-1943. The sender wanted Wright's help as Manhattan gave birth to another museum. "Could you ever come to New York," the letter began, "and discuss with me a building for our collection of non-objective paintings[?]"[1]

Looking at the handwritten letter, dated June 1, Wright didn't recognize the graceful, rolling script on the blue stationery. He also drew a blank on reading the signature, but if the writer's name sparked no recollections, Hilla Rebay's association did, as the title appended was "Curator of the S. R. Guggenheim Foundation." Certainly Wright knew the name Guggenheim. And he knew it meant money, New York money, and lots of it. A scion of Meyer Guggenheim, Solomon Richard had inherited a handsome share of his father's immense copper mining and smelting fortune, and, a savvy businessman himself, had greatly increased his wealth.

The letter could hardly have arrived at a better time. Fewer than five Taliesin fellows remained in Spring Green that summer. Some had enlisted in military service after the attack on Pearl Harbor. Others resisted the draft, seeking conscientious objector status, and in several cases, their principles, reinforced by Wright's strident isolationist stance, had resulted in imprisonment. The war had meant a dearth of new construction, and even a Wright-designed housing project for defense workers, planned for Pittsfield, Massachusetts, had been canceled. Wright's vocal opposition to the war had won him few friends; when he tried to get Broadacre City, his sprawling plan for rethinking the American town, designated a "worthy national objective," his petition met with silence from the White House.[2] As a result, the remaining Taliesin fellows spent more time tilling victory gardens than manning drafting tables.

On reading the entire letter, Wright found Rebay's note described a singular commission. That he had never designed a museum posed no impediment to the intrepid Mr. Wright; nor, it seemed, did the writer desire a traditional gallery. "I do not think these paintings are easel paintings," the letter explained. "They are order creating order and are sensitive (and corrective even) to space. As you feel the ground, the sky and the 'in-between' you will perhaps feel them too; and find the way."

This was the sort of challenge Wright could embrace. It wasn't simply a request for a design; the writer seemed to understand Wright's character. "I need a fighter, a lover of space, an originator, a tester and a wise man," Wright read. "I want a temple of the spirit, a monument! And your help to make it possible."[3]

Gratifying to read, the words also piqued his curiosity. But as usual, Wright had limited funds. To avoid the expense of a New York trip, he decided to respond by issuing what had become his standard invitation. He could play the master's role at Taliesin once again, the welcoming host and, not incidentally, the tour guide who revealed to his guest the Wright manner very much on display at his Spring Green property.

His reply, then, inverted the invitation: "Why don't you run down here for a week end? Bring your wife. We have room and the disposition to make you comfortable."

The Baroness Hilla von Rebay promptly and politely declined. "I am not a man," she advised Wright, adding, "I built up this collection, this foundation." More important, she explained, "Mr. Guggenheim is 82 years old and we have no time to lose ... Mr. Guggenheim is soon leaving for the summer and is seldom there in the winter. It is not easy."

The second note prompted Wright to move quickly. Within days, he boarded a train for New York, and less than a fortnight later, a formal letter of agreement was executed. It required Wright "to furnish preliminary studies, complete plans, final specifications and supervision necessary to the erection and completion" of the new museum. The construction cost was to be not more than $750,000, and Wright's fees were not to exceed 10 percent of the actual cost.[4]

The man who repeatedly professed a loathing for urban streetscapes had suddenly received an assignment in the nation's largest city. Though the fees represented a return to solvency for the financially straitened Frank Lloyd Wright Foundation, that seemed less important to the impecunious Wright then the chance to design a building that would again remind the world—and the likes of Philip Johnson and his International cadre—of Wright's genius. For a man well past the expected age of retirement (Wright turned seventy-six that June), the task of designing a home for what was then to be known as the Museum of Non-Objective Painting amounted to the perfect birthday present.

II.

1928–29 ... New York City ... Carnegie Studios

UNLIKE THE TRIUMVIRATE of women who founded MoMA (Mesdames Rockefeller and Sullivan, together with Miss

Bliss), Hilla Rebay (b. 1890) was an artist in her own right. The daughter of a German army officer, Hildegard Anna Augusta Elizabeth Freiin Rebay von Ehrenwiesen grew up in comfort in her native Alsace. At nineteen, she enrolled at the Académie Julian in Paris, where she studied drawing and painting.

By age twenty, she knew art would be her life's work. Her training prepared her to be a portraitist, but after moving to Munich in 1910, Rebay found she reveled in what she described to her mother as the "luxuriousness of color."[5] During the next decade, her peregrinations took her to London, Zurich, back to Paris, and on regular excursions to her family home in the Alsace countryside, then part of Germany. Her artistic inclinations led her steadily away from reproducing what she saw in the world and into the realm that, in 1911, Wassily Kandinsky labeled "non-objective painting."

As Philip Johnson would discover in the next decade, Berlin in the 1910s offered a heady mix of art and culture. While the upper echelon of the capital's society made for a ready market for portraits painted by the wellborn Rebay (she inherited the title of Baroness Hildegard Rebay von Ehrenwiesen), the city's diverse culture fostered new forms of art. Rebay found congenial company amid a subculture of avant-garde writers, filmmakers, painters, and other artists.

Hers was a compelling presence, despite her small stature. With thick blond hair, dark eyes, and intense seriousness—lightened, occasionally, by a radiant shy smile—she attracted well-placed suitors from her parents' world. But she chose companionship instead from the ranks of struggling artists. For a time, Rebay took as her lover the artist Hans (Jean) Arp (of mixed parentage, he was known by both German and French Christian names). Arp introduced her to paintings by Paul Klee, Marc Chagall, and Franz Marc, artists who made increasingly less literal images and experimented with color. Rebay was influenced by Arp's friends the Dadaists, among them Tristan Tzara and Kurt Schwitters.

During the Great War, Rebay herself painted large oils and tiny watercolors. While some early images portrayed recognizable elements of dance, her work increasingly focused on form, as the figurative dissolved, giving way to colorful abstractions. To earn money, she still painted people, pleasing the well-to-do who could afford images of themselves and their loved ones, but the art she made to please herself featured lines, planes, dots, and geometric figures. Like Kandinsky's, her works often bore titles linked to musicology, including *Composition*, *Allegretto*, *Fugue*, and *Capriccio*. Gaining the respect of her peers, her work hung on gallery walls in Cologne, Zurich, and Berlin.

During the war she fell in love with another painter. By 1917, she shared her life with Rudolf Bauer, but their time together was far from idyllic. Despite the influence she had on his development, Bauer held her work in low regard. Their off-and-on relations proved difficult for Rebay. Over the next decade, she had recurring headaches, throat ailments, and various illnesses, including a life-threatening bout with diphtheria. She repeatedly contemplated suicide. She lived for a time in Italy, in part to escape Bauer, who had come to rely upon her for living expenses. Though she felt diminished by him, she tirelessly promoted his work and revered Bauer as an artistic genius.

On the advice of friends, she crossed the Atlantic, arriving in America on the SS *President Wilson* in early 1927. She had $50 in her pocket, but aristocratic connections soon opened doors. The Baroness von Rebay found that New Yorkers seemed drawn to her, to her vital presence, and to her art. By autumn, an installation of her work at the Marie Sterner Gallery on Fifty-Seventh Street found numerous buyers. Not content with acquiring a Rebay collage and a painting, one collector, Irene Rothschild Guggenheim, sought out the artist. The two women became friends, and by the time the baroness sailed a few months later for a summer visit to Europe, the farewell messages in her stateroom included a bon voyage telegram from Irene Guggenheim.

After returning to New York in October 1928, the artist resumed work in her spacious one-room studio above Carnegie Hall. Though her calling was her non-objective works, she continued to accept other assignments, including one from a Manhattan dealer to copy a portrait of George Washington at the Metropolitan Museum.[6] More important, however, was a commission from Irene Guggenheim, who, with her husband, Solomon, occupied a large suite nearby in the Plaza Hotel. Mrs. Guggenheim wanted the baroness to paint a portrait of her husband.

He duly arrived at Rebay's tall-ceilinged studio with its ample northern light. Surrounded by Bauer's canvases, her own collages and paintings, and the works of other advanced European artists, the artist set to work over multiple sittings to record Guggenheim.

Theirs was an unlikely meeting of art and commerce. Rebay worked in oils to limn a recognizable likeness, a task that posed no particular challenge. A life-size Guggenheim emerged, a serious-seeming American businessman dressed in a tie and matching vest, jacket, and knee breeches of brown wool. Seated in a leather armchair, the subject looked to be at leisure, a man of late middle years, his legs casually crossed and his hands resting on his thighs. But the expression Rebay recorded belied the ease of his posture. His look is direct, fixed.

The baroness talked as she painted. Mr. Guggenheim may initially have been dubious about what he heard Rebay saying, but certainly he listened intently. During the preceding decade, the cause of non-objective art had nourished her, giving purpose to her life. Some observers labeled non-objective canvases "abstract," but Rebay, Bauer, and Kandinsky resisted the term. They saw their work not as abstracted from another source but as something entirely original. As Rebay had told Bauer in their early months together, "Reason and conscious intellect are of no help on our work, since it is based on feeling, and feeling corrects itself."[7] As Bauer put it, "The creations of the spirit must be non-objective."[8]

When Rebay explained her passion for this new art, Guggenheim grasped that the paintings held a powerful spiritual sway over the baroness; this art amounted to a religious vocation. She believed the most gifted of the non-objective artists had an ability to channel God, making the paintings of eternal importance. She insisted that they needed to be seen, the word of them spread. For Rebay, they carried a message of "rhythmic action, spiritual uplift, exquisite joy."[9]

The heat of her arguments warmed Guggenheim's interest in this new art, but her mystical beliefs in the power of nonrepresentational art made it all the more ironic that the painting of an entirely traditional portrait of her new friend "Guggie," as she soon called him, would be the pivot point in her life. When he had arrived in Rebay's studio overlooking Fifty-Seventh Street, his taste in painting began with Old Masters and ended with the rural landscapes of the mid-nineteenth-century Barbizon School and early Impressionists. But her passion, together with the non-objective works he saw in Rebay's Carnegie Hall studio, enlarged his artistic universe. In the coming months and years, she would become his guide, his sole adviser on

Solomon R. Guggenheim: businessman, philanthropist, and art collector.
(Underwood Archives/Getty Images)

a quest that, until he met her, had never entered his mind. Against the odds, Rebay converted Guggenheim. He would, in turn, enable her to become a curator and the founding director of a great museum.

Yet these transformations were a consequence of more than one woman's passion, an old-world title, and her skills as an artist. As Guggenheim himself soon explained, a lingering sense of rejection from his own youth predisposed him to his improbable shift.

Rebay traveled to Europe with the Guggenheims in 1929 and again in 1930. An artistic insider in the Old World, she easily gained entrée for her patrons to artists' studios to buy fresh works for their rapidly growing collection of the new art. She wanted them to understand the rich creative culture, and one July evening in 1930, the Guggenheims dined at the home of Walter Gropius in Berlin.

Arriving overdressed for the occasion, the Guggenheims were a little taken aback at the unfamiliar Bauhaus furniture, all skeletal chrome tubes and strips of leather, a stark contrast to the traditional chair in Guggenheim's portrait. Seeking to make her guests feel welcome, hostess Ise Gropius inquired of Mr. Guggenheim how he had become interested in modern painting. Rebay stood by, translating.

In English, Guggenheim explained that, as a young man, he had devised a new method of extracting copper. But his father, Meyer Guggenheim, had dismissed the idea. For the younger Guggenheim, the experience embodied a life lesson. As he explained to Mrs. Gropius, one should "never underestimate the works of those people who tried totally different methods." Solomon Guggenheim translated the notion to the art he had begun to collect. It was totally new—and he wished to support it.[10]

By the time Frank Lloyd Wright first met Guggenheim in 1943, the Baroness von Rebay had invested the industrialist's money well, collecting a remarkable array of contemporary art. For a time, its owner had contemplated a bequest to the Metropolitan Museum, but guided by Rebay, he had long since decided upon his own museum. Now he wanted a suitably unique building in which to house it.

III.

1939–43 . . . New York City . . . 24 East Fifty-Fourth Street

WHO WOULD BE the best architect for such a plan?" Baroness von Rebay had wondered years earlier, in 1930.[11] Having already won her benefactor's approval to think such thoughts, she confided in Rudolf Bauer, whose work she continued to revere, of her dream of a "Temple of Non-objectivity."

With Guggenheim's money to back her, Rebay thought big. In a long letter to Bauer, she described a temple "built in a fabulous style." She specified a restful entrance room: "[It] must have blue ceiling lights, like Napoleon's Tomb in Paris; a room . . . where one can get away from the noise of the streets before entering the temple of art." The galleries (she called them "exhibition halls") were to be "festive, yet cozy," with the music of Bach audible everywhere. She also wanted a library, a hall for lectures and musical performances, and a shop for the sale of reproductions "at cost." This was, after all, an evangelical endeavor. And it had to be in New York, "truly the only possible city," according to Rebay.[12]

The name Frank Lloyd Wright had been far from the first to come to mind; in fact, the concerns he expressed to Mumford years earlier about "reading my obituaries" proved very real. Rebay had known of his work since at least 1931, when she saw a Wright retrospective in Berlin, but Rebay later claimed that she thought he was dead.[13] In any case, her first instinct had been to look to Europe.

The extraordinary series of studio visits during the summer of 1930 netted the rapidly expanding Guggenheim collections many works of art. The Guggenheims and their guide met Marc Chagall, Piet Mondrian, and Fernand Léger in Paris, Kandinsky at the Bauhaus, and Bauer in Berlin. Rebay arranged for her American friends to meet several architects, too, and in addition to dining with Gropius, they made the acquaintance of Le Corbusier, who, Rebay learned, dreamed of establishing "the 1st truly modern museum."[14]

Mondrian recommended that Rebay consult architect Frederick Kiesler in New York. The expatiate-Austrian Kiesler dismissed Le Corbusier as "journalistic," but impressed the baroness with "his plan for a new museum that has no windows." As Rebay reported, "[It] is 14 stories high [and] *very, very* interesting."[15] Rebay consulted with German architect Edmund Körner, with whom she discussed "matching the museum to the painting, to the galleries, just as one custom-creates the frame around the picture."[16] Other names were bandied about, including Alvar Aalto, Marcel Breuer, and Richard Neutra. Before Wright was consulted, Rebay and company considered Walter Gropius (Bauer dismissed him as "too small-time") and Miës, whose "incredible glass structures" seemed ill-matched to a museum.[17]

Another kind of conversation altogether began when, in 1935, the Rockefellers and Mayor Fiorello La Guardia developed a master plan for a cultural pedestrian avenue that would link Radio City Music Hall and the MoMA with a proposed new home for the Metropolitan Opera—along with a Guggenheim museum. The plan for the Municipal Art Plaza stalled when rapidly rising land prices intimidated even the Rockefellers, though the discussions did prompt Solomon Guggenheim to initiate the legal formalities that led to the establishment of the Solomon R. Guggenheim Foundation on June 25, 1937. The founding document stated explicitly that one of the foundation's aims was to open a museum.

Although it proved another false start, an idea Rebay floated that same year gave a new shape to the vision of a new museum. Rebay broached the idea of an exhibition for the forthcoming 1939 New York World's Fair. Until then only a few New Yorkers had seen the Guggenheim collection. As early as 1930, Rebay had hung a selection in the couple's second-floor apartment at the Plaza—it ran the full length of the Fifth Avenue side of the hotel—which had been redesigned with Art Deco furnishings. A few canvases had been lent to Alfred Barr at MoMA for 1933 and 1934 exhibitions.[18] But by the late thirties, the collection approached a thousand works, many of them paintings by Bauer and Kandinsky, but with numerous other artists represented, including Fernand Léger, Marc Chagall, Paul Klee, Amedeo Modigliani, Georges Seurat, and László Moholy-Nagy.

In thinking about the 1939 event, Rebay herself put on paper her mind's-eye image of a special Guggenheim pavilion. It consisted of a dozen glass-roofed wings that extended like spokes from a central court-yard. Although the plan for the temporary structure in Queens never made it beyond her rough sketch on a piece of stationery, Rebay's rendering anticipated a future circular building on a rectangular plot.

By the time Rebay's letter prompted Wright's trip East to meet her and Guggenheim in 1943, the Museum of Non-Objective Painting had had a public New York home since 1939, a low-rise commercial building at 24 East Fifty-Fourth Street. In the late thirties rumors of war—and its eventual outbreak in Europe—had temporarily ended talk of building an all-new museum. But Rebay had transformed a rented retail space into galleries. With the help of architect William Muschenheim, who had been featured in Johnson and Barr's 1931 show *Rejected Architects*, she had adapted a forty-foot-wide storefront, which consisted of two floors plus a mezzanine on a hundred-foot-deep footprint.

The galleries surprised viewers. Many of the walls were hung with pleated gray velour drapery fabric, and the floors were covered with plush carpeting in a matching hue. For the first time in a gallery, newly available fluorescent lighting was used, the tubes concealed in the ceiling recesses. At Rebay's striking installation for the exhibition she called *The Art of Tomorrow*, the canvases were hung below eye level, many of them snug to the baseboard.

She wanted gallery visitors to take a seat on the oversized ottomans provided. Rebay looked to set the mood: In an austere setting, with piped-in Bach and Chopin playing, the visitor could contemplate the visionary pictures. The paintings were the indisputable focus, set off by their broad, bolection-molded frames covered with silver leaf.

The new museum got mixed reviews. The *Times* critic thought it "theatrical."[19] On his visit in 1943, Frank Lloyd Wright thought that

Rebay's installation and, in particular, her calculated effects with the bulbous frames, amounted to little more than "a hideous lumber-yard."[20]

With his unshakable confidence, Wright knew he could do better.

IV.

Fall 1943 . . . New York City

THE WOMAN THAT Frank Lloyd Wright met cut a formidable figure. Though she had grown stout with the years, the square-jawed and dark-haired Hilla Rebay carried herself with a confidence enhanced by her joint status as a European aristocrat, an artist well-known among the avant-garde, and the woman entrusted with Mr. Guggenheim's museum dreams. Though not yet a citizen—she had briefly been detained as an enemy alien earlier in the war—she spoke precise English, despite an unmistakable German accent.

The fifty-three-year-old baroness was charged with imparting to Wright her vision for the museum—and she had grown accustomed to being listened to. She explained the exhibition halls would display a collection that consisted not merely of her favored non-objective works but also, as she put it, "paintings with an object." These included such works as the elongated faces and nudes of Amedeo Modigliani, the primitivist canvases of Henri Rousseau, pointillist works by Georges Seurat, and the richly remembered dreamscapes of Marc Chagall, all of which, in Rebay's view, anticipated the non-objective. She told Wright she wished non-objective and objective works segregated one from the other, but that she wanted more than just galleries, insisting that the building's program also include a theater for film, studios for working artists, and even an apartment on the premises for herself.

Despite such requirements, Wright's assignment remained surprisingly vague. In writing to him in the days before he signed the contract, Rebay described a vision less concrete than spiritual. He was, she advised, "with infinity and sacred depth [to] create the dome of the spirit: the expression of the cosmic breath itself."[21] The man with money was similarly unspecific. "No such building as is now customary for museums," Guggenheim told Wright, "could be appropriate for this one."[22] They might know it when they saw it, but perhaps appropriately, the proposed museum they held in their minds remained a non-objective form.

For Wright, the greatest unknown was the site. He prided himself on responding to a place, on devising organic solutions that affixed a building to its setting. This new assignment came without a location. Instead, the contract specified a budget to acquire land ($250,000, not so large a sum given Manhattan prices) and a worrisomely short deadline by which to accomplish it. If by July 1, 1944, no site had been acquired, his contract automatically terminated.

Despite the entire world being at war—American troops fought their way atoll to atoll across the Pacific and the Allies conducted carpet-bombing raids over Germany, with devastating results—Wright had a compelling incentive to go shopping.

He preferred building in the open, but here his assignment was the teeming streets of Manhattan. Wright reached out to Robert Moses. A builder of bridges and parkways and Wright's cousin by marriage, Moses regarded himself as the man who could do for New York what Baron Haussmann had done for nineteenth-century Paris. Moses was perhaps uniquely suited to recommend sites in the vicinity, and within days, Moses himself took the wheel to chauffer Wright and Rebay to an eight-acre parcel in Riverdale, just north of Manhattan. The hilltop, part of a new park Moses was creating, overlooked Spuyten Duyvil, the turbulent confluence of the Harlem and Hudson Rivers.

For Wright, the prospect seemed the perfect departure from the dense Manhattan cityscape. Easily reached by car—which he, along with Moses, believed was key to the American future—the site, as Wright wrote to Guggenheim, seemed "a genuine relief from the cinder heap old New York is bound to become."[23]

Wright had in the past tried to persuade clients to relocate their dream buildings to remote sites in keeping with his organic vision. In 1936, upon seeing the industrial setting for the Johnson Wax Headquarters, Wright invited Herbert Johnson to make his business part of Broadacre City; recognizing the unreality of the request, Olgivanna had prompted her husband, "Give them what they want, Frank, or you will lose the job."[24] Just as the Johnson Wax Administration Building rose where the client wanted it, Wright's plea, in 1943, was rejected when Guggenheim and Rebay dismissed the Bronx site as too remote, since Riverdale was a full ten miles north of the existing midtown home of the Museum of Non-Objective Art.

Moses suggested alternatives, including lots on which two town houses sat on Park Avenue, between Sixty-Ninth and Seventieth Streets. But the asking price was twice the allotted budget. Next, two sites near MoMA were rejected. The possibility of sharing the same block with the J. P. Morgan Library, on the corner of Thirty-Seventh Street and Madison Avenue, ended when the property was sold to another buyer.

During these weeks, as the Wrights made repeated visits East, a bond developed between Hilla Rebay and not only Wright, but Olgivanna and their daughter, Iovanna. Rebay's belief in the mystical extended to omens, and she told seventeen-year-old Iovanna that, during her search for an architect, a book had fallen off a shelf, striking her on the head. The book was about Wright.[25]

Rebay's years of recurring maladies—incapacitating headaches, persistent throat pain—had led her to seek out exotic remedies, some of which she recommended to the Wrights. Utterly convinced that dental problems and tonsils had an insidious impact on the spirit, she persuaded Wright to have all his remaining teeth removed and replaced by dentures; she assured him that the extraction of the "dead teeth" would "purify" his blood. Olgivanna agreed to have teeth extracted, too, but the removals stopped when Rebay proposed teenaged Iovanna as the next candidate. "Hilla is not going to get her teeth as well," Olgivanna told Wright within earshot of one of the apprentices. "Frank, this is a building for which you, for which

FIG. I Frank Lloyd Wright in a contemplative pose, shortly before construction began at the Guggenheim Museum. (New York World-Telegram & the Sun newspaper *Photograph Collection, Library of Congress/Prints and Photographs*)

FIG. II Philip Johnson, Post-Modernism's Moses, with his tabletlike model of the AT&T Building, in the image used on the cover of the January 8, 1979 issue of *Time*. (*Ted Thai, The LIFE Picture Collection/Getty Images*)

FIG. III Wright's rambling homestead near Spring Green, Wisconsin, famously set at the brow of the hill and reflected here in the placid waters of the man-made pond. (*Roger Straus III*)

FIG. IV For Wright, Taliesin was an architectural laboratory, a place for testing his ideas. The "bird walk," a forty-foot cantilevered terrace that extends into space like a great diving board, anticipated the broad "trays" he incorporated into his design for E. J. and Lilian Kaufmann. (*Roger Straus III*)

FIG. V As seen from the meadow below, here is Miës's restored Tugendhat House with its defining horizontal band of tall windows. *(Donald Gellert)*

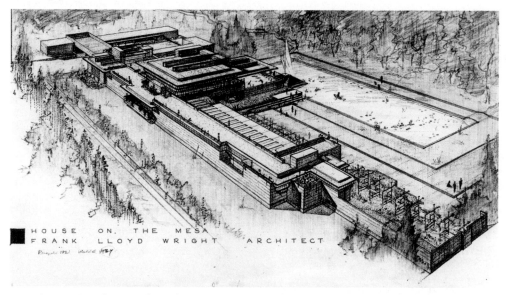

FIG. VI A perspective drawing of Wright's House on the Mesa, which was displayed at the 1932 *Modern Architecture: International Exhibition*. Although Wright recycled some of its elements over the years, this design was never constructed. *(The Frank Lloyd Wright Foundation/Art Resource, NY)*

FIG. VII Wright's desert village, dubbed Taliesin West, in the Sonoran Desert in Arizona. (*Roger Straus III*)

FIG. VIII For Philip Johnson, Wright's Taliesin West was the perfect exemplar of what the younger man called the "processional element in architecture," inviting the visitor to enter, engage, and experience the place. (*Roger Straus III*)

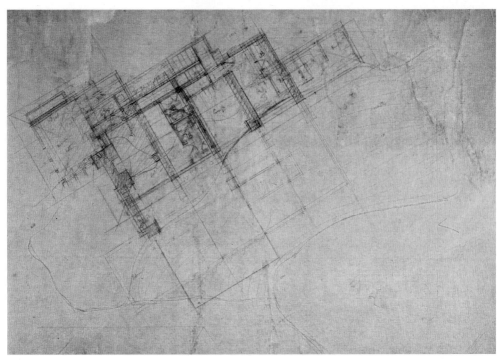

FIG. IX Wright's first rendering of Fallingwater, from the ground up, hurriedly sketched, on September 22, 1935, as E. J. Kaufmann motored toward Spring Green for lunch. (*The Frank Lloyd Wright Foundation Archives, the Museum of Modern Art/Avery Architectural & Fine Arts Library, Columbia University*)

FIG. X Not only its terraces but even the stairs to the stream are suspended above the waters of Bear Run. (*Roger Straus III*)

FIG. XI and **FIG. XII** Fallingwater's extraordinary changeability is clear from these two images. One echoes the from-the-streambed composition of Bill Hedrich's classic 1937 shot of Fallingwater (*above*); the other conveys something of the experience the visitor has upon approaching the house via the access road. (*Roger Straus III*)

FIG. XIII Wright's detailed early drawing of the Guggenheim Museum, which is both an elevation and a section. Note the word *ziggurat* and the little thumbnail views in the detail, below. (*The Frank Lloyd Wright Foundation Archives, the Museum of Modern Art/Avery Architectural & Fine Arts Library, Columbia University*)

FIG. XIIIa

FIG. XIV By late autumn 1957, the museum had risen well above the construction fence that lined Fifth Avenue. (*Gottscho-Schleisner, Inc., Library of Congress/Prints and Photographs*)

THE MASTERPIECE

FIG. XV Wright's (and draftsman Ling Po's) drawing titled "The Masterpiece," dating to 1958, with the yo-yo girl leaning into the Guggenheim's great rotunda. (*The Frank Lloyd Wright Foundation Archives, the Museum of Modern Art/Avery Architectural & Fine Arts Library, Columbia University*)

FIG. XVI The Glass House interior, as photographed in 1949. In part, it is a Johnsonian exercise in taste, with the MR furniture, the Nadelman twin figures, and the delicate Giacometti standing figure. (*André Kertész/Condé Nast via Getty Images*)

FIG. XVII Philip Johnson's most essential work, the Glass House, in New Canaan, Connecticut, as recorded in 2006, one year after his death. (*Carol M. Highsmith Archive, Library of Congress/Prints and Photographs*)

FIG. XVIII The first vision of the Farnsworth House, executed by Miës van der Rohe and delineator Edward Duckett. (*Hedrich Blessing Collection/Chicago History Museum/Getty Images*)

FIG. XIX Unlike Johnson's earthbound house, Miës's glass home for Edith Farnsworth stands atop piers, giving the illusion of floating above the grassy site near the Plano River. (*Carol M. Highsmith Archive, Library of Congress/Prints and Photographs*)

FIG. XX A view of the "great workroom" at the Johnson Wax offices in Racine, Wisconsin, with its memorable, treelike support columns of poured concrete. (*Jack Boucher, HABS, Library of Congress/Prints and Photographs*)

FIG. XXI As photographed in 1958, the Seagram Building (*left*) framed by its modernist sister, Lever House, looking southeast. (*Andreas Feininger/The LIFE Picture Collection/Getty Images*)

FIG. XXII Wright's Romeo and Juliet Windmill, an eye-catcher visible far and wide from its hilltop overlooking the Helena Valley, Wisconsin. (*Roger Straus III*)

FIG. XXIII Johnson's geometric exercise—a squared-off spiral stair to nowhere—in honor of his friend Lincoln Kirstein. (*Photo by Grace Hough courtesy of the Glass House*)

FIG. XXIV The aging Philip Johnson, still in residence after almost fifty years, leaning against the brick mass of the Guest House, with his more famous prismatic domicile behind him. (*John Dolan*)

we, have quite literally given our blood."[26] She did not exaggerate, as the Wrights had tried another of Rebay's unusual regimens, throat leeches, intended to draw out the poisonous "old" blood to encourage the new. Wright found the leeching "lower[ed] one's vitality for a week or two."[27]

With the passing of the summer and autumn, Wright's frustration rose. The search for a suitable piece of property produced nothing, but, Wright reported, his imagination was becoming crowded with ideas. He confided in Rebay, "I am likely to blow up or commit suicide unless I can let them out on paper."[28]

With the year ending, Wright took stock. On December 30, 1943, he telegrammed Rebay that he thought that BY CHANGING OUR IDEA . . . FROM HORIZONTAL TO PERPENDICULAR WE CAN GO WHERE WE PLEASE."[29] On New Year's Eve, he assumed a businesslike tone in writing Guggenheim. "It now seems probable, that our desire for a horizontal building is incompatible with real estate values."[30] Quite against his usual practice, Wright now accepted the need to take a more vertical approach in finding a solution suited to a city where towering skyscrapers were fast becoming the rule.

He offered Guggenheim no specifics, but seated at his drafting table as the snow accumulated outside Taliesin's frosted windows, he set aside earlier unfinished sketches for a low, horizontal building. He began to give his newly vertical thinking tangible form.

v.

January 1944 . . . Spring Green, Wisconsin . . . Taliesin

WITHOUT A SPECIFIC New York site to explore, Wright had no choice but to imagine one. Given what he knew of Manhattan real estate prices and his clients' demands for a complex building program, he calculated that a lot roughly 125 feet by 90 feet might be affordable and workable. This theoretical site resembled the plot near the Morgan Library that had been considered. Wright also decided such a corner site was essential.

Though he told Rebay he was "busy at the boards," he didn't tell her in his letter of January 20, 1944, that he had worked out the essentials of a design that he would be soon be ready to show. A man who prided himself on putting pencil to paper only after an idea had begun to jell in his mind, Wright's design for the large multipurpose building emerged with surprising speed.[31]

It wasn't without precedent in his oeuvre. Since the early stages of his career, Wright had acknowledged that geometric shapes exercised "spell power" over his imagination. According to Wright, the square represented integrity, the triangle implied structural unity. Wright said he found the cube comforting, the sphere inspiring. Many years earlier, musing on what could happen when such "architectural themes" as the circle, the square, and the octagon were combined, he asserted that the inherent possibilities ranged from the Shakespearean to the "symphonic."[32]

In designing Mr. Guggenheim's museum, Wright chose a three-dimensional shape that, though it had fascinated natural scientists, mathematicians, and the likes of Christopher Wren for centuries, rarely inspired buildings. But it seemed to have currency in the Guggenheim circle. Rebay herself may have broached the idea to Wright; Bauer perhaps suggested it to her.[33] Le Corbusier's thinking could have influenced both when, circa 1930, he shared with Rebay his plan for the beehivelike Musée Mondial, an unbuilt swirl-within-a square for a Swiss site.

Such writers as Emerson and Goethe had long since identified the spiral as a transcendent form, regarding it as a potent metaphor for movement and growth in both nature and man's mystical capabilities. That a mere line could rise into a three-dimensional figure possessed a certain magic. Yet in terms of built works, the spiral's history was limited.

In Wright's rush at New Year's and after to make a design for Mr. Guggenheim—Wright was acutely aware that the months were passing, his contract expiration date approaching—he recognized that this geometric eccentric might suit the task of designing an utterly unique structure. He was to design a new museum for a new kind of art; that art sought to look beyond the quotidian. If most museum buildings had yet to declare their independence from the palatial traditions of the treasure house, his would do exactly that. He prided himself on making creative leaps that left traditional forms looking outdated.

As he worked at his drafting table during those early weeks in January, he corresponded with his clients in New York. He warned them to ready themselves for a shock: "The whole thing will either throw you off your guard entirely or be just about what you have been dreaming about!"[34]

Wright's glance had fallen upon the spiral before. When he revised his Taliesin stationery a few years earlier, the Taliesin logotype had become a deceptively simple figure within a red square—though drawn in the style of ancient Greek fretwork, the rectilinear logo was actually a double spiral.

His experiments with the spiral went back to the mid-1920s, when he proposed a wedding-cake-like design for Sugarloaf Mountain near Frederick, Maryland. Called the Gordon Strong Automobile Objective and Planetarium, the structure was to have been an odd combination of access road and destination. In Wright's renderings, a cantilevered roadbed in the form of a helix wound its way to the top of a structure that capped a mountain. From its scenic overlook, drivers and passengers would take in the panorama of the Blue Ridge Mountains, and once out of their cars, they could explore the interior of the immense structure, a large dome containing natural-history exhibits as well as a planetarium.

The Automobile Objective never progressed beyond drawings, but twenty years later the spiral idea found new purchase in Wright's imagination. He intimated as much to Rebay in his letter of January 20. "A museum should be one extended expansive well proportioned floor space from bottom to top," he wrote in a breathless, unpunctuated rush. Without disclosing the character of his geometric thinking, he elaborated slightly: the building should be suitable, he wrote, "[for] a wheel chair going around and up and down, throughout."

Turning the earlier plan for the Automobile Objective inside out, Wright transformed the idea of an exposed roadway cantilevered on the exterior into an interior walkway, an unbroken ramp that encircled an atrium. The inward-looking design was an old theme for Wright; other urban buildings of his, such as the administration building for the Larkin Company in Buffalo, New York, and the Unity Church in Oak Park, Illinois, closed out the streetscape. For the Guggenheim, Wright imagined an interior ramp that would resemble a continuous circling balcony; inside, sealed with a continuous ribbon window high on the wall, the walkways overlooked not New York but a towering interior space that Wright called a "crystal court."

Unlike the legendary Sunday morning nine years before when Wright rendered the waterfall house, Wright developed variant designs for the Museum of Non-Objective Art over a period of several weeks. The drawings shared basic elements, in particular a seven- or eight-story tower, consisting of the rising galleries and the central court. An attached, four-story wing extended to one side for storage, classrooms, and Rebay's apartment. Below the main tower was to be a basement auditorium.

The first take that Wright and his boys finalized as a presentation drawing wasn't a spiral at all; rather it was a stack of identical, hexagonal galleries with level floors.[35] The geometry of an alternate version resembled Wright's Automobile Objective, with its tower a rising spiral of diminishing diameter. But the next two embodied one of the most original ideas of Wright's career, altering the dynamic entirely.

Wright's startling insight was to invert the cone; if Rebay and others had dreamed spiral dreams, certainly none of them imagined a mass that, rather than tapering on ascent, expanded from one story to the next. Wright envisioned a cyclone, a building with a radius that increased with altitude, capped with the dome Rebay requested. It was unprecedented in the history of architecture.

In late January, he wrote to Rebay. He told her he would remain in Wisconsin, delaying his anticipated annual departure for the warmth of

Scottsdale, until he completed the "preliminary exploration" for her building.[36] Indeed, by mid-February, the walls of a room adjoining the drafting room at Taliesin had become the setting for a display of the preliminary drawings for the museum, where another client reported seeing no fewer than eight colored sketches of the proposed Guggenheim museum.[37]

As with the Kaufmanns' Bear Run home, one drawing that Wright himself executed (some of the presentation drawings were the work of other Taliesin hands) presaged the future museum in a manner that can, many decades later, only be described as visionary. Unlike the Lilliputian view that signaled Fallingwater's coming-out with its publication in 1937 in the *St. Louis Post-Dispatch*, the museum likeness was not a perspective but an unusual combination of sectional drawing and elevation.

Executed on tracing paper, the sheet has a fragility despite being slightly larger than the perspective drawings that would eventually accompany it to New York (it is roughly twenty-six inches high and thirty inches wide, compared with the stack of twenty-by-twenty-four-inch perspectives on brown paper). The medium is different, too, of pencil and colored pencils rather than ink and watercolors. Yet the cartoon—it is more study than finished artwork—takes the viewer on a journey into the future building as the others do not.

Wright drew a front elevation; but he also bisected the building, dropping the guillotine of his section line along an axis parallel to the street. The sketch thus reveals both the rising mass of the tower and its inner volume as the ramp expands and rises beneath a shallow glass dome (see Fig. XIII). Since the drawing demanded a certain architectural sophistication to apprehend it, Wright set aside his square and triangles long enough to freehand a pair of small, thumbnail views to assure that his clients understood what they were seeing.

With his felicitous gift for describing his work, Wright added a provocative title, lettering the word *ziggurat*, alluding to the ancient Mesopotamian tower. In an afterthought, he added the German *Zikkurat*, perhaps out of respect for the German-born baroness. Then, as a fresh idea struck, he added a third title.

Penciled in with less precision than *ziggurat* or *Zikkurat*—Wright may been simultaneously writing and working out the letter sequence—*taruggitz*, in that fleeting moment, seemed to Wright a suitable label. Just as he inverted the Tower of Babylon, he reversed (more or less) the word *ziggurat*.

Wright brought the drawings to New York and permitted Rebay to glimpse them that March "for a short half hour"—and the spiritualist curator immediately liked Wright's unique architectural vision.[38] His inversion meant that her Museum of Non-Objective Art, though it defined an interior space, also implied ascendance. Wright's widening gyre, rotating and rising to the heavens, conveyed the sense that no building could truly contain the art that carried such meaning for Rebay. However, the curator in her did have concerns about the adaptability of the building for the exhibition of the paintings; she gave Wright notes about reconfiguring interior spaces.

Before refined drawings could be completed, however, the long-hoped-for property purchase came to pass, when an empty lot at the southeast corner of Fifth Avenue and Eighty-Ninth Street was acquired by the Guggenheim Foundation. The plot was shorter and deeper than the one Wright had specified for his drawings, but the overall area was much the same.

The true moment of confirmation occurred in July. After her initial approval, Rebay admitted to having second thoughts; Wright, angry that she listened to "a group of small critics whispering to you concerning something about which they can really know nothing," went to see Mr. Guggenheim.[39] He traveled to New Hampshire to meet with the vacationing Guggenheims. He carried a sheaf of plans, duly revised.

Guggenheim paged through the drawings as Wright and Rebay watched. Some of them were elaborately painted illustrations. One, a so-called night rendering, had been drawn on black board with colored inks and tempera, suggesting the lanternlike quality the museum would have at night. Another portrayed the building cloaked in a rosy hue that Wright favored. ("Red," he had assured Rebay, "is the color of Creation"; she did not agree.)[40]

After reaching the bottom of the pile, Guggenheim began again, working his way through the drawings, starting with the topmost, the tracing sheet that was both a section and an elevation. He concentrated on the drawings without so much as looking up at the architect and the curator waiting nearby.

Ever the deliberate businessman, Guggenheim said nothing, then made another pass through the portfolio Wright had brought.

Finally, Guggenheim raised his gaze. There were, Wright reported, tears in the man's eyes.

"Mr. Wright," he said, "I knew you could do it. This is it."[41]

Wright may have recounted the story to his advantage, but his version, whatever its added colorings, aligns with the facts. After his time with Wright in New Hampshire, Guggenheim dispatched to Spring Green a check for $21,000 for the acceptance of the preliminary plans, decreeing Wright's design "entirely satisfactory."[42] A model was commissioned, and with the plot purchased and Mr. Wright's scheme approved, work on construction drawings could begin.

Mr. Guggenheim and Baroness von Rebay, it seemed, would get their museum.

VI.

The Plaza . . . Fifth Avenue, New York City . . . Autumn 1945

WORD OF WRIGHT'S Manhattan project emerged gradually. In 1944, Rebay announced the acquisition of the property at Fifth Avenue and Eighty-Ninth Street, but few people seemed to be listening. By the time the press got a glimpse of Wright's sketches for the new museum at a press luncheon at the Plaza Hotel on July 9, 1945, Wright had modified the plans again, dubbing the secondary structure adjacent to the tower the Monitor. But the reporters seemed as interested in a vacuum mechanism at the entrance as in the architecture (*Life*: "On entering the building, visitors will cross a floor grill where suction will pull dirt from clothes, help keep museum clean").[43]

In September 1945, the volume of talk concerning Wright's spiral rose measurably. A second Plaza press conference, this one attended by Mayor Fiorello La Guardia and sixty-eight members of the press, engendered national publicity as the country shifted into peacetime mode with World War II finally over. Wright came to New York with a substantial set of working drawings—forty-two sheets, thirteen of them structural, all signed and dated by Wright on September 7, 1945.[44] With paintings

Team Guggenheim: Mr. Wright, the baroness, and Solomon Guggenheim at the September 1945 New York press conference with the just-executed model.
(Margaret Carson/*New York World-Telegram & Sun* Collection)

from the Guggenheim collection hung on the walls around him, Wright offered the public a look at the laboriously made Plexiglas model, also freshly arrived from Taliesin. Sections of Plexiglas had been heated in order to shape their curves, then painted a cream color. The labor-intensive fabrication, Wright told Guggenheim, had cost nearly $5,000, almost double what Wright had originally estimated.[45] He also attached a new name to his project: Wright claimed to have designed "The Modern Gallery."

He posed for *Life* magazine with his big-as-a-bathtub model on the floor at his feet. In the magazine's next issue, the lead article opened with a full-page photograph of "America's most distinguished architect" looking doubtfully at the camera. He held the building's dome in his hands, its surface scored to suggest the intricate glass tubes Wright planned to use. The accompanying text proclaimed, "When it is completed, probably in 1947, at a cost of $1,000,000, it will be the most unconventional building in New York City."[46]

Wright was in pontification mode when he addressed the group of editors at the Plaza that Thursday in September, announcing, "This building is built like a spring." He swung the front of the model open to reveal its dollhouse interior. "You can see how the ramp, which is coiled in the shape of a true logarithmic spiral, is one continuous piece from top to bottom, integral with the outside wall and the inside balcony." Gently patting his brainchild, he told the surprised audience, "When the first atomic bomb lands on New York [the museum] will not be destroyed. It may be blown a few miles up into the air, but when it comes down, it will bounce."[47]

The outrageous Wright made good copy, but some members of his audience, on returning to their desks, labeled his building "strange" and "bizarre." At least one thought that the model looked like "a big, white ice cream freezer."[48] In the January issue of *Architectural Forum*, readers got a more fulsome view. Its editors predicted that, on ascending the circular glass elevator shaft and on descending the gallery ramps of the completed building, people "will have had their first real experience of what architecture can be like."[49]

At the September 1945 press luncheon, a reporter from *Time* asked Wright whence the building's form had come. The architect replied that he drew his inspiration from the Middle Eastern ziggurat, but that he inverted it because "the ziggurat is pessimistic." His variation, he claimed, would produce a building that was "an optimistic ziggurat."[50]

As years passed, Wright's optimism would be tested. In 1946, an adjacent plot of land was acquired; the first parcel, which included the southeast corner of the intersection of Fifth and Eighty-Eighth, gained thirty feet of frontage on Fifth Avenue and an Eighty-Eighth Street access. However, the L-shaped parcel still left the building on the corner of the block in other hands. When Wright turned eighty the following year (admitting only to seventy-eight), construction had yet to begin. Guggenheim believed that, following a postwar rise in prices, construction costs would come down, but no such depression had come.

In 1948, exactly ten years after the issue dedicated to Wright introduced the house at Bear Run to the architectural public, Henry Luce and *Architectural Forum* editor Henry Wright handed Wright the reins again. As the editor's note up front points out, "This issue was completely designed and written by [Wright]; the plans and sketches appear as they were drawn by the 50 young men who now compose the Taliesin Fellowship."[51] To prepare the January issue, the editor had journeyed to Taliesin, meeting again with Jack Howe and Wes Peters, apprentices he met a decade earlier (Peters by then was married to Olgivanna's daughter by her first marriage, Svetlana, and had become very much a part of the Wright family).

Henry Wright knew the drill: "Things haven't changed much. Everybody still gets up for breakfast at six; everybody washes his own dishes and takes turns cooking. There is still a movie in the theatre on Saturdays, dinner and music in the Wright living room on Sundays, lots of good talk every day when the drafting room knocks off for tea at 4:30." But the focus, the editor wrote, always came back to "the silvery-haired

Master, [sitting] at his own drafting table, in front of the roaring wall-size fireplace . . . turning his enormous dreams of life for Free Men into the reality of structure—his force and vitality undiminished."[52]

When his turn came, Frank Lloyd Wright wrote in the magazine of his Fifth Avenue museum-to-be, "The Museum for the Solomon R. Guggenheim Foundation will be built someday . . . Construction of the building is awaiting favorable building conditions."[53]

As events unfolded, however, Wright's optimistic ziggurat lost whatever momentum it had in November 1949. Wright had written to Rebay in June, complaining, "The cosmos sweeps onward and upward while we crawl on the surface like flies on a transparent window-pane."[54] His stairless structure met a new level of stasis when, on November 3, the once-imposing figure of Solomon Guggenheim, weakened by a battle with cancer, succumbed, at age eighty-eight.

Wright remembered the older man respectfully—by then Wright himself was well into his eighty-third year—and described Guggenheim as "the only American millionaire whom I knew or had heard of who died facing the Future. All others cuddle up to the past."[55] For some years to come, however, the future home for non-objective art that the dead man envisioned made little progress aside from the new name that Wright coined. He took to calling his ziggurat the Guggenheim Memorial.

CHAPTER 11

Philip Comes Out Classical

It seems I cannot be but Classically inspired; symmetry, order, clarity above all.
—Philip Johnson

I.

Migrating to New York . . . The Return of Peace

IN MARCH 1943, thirty-six-year-old Philip Johnson had been drafted into the army. He served just eighteen months and never saw combat, remaining a private charged with menial duties on bases in the United States. Heading home from Camp Atterbury in Columbus, Indiana, Johnson, once again a civilian, stopped to visit his first friend from architecture school, Carter Manny.

Johnson had been granted a medical discharge when symptoms of his earlier nervous disorders had resurfaced. This time around, the manifestation was "itching of the nerve ends." When dining with Manny and his wife, Johnson periodically rose from the dinner table to rub his back on a nearby doorjamb to scratch the itch.[1]

His army service had done nothing to quell his interest in architecture, and soon Johnson wrote Manny to describe another stop on his postservice travels. After returning to New York, he reported, "I was restless so I hiked off to Chicago to see Miës." Then he took a detour to Wisconsin. "Went to Racine to see the *Meister's* work."[2]

He came away from his visit to the S. C. Johnson and Son headquarters with contradictory feelings. He described Wright's office building as "very exciting," but its "details execrable." Further, he thought its "color and shapes very good," but the "entrance geared too low and too 'in behind' for me." Despite those initial mixed reactions, however, his seeing Wright's highly original office space precipitated a gradual shift in Johnson's view: Over time, that building in Racine would become, in Johnson's estimation, Wright's "greatest work." Years later he described it in an interview.

> It has the greatest interior in the country of any period. The idea of using those lily-pad columns and letting the light filter down between them is such a surprise, such a unique, absolutely unique way of doing a big space, you see, that you can't think of a better, more interesting space because the columns give you the rhythm, the light is perfectly divided, and yet the columns cut the feeling of space into small enough units so that you [don't] feel silly at a typewriter. You can't go into Grand Central Station and start typing a letter. It's that kind of big space. But this is. It's intimate and big.[3]

Johnson's Wisconsin foray had been a transition moment: The admiring skeptic had begun to be a believer in Wright's new work.

Choosing to settle again in Manhattan, Philip Johnson put his little Cambridge house on the market, selling it for $24,000, roughly what it cost him to build. At Alfred Barr's invitation, he rejoined the MoMA team, again as director of the museum's Department of Architecture (John McAndrew had departed to spend the war years in a government post with the Office of Inter-American Affairs, but would resurface after the war as director of the Wellesley College Museum). MoMA's architecture department had separated from the Department of Industrial Art, which had become the fiefdom of Edgar Kaufmann jr., who had left retailing in Pittsburgh to return to New York. Johnson invited Carter Manny to come East to be his assistant at MoMA, but as the father of a newborn daughter, Manny declined. He couldn't afford to live on the modest salary of $4,000, especially after having spent several months paying his way as an apprentice at Taliesin.

Still, the old connections would briefly fire when the MoMA presented a small show of a new Wright house. After Johnson managed a trip to Taliesin late in the summer of 1945—in a thank-you to Wright dated September 25, he described his visit as a "wonderful weekend"[4]—a conversation commenced that led to an exhibition for 1946. Called *A New Country House by Frank Lloyd Wright*, the show's most essential feature would be a large model, executed in three-eighths scale (its base measured six feet by twelve). Designed for E. F. Hutton executive Gerald M. Loeb, the home was planned for a hilltop in Redding, Connecticut, but the actual house was never built.

Even building the model proved complicated and expensive. Unhappy with the demands for more information made by the cabinet shop Johnson had commissioned to make it, Wright decided to produce the model himself at Taliesin. Edgar Kaufmann jr., wise in the ways of Mr. Wright and his former colleagues in Spring Green, assisted with its completion. After delivery, however, Wright dispatched a bill for costs incurred, since several Taliesin apprentices had worked all hours to complete the work. Johnson arranged for this invoice to be paid, then wrote to the client and patron, thanking Loeb for his role in smoothing Wright's feathers, ruffled as they usually were when interacting with the MoMA. "It was very generous of you to settle the Frank Lloyd Wright affair so literally. I believe it was the right policy to help him in any possible way, and . . . I am glad to avoid the acrimonious telephone battles that would ensue had we not paid him."[5]

Regardless of its associated headaches, the little exhibition amounted to another step in Wright and Johnson's maturing acquaintance. As Johnson remembered it, he put "those double-vision things, stereopticons . . . all over the room." Hung at eye level, they accompanied the model. "That's all there was in the room." With the financial disagreement resolved, Wright telegrammed Johnson with an invitation to Taliesin: BREAK YOUR CHAINS, CHOOSE A TRAVELING COMPANION AND STAY AWHILE.

"So I got to know him better," remembered Johnson.[6]

For Johnson's old collaborator Henry-Russell Hitchcock, the regaining of Wright's good graces began earlier. After Wright's earlier unreasonableness led to the cancellation of the MoMA catalog for the 1940 exhibition, the Master had looked for a way to create a new book independent of the museum. He wrote to his publisher, Charles Duell, explaining that he wished "to record and explain the Museum of Modern Art Exhibit [of 1940]."[7] He had a title—the one he had tried to persuade Barr and McAndrew to adopt—and a new collaborator.

Hitchcock traveled to Taliesin in May 1942 to examine photographs and drawings, and in 1942 Duell, Sloan and Pearce published *In the Nature of Materials*. Taliesin apprentices reported a surprisingly untroubled Wright-Hitchcock collaboration, despite Wright's usual attitude. He announced to the reading public that "[Hitchcock's] opinions on architecture I have distrusted as being far too academic, but since it is safer to trust one's point of view to one's enemies than to one's friends, I asked him to record the show."[8] The book immediately became an essential title in the growing Wright bibliography and remains in print almost seventy-five years later.

In the postwar years, both Hitchcock and Philip Johnson made pilgrimages to Wright's "desert camp," Taliesin West in Scottsdale, Arizona. For Johnson, as at Johnson Wax, his encounter with another Wright work would require him to further adjust his thinking.

At the invitation of a veterinarian-turned-hotelier named Dr. Alexander Chandler, Wright and his extended Taliesin family had spent their first winter in the Southwest in 1928–29. Chandler's dream of a desert Venice never came to pass—the completed plans were among the many that were stowed away in flat files after the crash of 1929—but Wright's "ephemerid," as he called it, a temporary camp on a rocky plateau overlooking the site of the proposed hotel, had been a harbinger. That first desert outpost consisted of a dozen-odd cabins built on wooden platforms with partial walls and canvas roofs. Inspired by the rosy hue of the desert, Wright ordered the little buildings painted a dull red.

After Black Tuesday, the notion of permanent winter quarters for the Fellowship in Arizona remained in abeyance for almost a decade; it came fully to life only when, in December of 1936, Wright was suddenly reminded that he wasn't as ageless as he sometimes seemed. After a prolonged bout with pneumonia, he took his doctor's advice to find a more clement climate for the winter months and purchased eight hundred acres in the Paradise Valley in the shadow of the McDowell Mountains. In January of 1938, he and a band of Taliesin fellows established an encampment there in the Sonoran Desert for the winter months; each year thereafter Wright led an annual migration west. From roughly November to April, the desert camp that came to be known as Taliesin West would be home.

Johnson first visited after World War II. By then, Taliesin West was a campsite made permanent. The Arizona setting had put different demands on Wright, but he applied the basic tenets of his philosophy of architecture to the hot and arid landscape. He needed housing for his immediate family; an office and studio; a structure to function as a workroom for drafting and teaching; communal areas for the kitchen and dining room; and spaces for musical and film entertainments. All of these were to be integrated into the natural features of the mesa.

Wright employed rudimentary materials—rubble stone, poured concrete, rough-sawn redwood, and canvas. He wasn't bashful about describing his accomplishment: "Our new desert camp belong[s] to the Arizona desert as though it had stood there during creation."

The armature was an L-shaped exterior hallway. The leg of the L ran east-west, extending from Wright's office at the northwest end to his private quarters at the other. In between was the largest space in the complex, the drafting room, and common spaces for food preparation and consumption. The foot of the L was another open artery that ran from the front to the rear of the complex, passing through a breezeway or loggia that separated the Wright family living quarters from the central core of the community. To the rear of the main structure was a movie theater and gallery, along with quarters for apprentices with their own enclosed courtyard.

The assemblage of structures was set upon an angular footprint of concrete pads, terraces, and gardens. The low masonry walls were built trapezoidal in section, wider at the bottom than the top. To shape them larger stones had been set flat-side out at the base of concrete forms, with large boulders used as fill in the center. Smaller stones and a thin slurry of concrete were then poured into the forms to cement the stones together, producing a conglomerate. With the forms removed, cement obscuring the faces of the large stones was chipped away by hand and the stone acid-washed, producing what Wright termed "desert masonry rubble walls" (see Fig. VII and Fig. VIII).

The final touch was the expanse of canvas between the brown-stained redwood beams. Individual sheets of canvas were stretched over wooden frames that were then mounted as panels, some of them operable. Wall flaps functioned as doors and windows, opening and closing to permit airflow during the heat of the day and to retain warmth during the cold desert nights.

When Johnson visited the first time, Taliesin West was unlike like anything else he had seen: He regarded the place, despite its being the work of an aging imagination, as a revelation. "No one understands the third dimension as well as [Wright]," Johnson would soon write for an international audience in the pages of *Architectural Review*. "His buildings can rarely be appreciated correctly except at first hand. A photograph can never . . . record the cumulative impact of moving through his organized spaces, the effect of passing through the low space into high, from narrow to wide, from dark to light (Taliesin, Taliesin West, Johnson Wax Co)."[9]

Philip Johnson made periodic trips to both Taliesins, and after one visit to Spring Green, Wright wrote to him, "You are always a welcome inmate. Nice to see you again, and the sooner the better. We don't have to see eye to eye to love each other do we."[10]

Theirs was a slow-evolving camaraderie, and Johnson, for a man who had designed so little, had surprising standing in Wright's estimation.

The older man clearly recognized Johnson wished to play with the big boys. On the occasion of a Johnson visit to Scottsdale, the Meister seated the balding but still youthful Johnson at the head table for one of the community's regular black-tie dinners. With the apprentices seated around them, Wright instructed, "Philip, sit here," indicating a small chair near his own. Then, in a stage whisper, Wright announced to the room, "The prince visits the king."[11] Johnson was not amused.

In private, Johnson was known to dismiss as "nonsense" Wright's assertions that the Scottsdale settlement was "'created by its site,' and the 'horizontal line' being 'the line of life.'"[12] Nevertheless, Taliesin West would inhabit Johnson's imagination in a way that Chartres had done in earlier years, a frequent point of reference for him in his public utterances.

II.

Autumn 1945 . . . New Canaan, Connecticut . . . Escape from New York

NOW BALD, HIS pate rimmed with graying hair, Philip Johnson, age thirty-nine, decided the time had arrived to build a house in the country. One fine fall day, the newly domesticated Johnson, together with Jon Stroup, his first live-in lover, embarked on a scouting mission. The handsome Stroup, ten years Philip's junior, was an editor at *Town & Country* and a freelance writer. Together they headed north and east from Manhattan, bound for New Canaan, Connecticut.

By prior arrangement, they parked on Ponus Ridge Road, where a remnant of a stone wall lined the shoulder, flattened by frost and half-obscured by decaying leaves. A gap in the disorderly wall gave access to the property they had come to see, which descended a gradual slope.

No longer suppressed by either farmer's plow or grazing livestock, low scrub bushes, new-growth ash, and other trees had reclaimed the land.

The two men separated, the better to explore the five-acre parcel, but Stroup came upon the inevitable building site first.

As he meandered down the hillside, working his way through the thicket of saplings and brush, he entered an open, level area, perhaps a hundred feet in breadth and roughly as long. It seemed more like the site of an abandoned croquet pitch than a forest clearing. If the break in the tree cover and sudden appearance of sky overhead surprised Stroup, more remarkable was the downhill vista.

Striding across the clearing, he stopped on reaching the western edge, where the terrain fell steeply away. He looked down upon immense boulders, left many millennia earlier by a departing glacier. They formed a natural riprap retaining wall that lined an intimidating eighty-foot drop.

The view to the horizon might have been the work of a photo stylist seeking maximum depth of field. Mature trees framed the view in the middle distance. Looking beyond the trunks of the century-old oaks, Stroup took in a commanding view of a narrow valley, its floor defined by a meandering stream. As if from the prow of a ship, a view of the Rippowam Valley opened before him, deep and distant.

He called out to Johnson, "You can see almost to New York!"

His companion soon stood by his side.[13]

"I liked it immediately," Johnson later remembered, "and didn't look any further."[14] He knew he wanted the land and exactly where the house would go ("The setting on the hill I picked in the first five minutes").[15] Within an hour, Johnson reached a handshake agreement to buy the property on what is today Ponus Ridge Road.

———

ON PHILIP JOHNSON'S return to New York after his stint in the army, he had rented an office, a one-room space at 205 East Forty-Second Street. He understood there would be little new work until the proscription on wartime construction was lifted, but the extra rent bill seemed a small matter. He was a well-connected New Yorker, with many wealthy friends and contacts who would desire new houses with the return of the peace, and Johnson confidently anticipated postwar projects and the launch of his new career.

With the fall of Germany in May 1945, commissions had indeed begun to come his way, and conscious of his modest drawing skills, Johnson sought out a friend from Harvard to help execute polished renderings and finished plans.

Like Johnson, Landis Gores was an Ohioan who majored in classics as an undergraduate (in Gores's case, at Princeton). He had enrolled, in 1939, at the Harvard Graduate School of Design, and upon meeting in Cambridge in autumn 1940, the two men found their architectural tastes overlapped.

Gores remembered the two of them as "solitary mavericks."[16] Both were skeptical of Walter Gropius and shared an admiration for Miës, who, before accepting a job offer at Chicago's Armour Institute, had rejected Harvard's advances in 1937 when he learned there was another candidate for the job. Harvard had hired that man—Gropius—in part because he was reasonably fluent, unlike Miës, who couldn't compose an English sentence.

During the summer of 1945, Johnson contacted Pamela Gores, inquiring whether her husband, still on active duty, might want to join Johnson's practice once Landis returned to civilian life. Gores had spent the war in the Code and Cypher service of British Military Intelligence, helping break the codes of the German high command. When he learned of Johnson's invitation, he welcomed the offer. On the day before Thanksgiving 1945, Landis Gores moved his drafting materials into the two-desk office.[17]

Another GSD man who migrated to Manhattan, Eliot Noyes, had been the first of the Harvard men to consider building in New Canaan. After a prewar stint at Gropius's and Breuer's Cambridge architectural offices and then serving briefly as MoMA's director of the Department of Industrial Design, Noyes (GSD, class of '38) had found postwar work with Norman Bel Geddes. But in early 1945, piloting a rented plane, he had scouted the New York suburbs, and looking down upon the rolling landscape of Fairfield County, Connecticut, he spied the place he wanted to settle his family.[18] He had soon set to work building a flat-roofed house. Noyes's real estate broker had, in turn, introduced Johnson to the road that ran along Ponus Ridge.[19]

Two other men made similar journeys from Massachusetts. After spending a decade at Harvard, Professor Marcel Breuer hung out his architectural shingle in New York in 1945, and John Johansen (GSD '42) caught on with the firm of Skidmore, Owings & Merrill. With the war over, as Noyes expressed it, all were eager "to get back into the world of doing things."[20]

They would singly and collectively decide to do some of the most important of those things in New Canaan, and these men—Johnson and Gores, Johansen and Noyes, and their favorite professor, Marcel Breuer— would later come to be referenced in architectural texts as the Harvard Five. They constituted a loosely linked brotherhood of Modernists in the postwar years, when all of them moved to New Canaan to build houses.

Located at the terminus of a branch line of the New York, New Haven and Hartford Railroad, the town welcomed a great many former soldiers adapting to peacetime. The quiet leafy streets of the conservative Yankee town and its eight thousand inhabitants (ca. 1945) would see its population double in the postwar years.

The Cambridge arrivals in particular altered New Canaan's traditional architectural look, long characterized by New England vernacular houses, which tended to be wood-framed and antique, with many homes dating to the eighteenth century. When Johnson arrived, it was a countrified version of his old Ash Street neighborhood, but the next decade would see the construction of nearly a hundred houses in a Modernist manner, many of them works of the Harvard Five.

Construction began in 1947 on Breuer's long, low house. The upper floor with the principal living spaces was cantilevered on all four sides over the lower level at grade. Breuer used steel cables, as he put it, to realize "one of [man's] oldest ambitions: the defeat of gravity" (and to build a substantial house affordably on a reduced footprint).[21] That same year Landis Gores bought four acres on Cross Bridge Road. Johansen followed, in 1949, establishing his architectural practice in town and building a house on Ponus Ridge Road. That home, with its wall of glass and bedrooms relegated to the basement level, was completed in 1951.

III.

1945–47 . . . New York City . . . At the Drafting Table

A S W I T H M A N Y apparently simple things, Johnson's Glass House achieved its transparency only by repeated reductions and reimaginings. The French phrase applied: *L'art difficile d'être simple.* Johnson was trying to master the difficult art of the simple.

As office colleague Gores recalled, the conceit of a glass-walled house surfaced in Johnson's mind as soon as he bought the property in 1945. However, as they knew of no technical solution at that moment for implementing the idea of a house with walls entirely of glass, they began with another approach. Within weeks of the real estate settlement in late 1945, Johnson and Gores began producing drawings for a dwelling that integrated plate glass and structural masonry.

In a letter to Henry-Russell Hitchcock early in the process, Johnson spoke of "trying to be Classical without the grammar."[22] A year later, he acknowledged the range of his sources. After describing the several architectural projects occupying him, he concluded, "The most interesting is my own house on a steep hill in New Canaan which is turning out half Persius [a reference to nineteenth-century German neoclassicist Ludwig Persius] and *half Wright.* The Wright influence came from a two week stay the master made a month ago. We got along swell. So the house drips over the ravine like the California numbers."[23] But the impact of Johnson's time with Wright proved fleeting.

Early in the design process, a combination of two buildings gained favor. In preliminary sketches, partitions divided the primary structure into traditional rooms. Johnson established some ground rules, one of which was: *No roof overhangs.* Gores disliked that limitation (his own New Canaan house, completed in 1948, would be unmistakably Wrightian, with cantilevers, shading cornices, and handcrafted grillwork). The coming months would bring a few clients to the door, and Johnson's first nonfamily commissions; the Booth House in Bedford Village, New York, and the Farney House, on the beach in Sagaponack, Long Island, were completed in 1946 and 1947. But work on the design for Ponus Ridge occupied the two architects during countless unbillable office hours over many months.

Having now turned forty, Johnson wanted the project to help launch his new, midlife career. Given its context—the fertile Modernist environs of New Canaan—he knew he must make a statement that distinguished him from his cohort.

Johnson kept thinking and Gores kept polishing his friend's ideas on paper. With each new approach, Johnson began with rough, freehand sketches in soft, dark pencil. As a plan matured, the drawings got more sophisticated, with thinner lines, dimensioning, the indication of wall thicknesses, and an occasional section drawing. As one variant of the Ponus Ridge Road solution succeeded another, the sets of superseded drawings were bound in folders and stowed in a vertical file near the desk occupied by the young firm's part-time secretary. One was labeled CENTRAL COURT PLANS, 1945–1946. In those renderings, Johnson tried out variations of the Cambridge house on Ash Street. But the designers soon abandoned that tack. For a time, the strictly rectilinear structure began to gain curvilinear elements, but nothing remained fixed for long.

A solution satisfactory to Johnson did not emerge for two years, during which twenty-seven distinct schemes were tested and three times as many minor variations sketched.[24] Johnson, rather like an actor let loose in a costume shop, tried on forms borrowed from others, impatient to find one that suited him. French neoclassicist Claude Nicolas Ledoux (1736–1806) was among his sources, as Johnson confided to his epistolary friend J. J. P. Oud.[25] Some renderings incorporated sturdy Richardsonian arches (H. H. Richardson would always remain at the top of Johnson's most-admired list). At one stage, memorialized in a file labeled CIRCLE VERSIONS, 1946, a basement plan gained a circular stair inside a large cylinder that resembled a painting by the Suprematist painter Kazimir Malevich, a stark geometric statement that also featured a circle within a larger rectangle. Later that year Johnson sketched a plan with two abutting rectangular elements that were offset as if one had slid out of alignment. Other versions assumed L-shapes.

One early sketch looked like a page from a Wright portfolio of his middle-class Usonian plans. It included a pergola as a line of access to a set of overlapping masses. It, too, was soon superseded and simplified, as Johnson's restless imagination moved on.[26]

During this time, Johnson lived a double life. After spending his mornings at his Forty-Second Street architectural office across the street from the Daily News Building, the energetic Johnson made his way uptown to the MoMA and his role as director of the Department of Architecture. As of 1946, he focused his curatorial energies on the development of one major exhibition in particular. He felt no one else could do justice to the work of Miës van der Rohe—according to Gores, Johnson still maintained a "proselytizing devotion" to the expatriate German.[27] Johnson would curate a show, he decided; then he persuaded Miës himself to install it. The *Miës van Der Rohe* exhibition was to open in September 1947. The accompanying book would bear Johnson's byline.

The planning and research for the exhibition and catalog meant frequent travel to Chicago to interview and consult his subject. The Armour Institute campus, now known as the Illinois Institute of Technology (IIT), was a Miësian work-in-progress. Built on a cleared urban site, the community of low-profile, rectangular buildings would feature prominently in the show and in one of the book's chapters. Yet the emergence of the campus wasn't what galvanized Johnson. His Voilà! moment occurred when he encountered an as-yet-unbuilt house Miës had designed.

A Chicago physician and research nephrologist named Edith Farnsworth also desired a country house. A woman of independent means, she purchased nine acres of alluvial farmland near Plano, Illinois, sixty miles from Chicago. Before earning her medical degree, she had studied English literature at the University of Chicago, music theory at the American Conservatory of Music, and trained under violin virtuoso Mario Corti in Italy. Given her artistic inclinations, she wanted a role in planning her house.

After dismissing another architect who insisted he must retain complete artistic freedom, Dr. Farnsworth met Miës, in early 1945, at a small dinner party. He impressed her, and she invited the "massive stranger," as she described him, to survey her riverside property. The two then made a series of Sunday visits to her property on the Fox River.

One afternoon early in the spring of 1945, with no design yet put to paper, Dr. Farnsworth raised the issue of building materials, asking Miës what he had in mind. Glancing around them at the rising ground, the river, and the meadow grasses, the usually taciturn Miës told her abruptly, "If I were to build here for myself, I think I would build in glass because all the views are so beautiful that it is hard to decide which view should be preferred."[28] The insight prompted Miës, uncharacteristically, to daub a watercolor elevation of a one-room glass house, in April of 1945. In a few watery strokes atop a simple pencil sketch, a transparent box appeared, seemingly suspended over the horizon line, dwarfed by the suggestion of three billowing trees in watercolor wash. The all-glass structure, outlined by white steel, stood atop piers (see Fig. XVIII). Almost six years would pass before the house was completed, in March 1951, but little would change from that first rendering.[29]

When Johnson learned of the project in Miës's Chicago office, the impact on him was immediate. He saw not only renderings but the model of Dr. Farnsworth's see-through house, which sat on Miës's desk at IIT. An all-glass belvedere *could* be executed, Johnson realized. By midsummer 1947, the Johnson and Gores office produced its own miniature, an eighth-scale model of Johnson's design for his own, soon-to-be-world-renowned house.

IV.

1947–49 . . . New Canaan, Connecticut . . . A Plan Emerges

ULRICH FRANZEN SENSED the creative buzz. Their fellow student from Harvard days, he visited Johnson and Gores at their office during the drafting that resulted in the Glass House. "I was terribly jealous when I first saw [the plans]," Franzen recalled later. "When architects get jealous, it always means there's something special going on."[30]

The house would not be a simple lift of Miës's design for Dr. Farnsworth. At first Johnson did mimic Miës's basic glass-box scheme with its eight supporting posts, but over many months, Gores made multiple variations at Johnson's orders. Four- and six-column plans were drawn and rejected. The cantilevered corners of the Farnsworth plan disappeared. The New York duo reconsidered the use of arches, but the reappearance of the traditional masonry elements proved short-lived.

Johnson decided to plant his box on a two-step brick podium laid up at grade (unlike Miës, whose Farnsworth House would stand atop steel stilts, five feet three inches above the ground). Instead of Miës's nearly invisible mitered-glass corners, the Glass House would have I-beam posts that unmistakably delineated the corners; together with the complementary wide steel beam at the cornice line, the result was akin to a plain black frame on a photograph. Miës's open floor plan remained, as traditional floor-to-ceiling walls were banished. The Malevich-inspired cylinder reemerged, but this time, in a borrowing from Miës, it contained not a stair (the Johnson house had become one story) but enclosed a shower bath and the firebox and flue of a fireplace. By October 1947, the basic elements were decided.

During that autumn, Gores, a superb draftsman, began the working drawings. Johnson hired a reputable New Canaan contractor, though the steel and glass specifications went to a New York City specialist firm for fabrication. After a martini-moistened picnic in the spring sun on March 20, 1948—the four celebrants were Pam and Landis Gores, Johnson, and his sister Theodate—construction began at the prow, where stakes already demarked the soon-to-be-dug foundations for both the main glass box and an accompanying brick box that would house utilities and guest quarters. The master set of plans was dated March 23, but drawings from Gores continued to arrive, signed and dated individually, including some full-size renderings of steel details for mullions, cornice, corner posts, and doorjambs. Precise finishes were required, as were additional mechanical details, and Gores was occupied at his drafting table, delivering drawings into the summer, all annotated with dimensions and notes in Gores's precise hand, the letters and numerals so small as to almost require a magnifying glass.

The primary structure would occupy a rectangular footprint thirty-two feet by fifty-six, its flat roof enclosing a ten-foot-six-inch-high ceiling. Vertical I beams defined the corners, and two more pairs punctuated the long sides, suggesting a division of the house into three symmetrical bays. But the dark gray steel piers would frame the walling, which consisted solely of a plate-glass skin that stretched around the 176-foot perimeter. Textured ironspot brick arrived from Ohio for the podium, the interior bathroom drum, and the floor, which would be laid in a herringbone pattern atop the piping for an innovative radiant-heating system of the sort Frank Lloyd Wright often used.

The fortresslike second structure, constructed almost entirely of brick, soon rose ninety feet away; its apparent impenetrability would be the inverse of the glass structure's transparency. Its only door faced the Glass House; the windows, just three portholes, looked away through the rear wall. The Guest House, as the masonry structure was called (though, a few years later, Johnson would reinvent it as his master-bedroom complex), would often be overlooked and ignored like the publicity-shy spouse of a world-renowned celebrity. But it defined a space between the buildings that amounted to a courtyard. The assemblage thus resembled a Miësian court-house, though one far from a cityscape, isolated as it was on a rural promontory.

By summer 1948, Johnson could clamber atop the skeleton of what would be his own glass house, with its steel posts and beams spanned by a wooden roof deck. He found that the structure wobbled disconcertingly, but there was no turning back.[31] Reassurance soon followed as, upon the installation of the plate glass a few days later, the structure stiffened. No bracing would be required: The house of glass would indeed stand.

v.

1948–49 . . . New Canaan, Connecticut . . . Visiting the Site

DURING THE EIGHT months required to build the Glass House, Johnson visited the construction site periodically, alternating his Connecticut trips with weekends spent at the summer house at East Hampton, Long Island, that he rented with Jon Stroup and Theodate. His supervision on Ponus Ridge extended to landscaping work, mostly the selective clearing of trees, as he began his lifelong transforming of the acreage into, in eighteenth-century terms, a pleasure garden. At first his acreage looked, as Marga Barr remembered, "brushy, inchoate—a place that did not 'compose' in any way . . . How he foresaw what he could make out of it, is part of his genius."[32] More buildings, so-called follies, would come later.

With the house habitable by mid-November, Johnson spent the holidays quietly ensconced in his completed New Canaan home, getting acquainted with its nuances, establishing his patterns. The experience was a revelation, which Johnson later summarized: "[It's] the only house in the world where you can watch the sun set and the moon rise at the same time. And the snow. It's amazing when you're surrounded at night with the falling snow. It's lighted, which makes it look as though you're rising on a celestial elevator."

Johnson also found that—just as he had hoped—his unusual domicile became, almost overnight, the object of widespread public curiosity.

Even before the plate glass was in place, the rumor of an all-glass house lured onlookers, and flocks of uninvited visitors blocked traffic on Ponus Ridge Road, seeking to glimpse what one newspaper archly termed Johnson's "'private' residence."[33] While the congestion and the presence of New Canaan cops to direct traffic irritated his neighbors, the word of what was happening reached beyond the conservative community of early, clapboarded homes. Editors and reporters in New York recognized a good story, and as the din of construction noise faded, it was replaced by a different sound, that of the critics and architects gossiping. The magnetism of the Glass House far exceeded even Johnson's hopes.

The peculiar nature of the house compelled attention, and Johnson soon fielded an inquiry from the *New York Times*. In an article for the Sunday *Times Magazine*, a slightly bemused Mary Roche, the paper's home editor and interior design columnist, recited a few facts about a new kind of architectural experience. Mr. Johnson's house sounded rather peculiar, she told her readers, consisting as it did of one room, with neither movable windows nor partitions. She reported the largely empty glass box cost $60,000 to build, a sum four times the cost of an average house in 1949. "Certainly this is a very special house, satisfactory to its bachelor owner," she observed, "but of little use to a typical American family."

Johnson had personally shown Roche the house. She had clearly been beguiled by him and his project, even as she wondered at its oddity. "It feels like the outdoors, like a glade in the woods," she wrote. "For the majority, perhaps, it wouldn't work at all. But [the Johnson house] is an interesting demonstration of a different concept of living—a concept which regards cooking, eating and sleeping as casual variations of one central activity rather than separate activities in themselves."[34]

Two months later, in its October 1949 issue, *House & Garden* portrayed the house as an assault on tradition in the eyes of the "defenders of the Colonial House." As Mary Roche had done, however, the magazine took a measured stance. On the one hand, it reported that the "residents of Fairfield County have not yet recovered from their astonishment at the glass house which Philip C. Johnson recently designed and built for himself in New Canaan." On the other, the unsigned article continued, "The result is a truly original building of timeless elegance and classic simplicity, as well as a conclusive demonstration of the fact that modern building techniques have come of age."[35]

Johnson not only opened his house to the press, but he himself proved an open book, available to answer questions. He explained his thinking persuasively. Still more important, he permitted photographers to open their lenses. One double-page spread in *House & Garden* suggested the prismatic quality of the house, with the caption "The house with its massive brick cylinder rides across the horizon like a ship." The images, together with a floor plan, conveyed as words could not how different living spaces were delineated by a row of six-foot-high cabinets that hid Johnson's bed; an area rug that defined the seating area; a dining table and chairs in the southwest corner; and the low bar of the kitchen in the southeast corner.

The editors asked the inevitable question: Is *any* privacy possible in Mr. Johnson's see-through house? The answer was *yes*. Suspended from a track at ceiling level, curtains extended around the entire perimeter. Though far from a blackout shade, the translucent natural fabric, woven from the tropical pandanus palm, cut the glare and, when drawn, closed out peering eyes.

The *New York Sun* labeled Johnson's new abode "the all-glass-home!" Reporting on the continuing Sunday traffic jams, columnist H. I. Phillips gave Johnson a chance to defend his design ("Mr. Johnson insists . . . [the sheet glass] simply brings the outdoors indoors"), but the *Sun* writer couldn't resist poking fun: "In this type of bungalow, there is never a moment when you can be sure whether you are indoors or outdoors without looking at a thermometer or reaching to the floor to determine if you will come up with any wildflowers."[36]

Philip Johnson could afford to smile at such small witticisms. He grasped that, inevitably, the general public would be preoccupied with the oddity, vulnerability, and voyeuristic possibilities of a house of glass. But he lost little sleep over the ephemeral chatter, happy to ignore a joke or two from the workaday press writing for the common man. He focused instead on the need to manage the house's critical reception within the smaller realms of the architectural community and the museum world.

He had seen how Gropius and Breuer, upon first arriving in the United States, had designed houses for themselves as means of exhibiting their brand of new architecture, demonstrating for a conservative client base the new things they could do. Wright was another for whom showing off his own domicile was standard strategy; he welcomed his clientele into his homes, which were laboratories and showcases.

Johnson, however, would shape the formal discussion of the house in a way that no architect before him had done.

VI.

1949–50 . . . On the Printed Page

ARCHITECTS HAVE PUBLISHED their designs for centuries. Andrea Palladio's *I Quattro Libri dell'Architecttura* (*The Four Books on Architecture*, 1570) helped make him, arguably, the most influential architect of all time. The pattern books of Asher Benjamin spread the gospel of the Federal and Greek Revival styles to emerging towns in nineteenth-century Middle America. Frank Lloyd Wright had announced Fallingwater to great public acclaim in the pages of *Architectural Forum*.

Philip Johnson thought he could top Wright and everyone else.

Building a house of glass, he surmised, had been to invite the casting of stones. That insight prompted him to construct an argument that he hoped would be a preemptive barrier to deflect at least some of the criticism that might be sent his way by hostile critics in the architectural press. He decided to go beyond simply letting the New Canaan project speak for itself, which was what most architects did (and Wright had done with the Kaufmann house, accompanying a dozen-odd photos and two plans with a single page of text describing the Bear Run setting and the construction of Fallingwater). Instead, Johnson elected to take what might be called the provenance approach. He would buttress the launch of his second career by employing the skills learned in his first, writing of his own architectural work as a curator and critic.

He chose the most prestigious architectural journal of the day, the British-based *Architectural Review*, as the vehicle for his assay into shaping the professional perception of his work. He elected not to begin by trumpeting his domicile's unusual construction, but chose an understated title, "House at New Canaan, Connecticut." The publication of the piece was a departure for the magazine, which, when reporting on individual projects, typically published unsigned, shorter articles that were largely descriptive. But readers of the September 1950 issue of *Architectural Review* were warned from the start they were in for something different. As the magazine's editor explained in his introductory note, Johnson's house "is proclaimed by the architect [to be] frankly derivative."[37]

While Frank Lloyd Wright always looked to proclaim his originality, Johnson would cite his sources. He opened his allotted eight pages with a site plan, followed by a mix of other images. He invoked the ancient Greeks and Le Corbusier as the inspiration for the layout of the driveway and approach paths. The siting of his house he described as Schinkelesque, pointing out that his situation resembled that of the symmetrical five-bay country cottage that nineteenth-century German classicist Karl Friedrich Schinkel designed for Glienicke Park, near Potsdam, circa 1830.

Johnson identified geometric sources for his thinking, including the painted rectangles of two contemporary abstract painters (Malevich and Dutchman Theo van Doesburg); the spherical garden house of Claude Nicolas Ledoux (unbuilt, but drawn ca. 1780); and Miës's arrangement of rectangular structures at the Illinois Institute of Technology. Johnson briefly explained the linkages between his work and the others, some of them obscure.

The culminating moment of his exegesis on his sources accompanied a photograph of the model of the Farnsworth House (no image of Miës's glass house was available, as the actual dwelling would not be completed until 1951). Johnson plainly admitted borrowing the concept: "The idea of a glass house comes from Miës van der Rohe. My debt is therefore clear."

What Johnson *didn't* cite in his eclectic list of sources was also instructive. As a student of the architectural past, he knew sixteenth-century Hardwick Hall, in England's Derbyshire, with its then-unprecedented expanses of glass (which had inspired the oft-repeated rhyme "Hardwick Hall, more glass than wall"). Johnson was no stranger to the Crystal Palace, perhaps the best-known building of Queen Victoria's long reign; almost twenty years before, he had cited the 1851 exhibition building as a forerunner of the new architecture he and Hitchcock featured in the 1932 MoMA show. But he chose to omit both Hardwick and Joseph Paxton's oversize greenhouse in writing of the house at New Canaan.

When Johnson finally got around to revealing his house, the reader unexpectedly met not with a show-me shot like Hedrich's trout's-eye view of Fallingwater but an art photo by Arnold Newman, known for his portrait work. A cathedral-like copse of trees—actually, a reflection of the trees—overhangs a figure in silhouette at a desk. A hint of the structure was to one side, but the eighteen-foot sheets of sheer glass in the foreground and middle distance functioned like the lenses of a telescope, putting the seated Johnson, his back to the camera, at the image's vanishing point.

Memorable as it was, the photograph only hinted at the configuration of the house itself. Johnson explained himself, quoting Miës, "I discovered by working with actual glass models that the important thing is the play of reflections and not the effect of light and shadow as in ordinary buildings."[38] The words drove home the notion that Johnson was writing about an idea as much as a house.

Although he stated explicitly that the "Johnson House" was no "ordinary building," his article was also a masterpiece of understatement. He offered no manifesto; his text consisted solely of captions, all of them written in a breezy, first-person voice, with the confident and confiding air of a welcoming host showing his guests around his house. The informality was reinforced with nine more photographs of the Glass House (that name would soon be in general use), most of them the size of snapshots.

To the careful reader, the sum of the published parts, which also included a floor plan and a section drawing of an I-beam corner detail, amounted to a cogent, carefully constructed argument. Johnson was claiming a place for his house along architecture's timeline, and surprisingly, in establishing his coordinates, the Modernist avatar planted his flag in what was clearly classical territory. Moving from the ancient Greeks to the neoclassicists, Johnson embraced their symmetries. In his 1947 catalog for his Miës exhibition at the MoMA, Johnson had described the Farnsworth House as having "the purity of [a] cage,"[39] and while that phrase also suited his house, his arrangement of similar elements amounted to a stripped-down post-and-lintel frame that constituted an eight-column loggia.

The arrangement of the two principal buildings, with the Guest House parallel but offset with respect to the Glass House, formed a composition borrowed from the Acropolis. As Johnson explained, "The Greeks restricted the angle of approach to their buildings to the oblique and placed their monument so that only one major building dominated the field of vision from any given point."[40] As he later rephrased it, "Never approach a building head on: the diagonal gives you a perspective of the depth of the building."[41]

Johnson built his building on a plinth as the Greeks and Romans did, and its dark gray steel columns make it a temple in the woods. He borrowed from the classically inspired vernacular of local Federal Style architecture, dividing the walls of sheer glass with a belt of steel at roughly the height of a chair rail. The tipsy guest who walked into his Cambridge glass wall may have inspired it, but this visual cue was the equivalent of wainscot.

The critical vocabulary applied to classical buildings—*pure, clean, ordered, columnar, rational*—clearly fit, but a striking resonance also brought to mind another building, also built for an unmarried man, a belvedere that every serious student of the architectural past knew. Palladio's Villa Almerico was to be the retirement home for a papal prelate returning home to the Veneto after his days in Rome. Palladio centered four doors at the Villa Rotonda, as it is more commonly known, one on each elevation, at the cardinal points of the compass. Johnson had done the same. The Villa Rotonda is sited partway down a hillside, like the Glass House. Johnson's and Almerico's centralized pavilions were both designed to embrace the full 360 degrees of their surroundings.

Both featured an interior cylinder. In Vicenza, it was a grand, frescoed chamber, while in New Canaan Johnson chose a quite different scheme. He located his masonry cylinder off axis, but its protuberance through the roof was as defining in its stylized way—Johnson called it the "anchor"—as the dome at the Villa Rotonda. Among his many stated aspirations, Johnson had self-consciously adapted an earlier idea to his post–World War II house, explaining that his brick cylinder alluded to "a burnt wooden village I saw once where nothing was left but the foundations and chimneys of brick."[42]

To be sure, Johnson applied no porticoes to his glass house, unlike the four porches at the Villa Almerico. And Palladio's masonry monument, fully ordered and domed, differed greatly from Johnson's glass box.

The Glass House interior—perhaps the ultimate indoor-outdoor space—complete with Mies furniture, an area-defining rug (Johnson called it a "raft"), and the Arcadian Poussin canvas. (Carol M. Highsmith, Library of Congress/Prints and Photographs)

Nevertheless, the two are relations, reacting as they do to their sites in a formal way that alludes to the classical past.

In furnishing his house, Johnson kept to his own century, using the familiar Miës chairs and other pieces from his Manhattan apartment. By the time he repositioned them in a fixed and formal arrangement in New Canaan, the furniture, designed twenty and more years earlier, had become modern classics. Their groupings defined the uses of individual spaces in a way that, in a more traditional house, partitions would.

One element that had held pride of place in Johnson's Manhattan apartment didn't make the trip to Connecticut, since the Schlemmer canvas *Bauhaus Stairway* now hung at the MoMA. In New Canaan, Johnson chose to feature a quite different painting, one that he acquired specifically for his new house. As the only object that predated the twentieth century, it became a focus amid the sparse decorations, and with no wall on which to hang it, Johnson designed a metal easel for the old-master painting that amounted to a reference point for his newfound classicism.

Acquired at Alfred Barr's suggestion, the work, *The Burial of Phocion* (1648–49), was one of three known versions from Nicolas Poussin's studio. The artist depicted a classical landscape, an arcadian view inspired by poetry that, as a Harvard undergraduate, Johnson had studied in its original Latin. Figures are in the foreground, but the beauty of the canvas derives from its loving portrayal of an idealized Roman landscape, complete with temples and rolling hills. In New Canaan, it did not merely express Johnson's educated artistic taste but also suggested his larger vision of his home's place in its own setting.

At Johnson's house, Poussin serenity worked in tandem with the bucolic Connecticut landscape that surrounded it. In the fullness of time, Johnson's own composition at New Canaan would echo Poussin's: Johnson would increase his holding to forty-nine acres, adding many architectural features and follies and ruins, as Johnson's and Poussin's visions grew together.

———

NOT EVERYONE WAS persuaded by Johnson's attempt to establish his house's context. The first serious critical article about the house, which appeared in *Interiors & Industrial Design*, rather misleadingly described it as a Victorian bell jar, the "kind of glass bell used to protect Victorian clocks."[43] The writer, Arthur Drexler, dismissed the place as "less like a house than like a diagram drawn in the air to indicate a quantity of space."[44] Johnson, not so thin-skinned as Wright, was far from offended, and he soon invited the younger Drexler to join his department at the MoMA.

Of continuing concern in the Connecticut suburb were the cars and the explosion of foot traffic on Ponus Ridge Road. A local paper, the *New Canaan Advertiser*, gave voice, via lines of doggerel, to the feelings of many among the town's silent majority concerning the town's new architectural fame. By 1952, the town seemed to have a quorum—with dozens of new modern houses, New Canaan had become *the* Modernist place to see in the East. A house tour was arranged to satisfy the public appetite to get a closer look at Johnson's and the other new houses. But one pseudonymous wag, Ogden Gnash-Teeth, dismissed the new as "an architectural form as gracious as Sunoco service stations."[45]

Johnson seemed to derive pleasure from every turn in the conversation. One woman, on visiting the Glass House, told Johnson skeptically. "Well, it may be very beautiful, but I certainly couldn't live here."

Johnson's reply? "I haven't asked you to, madam."[46]

VII.

The Fifties . . . New Canaan, Connecticut . . . The Glass House

A S H E W O U L D later demonstrate at Yale, Frank Lloyd Wright was among the unpersuaded. He found the Glass House an occasional and convenient stopping place during the construction of the Sander House (1952), a commission on a rock outcropping in Stamford, another town in Fairfield County, Connecticut, and the Rayward House (1955), for which a portion of the Noroton River in New Canaan was dammed to create a pond and waterfall.

Ever watchful of his competition, Wright recognized that Johnson had truly joined their ranks. That may explain his tendency to belittle the place, but the Glass House must have seemed alien to Wright for many reasons. He liked to design not only a house but its furniture, patterned windows, decorations, light fixtures, candlesticks, and doorknobs. On Ponus Ridge, Johnson's house consisted almost entirely of factory-made materials, and most of the furnishings were the work of Miës van der Rohe.

Philosophical as well as practical differences separated the two men ("I was so anti-Wright at the time," Johnson remembered later).[47] Well before Johnson's birth, Wright declared war on what he called "the box," and to judge from architectural trends in the decades that followed, he was winning. Architects were blowing out walls, stretching roofs, mixing masses, and creating interior spaces that were distinguished less often by partitions, more often by usage. Wright loved to vary ceiling heights, to surprise people with contrasts of light and dark, of textures, of intersecting planes. Though Johnson had absorbed Wright's dislike of the boxy feel of partitioned rooms, at the Glass House he outflanked Wright, building a new version of a highly regular, flat-topped box in which all four sides were bilaterally symmetrical.

In his *Architectural Review* article announcing the Glass House, Johnson consciously cast himself as the anti-Wright. He made a point of distinguishing his use of his New Canaan acres from Mr. Wright's method. "My house is approached on dead-level," he wrote, noting parenthetically that, in contrast, "Frank Lloyd Wright, that great Romantic, prefers shelves or hillsides." Johnson cited no specific Wright designs as evidence, but Johnson knew from his visits that both Taliesin and Fallingwater stood on hillsides.

Their native gifts also set the two men apart. Wright came of age studying engineering at the University of Wisconsin and then working as a delineator for Silsbee and as Louis Sullivan's head draftsman in Chicago; Johnson spent a seven-year undergraduate sojourn at Harvard, an on-again, off-again intellectual adventure in classics and philosophy. Wright lived to draw pictures; Johnson's greater gift was in the realm of ideas, and the New Canaan house reflects that contrast. Johnson's friends often made light of his labored efforts at the drafting table, while Wright was an acknowledged master of the line with his T square, triangles, and colored pencils. As a young man Wright won the admiration of Sullivan and others by virtue of his intricate detailing, his ability to dress a building, while most of the drawings for the Glass House had been taped to Landis Gores's drafting table, not Johnson's. Even had Johnson executed them, the Glass House renderings, consisting as they did almost entirely of straight lines, would have posed little challenge to a student enrolled in Architectural Drafting 101. No majestic perspectives survive of Johnson's house.

Never a man to hold his tongue out of politesse, Wright repeatedly mocked Johnson's house—and Johnson kept begrudging track of Wright's words. In a West Coast speech delivered to a group of Washington architects in 1957, Johnson observed mildly, "Mr. Wright has been annoying me for some time."[48] But Johnson, a skilled and relaxed speaker, wished to elicit more than smiles and chuckles; it's clear from his words that Wright's gibes and jabs irritated him.

"[Wright] says that my . . . Glass House . . . is not a house at all—it's not a shelter, it doesn't have any caves, it's cold and it doesn't give you a feeling of comfort; it's a box. He once said—he's much cleverer, of course, than all the rest of us so you can't say these things as well as he does—that my house is a monkey cage for a monkey."

Johnson's pique was palpable, even though he knew that Wright on principle could not help but dislike a house entirely of glass. To Wright, Johnson's New Canaan oddity was akin to a ship without a bottom, the emperor without clothing, an opportunity wasted.

In his little discourse on Wright's reactions, Johnson found fault with Wright's thinking. Having himself drawn deeply on the architectural past, Johnson dismissed Wright's "contempt for the history books, for all architecture that preceded him." Wright's imperious insistence on his utter originality irritated Johnson. "Was he born full-blown from the head of Zeus," Johnson spluttered, "that he could be the only architect that ever lived or ever will?"

That said, Johnson gave Wright full credit for having "changed the course of architecture single-handed from 1900 to 1910." He described

Wright as "brilliant and cantankerous," then expressed wonder that "we can admire [Wright] at the same time we dislike him as much as I do."

Whatever the frustrations his old nemesis posed, Johnson nevertheless credited Wright with giving him a firm shove in the direction of his new career. As the 1950s began, Johnson juggled his roles as a curator at MoMA, a teacher at Yale, and an architect with a still-modest practice. But Wright recognized that the Glass House gave Johnson a new status. Thus, he posed Johnson a challenge.

"You can't carry water on both shoulders," Johnson remembers him saying.[49] "Philip, you've got to choose: Do you want to be a critic, or are you going to be a practicing architect? You can't do both."

Johnson admitted then that he needed to be bold. "Wright changed my life."

He needed to commit himself to being an architect. "Of course it was so obvious. But the fact is that [Wright] was the only one that said it."[50]

VIII.
Spring 1958 . . . New Canaan, Connecticut . . . The Glass House

THE TWO MEN shared a penchant for control. They knew how they wished their interiors to appear. Wright famously dictated to clients where the Japanese prints (which he had selected) were to hang and how the furniture (of his design) was to be arranged. Johnson forbade the use of pillows on his daybed; comfortable though they might be, they ruined the aesthetic.

When returning home one weekend afternoon from a neighbor's cocktail party, Johnson found someone had visited in his absence and left him a note. Written in what seemed a strange hieroglyphic, the message extended around the house in a continuous, descending line; for a stylus, the writer had used a cake of soap directly on the glass. More remarkable still, the visitor—soon revealed to have been Eero

Saarinen—had written his message *backward*. Once inside the house, his note was easily read.

The long note expressed Saarinen's delight and admiration for Philip's new house. Johnson welcomed the endorsement of Saarinen, as Eero, son of noted architect Eliel Saarinen, was already making his mark in architecture and furniture design. The price of the compliment, however, would be hours of labor removing the message with hose and sponge.[51]

Another unscheduled visit occurred in spring 1958. In town to inspect the completed Rayward House, Wright decided to make a call at Johnson's. After phoning ahead and being told they were very much welcome, Wright headed for Ponus Ridge, together with Mr. and Mrs. Rayward and Pedro Guerrero, Wright's favorite photographer and a resident of New Canaan.[52]

Wright headed the procession that approached on the white-pebbled path, and Johnson, framed in his open doorway, offered a wry greeting: "Mr. Wright, welcome to the monkey house."

According to Guerrero's recollection, Wright asked, apparently confused, "Why do you call it that?"

When Johnson replied that Wright had named it so, Wright was quick with a comeback: "No, Philip, I said you were capable of doing that, not that you had."

The sparring was under way.

The new arrivals joined an impromptu cocktail party, Guerrero recalled, and Wright made himself the center of attention. He was soon delivering a lengthy peroration on the evolution of architecture from the time of the caveman, positing that bunched bamboo tied with vines anticipated the classical column.

Refreshing his glass of whiskey at the bar, Wright considered *Two Circus Women*, a large figural sculpture. Executed by Elie Nadelman, the papier-mâché work rested atop a plain plinth. Johnson had described the bulky sculpture as "the type of foil which this kind of building needs," and the generous curves of the women and the work's textured surface contrasted with the hard lines and machine smoothness of the surrounding steel and glass.[53]

Johnson had positioned Nadelman's women with care, with the large sculpture anchoring a corner of the seating area diagonal to the Poussin canvas, indicating a separation between the sitting, eating, and food-preparation areas. But Wright, after mixing his drink, took exception to its placement. So he moved the women, who were attached at the waist like Siamese twins.

A short time later, when Johnson noticed that *Two Circus Women* was out of its accustomed place, he returned the sculpture to its original position.

When Wright went to freshen his drink a second time, he remarked on the repositioning. According to Guerrero's account, he reprimanded his host, "Philip, leave perfect symmetry to God!"[54]

CHAPTER 12

The Whiskey Bottle and
the Teapot

Here, gentlemen, you see something grave and silent. Standing there in the
disaster that Park Avenue has become, it looks as though it had just wandered
in from some higher and more integrated civilization.
—Vincent Scully

I.
Spring 1952 . . . Park Avenue . . . The Bronfman Job

WITH THE ARRIVAL of the 1950s, Frank Lloyd Wright's
design for the Guggenheim remained no more than a scale model
the size of a kitchen table. When the possibility of a new and different
New York commission came to his attention, he knew that, if he could
enthrall the Bronfman brothers as he had Hilla Rebay, he might claim
credit for two of the most significant new buildings in what even Wright
had come to recognize was the nation's cultural capital.

He approached Allan Bronfman, brother of Samuel Bronfman,
president of the Joseph E. Seagram and Sons corporation. Wright made
contact through a son-in-law, Kenneth Baxter, an executive at the
company. A year before, Seagram had purchased an entire blockfront on
Park Avenue for $4 million. It planned to raze the existing twelve-story
apartment building to construct a new corporate headquarters, having

outgrown its elegantly appointed executive offices on the fifteenth floor of the grand Chrysler Building. The Bronfmans had a reputation for doing things well. They had a site, money, savvy, taste, and a respect for architecture. Wright wanted in.

In his usual way, Wright's pitch to Allan Bronfman began with a dismissal of the precedents, the existing "half-baked" skyscrapers that lined New York's streets. Writing in March and again in April 1952, Wright promised a better design, something "that would enable you to astonish and delight the world." He told Bronfman and his colleagues that a building he designed would be the equivalent of a million dollars' worth of advertising. Anticipating concerns that they might think him too old, Wright added, "Great ideas are involved—so having them up in my sleeve, as the final grand act . . . I am eager to shake them out."[1]

The conversation ended almost before it began. To start with, the decision was not Allan Bronfman's to make. Perhaps more important, Wright's checkered reputation had long since registered with veteran Seagram executives. As one put it in an interoffice memo, "The roof [of a potential Wright building] will probably leak; the heating system and the lights probably won't work; he will make it extremely difficult to house your employees because he will place them where he wants them, not where they are practically located. When you get through (if you ever finish it) it will cost twice as much as any other building."[2]

No one entered Wright's name on the short list—or any list—of prospective designers for the House of Seagram. It would be a full two years before the hiring decision would be made, but Wright's failure to win the job did mean that New Yorkers would, in the latter half of the fifties, be treated to the remarkable spectacle of two entirely unlike landmark buildings rising simultaneously. It would be an undeclared competition, as Wright's spiral emerged as New York's most unique building and the Seagram tower a paradigm for the city's future. A battle was about to be joined between buildings soon nicknamed the teapot and the whiskey bottle.

Before the main event, Wright did succeed in shaking a design out of his sleeve, to be realized on Park Avenue in 1955.

Like Johnson years earlier, Maximilian Hoffman dreamed of bringing contemporary European design to an American audience. Only the preoccupation of the Austrian émigré and former race-car driver wasn't architecture. He focused on European automobiles.

In 1947, the first showroom of Hoffman Motor Car Company opened on Park Avenue with a four-passenger Delahaye in the window. The curvaceous coupe was the only car in Hoffman's inventory at the time, but he was soon selling BMWs, Coopers, Rovers, and Bentleys. He climbed back behind the wheel to win several races driving a specially modified Porsche roadster, helping inspire a new fascination with European sports cars in the United States. His business grew rapidly, and in 1951 he opened a second showroom, this one on Broadway's Automobile Row. Along its roughly half-mile length extending north from Fiftieth Street, neon signs invited passersby to check out mostly American marques, among them Hudson, Buick, Studebaker, and Cadillac.

After gaining major contracts to sell cars for Jaguar and Mercedes-Benz, Hoffman decided he needed an architect to design a more dramatic setting for his goods. Since their social circles overlapped, he consulted Philip Johnson. Hoffman was on his way to establishing a network of hundreds of dealers that extended to Beverly Hills, and though no student of architecture, he knew he wanted showy. It didn't take long for him to decide Johnson's glass-and-steel mode was "too cold" for his tastes; an understanding Johnson pointed him west to Wisconsin, recommending he consult Frank Lloyd Wright.[3]

When they met, Wright and Hoffman liked each other immediately. Long fascinated by the automobile—to Wright, fine cars embodied design, speed, and an aura of independence—he immediately accepted the commission, in December 1953, to design a new showroom at 430 Park Avenue. In return for his architectural work, he agreed to accept compensation in motorcars, not cash, and a gull-wing Mercedes 300SL was soon parked at Taliesin.

After a series of construction delays, Hoffman's new showroom opened in May 1955. The centerpiece of the thirty-six-hundred-square-foot ground-floor space was a rotating turntable, designed to accommodate three cars (the marques represented were Porsche, BMW, and Alfa Romeo). Its location, roughly two miles south of the proposed Guggenheim site, meant that New Yorkers got a foretaste of Mr. Wright's plan for upper Fifth Avenue. A perimeter ramp encircled the turntable, displaying several more vehicles as it rose to a cantilevered balcony. *Architectural Forum* admired the installation, commenting that its warm colors "contrast and complement the steely shine of the beautifully detailed but unrelenting industrial products."[4]

At last, after decades of discussion and an assist from Philip Johnson, a Wright site, albeit a modest one, finally arrived in New York.

II.

The Early Fifties . . . New York, Paris, and New Canaan, Connecticut

THE CHATTER SURROUNDING the Glass House gained Philip Johnson new visibility, but this recognition as an architectural practitioner was both good and bad.

A casual 1949 encounter at MoMA landed him a Rockefeller commission. Ascending with him in an elevator, museum benefactor and soon-to-be-trustee Blanchette Rockefeller asked Johnson to recommend an architect for a residential project on East Fifty-Second Street. It would function both as a guesthouse, convenient to the Rockefellers' duplex apartment overlooking the East River, and as a gallery space, since her husband, John D. Rockefeller III, thought Blanche's taste for contemporary paintings and sculptures not quite in keeping with his English furniture and Asian and Impressionist art.

Johnson began thinking aloud, offering the names of possible designers. But the casual elevator conversation rapidly changed course when Mrs. Rockefeller interrupted Johnson's talk of other designers.

"But, Mr. Johnson, you're an architect, aren't you?"[5]

So Johnson himself designed the house. Completed in 1950, his clever design sat upon the footprints of an earlier house and stable, which simplified the permitting. With its symmetrical glass-and-steel façade and interior garden, the town house was a descendant of Miës's thirties court-houses and Johnson's Ash Street home in Cambridge. Its street façade closely resembled the front elevation of Miës's ITT Library, a drawing of which Johnson had reproduced in his 1947 Miës exhibition.[6]

By the time the Rockefeller guesthouse was finished, Johnson had hired three draftsmen for the Manhattan office he shared with Landis Gores. Architecture had become his business, and as a working architect, Johnson signed his drawings "Philip Johnson, Designer." Then a knock at the door of his expanded Forty-Second Street offices brought Johnson back to reality.

A state official pointed out that Johnson was operating outside the law, since he had failed the state licensing examination in 1945 (and would fail twice more before passing).[7] Johnson was undeterred, and with the expiration of the lease on his Manhattan office space on December 31, 1950, he sent out announcements that he was moving to New Canaan. As he remembered later, "I wanted to be in a community of architects and the laws here in Connecticut regarding licensing were not as strict as in New York."[8]

———

AT AGE TWENTY-SEVEN, Phyllis Lambert looked to restart her life. Recently divorced from her husband, a banker named Jean Lambert, she kept his surname and remained in Paris. She sculpted in her studio and intrigued by architecture, traveled widely in Europe, photographing what she saw. It was no accident that she lived an ocean away from her domineering father, Samuel Bronfman.

In early summer 1954, Lambert happened across a photograph in the international edition of the *Herald Tribune*. The style and manner of the proposed new Seagram Building irritated her. When a letter from her father arrived enclosing a sketch of what was to be the headquarters of the family business, she was outraged. She wasn't alone: Back in New York, others thought the proposed design resembled an "enormous cigarette lighter" and a "big trophy."[9] Lambert's strong feelings inspired her to write a long, hectoring letter that stung its recipient ("Dearest Daddy"), a powerful man who rarely tolerated dissent from progeny or employees.[10]

The letter, dated June 28, 1954, would become an important epistolary moment in twentieth-century architecture. The densely typed, single-spaced letter went on for eight pages, with numerous cross outs, marginal notes, and several freehand sketches in Lambert's hand. From her insistent "NO NO NO NO NO" at the opening—the first, densely argued paragraph is some four thousand words long—it is an artist's cri de coeur, one that clearly signaled the arrival of an architectural conscience.

She dismissed the plan in hand as a "Flash Gordon job." Worse yet, she added, "It is CHEAP." For a company seeking to enhance a reputation tarnished by its role in selling liquor during Prohibition, a déclassé look would be particularly damning. In making her argument, she also invoked the Renaissance, Shakespeare, and quoted John Ruskin.

In one impassioned passage, Lambert drew an essential conclusion: "You have one alternative and one alternative only: you must put up a building which expresses the best of the society in which you live, and at the same time your hope's [*sic*] for the betterment of this society. You have a great responsibility and your building is not only for the people of your companies, it is much more for all people, in NY and the rest of the world."

Without necessarily bowing to her argument, the father invited his daughter-in-exile to return home. He placed a transatlantic call and solicited her help in choosing the marble for the skyscraper's ground floor.

Bronfman, whose business expectations extended to his sons but not his daughter, would soon be surprised that, on Phyllis's return, she parlayed his mundane decorating assignment into a great deal more.

He arranged for her to meet his trusted friend Lou R. Crandall, president of the dominant construction firm of the day, the George A. Fuller Company. By then she had also consulted Lewis Mumford, who had recommended Marcel Breuer as architect. Lambert began to assemble an informal list of other candidates, on which Louis Kahn's recent extension to the Yale Art Gallery got him a place. A meeting with Alfred Barr led her to Philip Johnson; he was leaving his curatorial post at the MoMA, Barr confided, to devote his time to building his architectural practice. Johnson's wide knowledge of contemporary design could be valuable, counseled Barr, and on meeting him, Lambert decided he was just the sort of cicerone she needed, a tour guide to the architecture of the day.

When she sat down with Crandall, he was impressed by what she had already learned, and he recommended that she research potential architects for the project. She should go and talk to them, visit their built works, then make a recommendation. He helped persuade Samuel Bronfman of the wisdom of such an approach, and the father set a deadline. His daughter had six weeks.

Acting as her intermediary, Philip Johnson invited Eero Saarinen to meet with Lambert at the Glass House. In a witty construct that pleased Johnson, Saarinen compiled three lists: one of architects who *could* but *shouldn't* design the proposed building; a second enumerating *should-but-couldn't* candidates; and finally the *could-and-shoulds*. Among the serious candidates were I. M. Pei, Walter Gropius, Paul Rudolph, the firm of Skidmore, Owings & Merrill, and Saarinen himself.

Accompanied by Johnson, Lambert visited architects and construction sites. Her railroad itinerary included stops in Boston (to see works of Saarinen and Gropius), Philadelphia (the Howe and Lescaze PSFS tower), and Detroit (Saarinen's General Motors Technical Center). In Chicago, Lambert visited Miës van der Rohe's apartment towers on Lake

Shore Drive and the ITT campus, then toured Wright's Johnson Wax building in Racine.

As the deadline approached, she narrowed the field to two architects. One was Le Corbusier, but his only built structure in the United States, the United Nations was, as Lambert saw it, "an emasculation" of his original design. Miës had more to show on American soil, and while riding a train bound for Chicago, Lambert told Johnson, "You know, I've made up my mind."

As he recounted the story, Johnson "didn't have a clue" as to which architect she liked best.

"Well, what?" he inquired impatiently.

"I've picked Miës van der Rohe."[11]

In Miës's work, Lambert confided in a friend, she saw "a play of depth and shadow by the use of the basic structural steel member, the I beam. This ingenious and deceptively simple solution is comparable to the use of the Greek orders and Flying Buttress."[12] Almost every architect they talked to had referenced Miës; having already gained the admiration of his peers, he had won Lambert's. "It became clearer and clearer that it was Miës van der Rohe who had so understood his epoch that he had made poetry of technology."[13]

Like a provident uncle, Lou Crandall again inserted himself into the conversation. Samuel Bronfman trusted Crandall's business sense, and Crandall advised that a collaboration with Miës was "doable." That may have decided Bronfman, but Crandall added another idea. If Miës was to be the choice, why not ask Johnson to be his associate? Johnson had at last gained his New York license, and he brought valuable skills, including a gift for publicity, his ease in New York society, and fluent German (Miës's English, though improved, remained rough at the edges).

Miës himself more than embraced the idea: He suggested a partnership. "Shall we make it 'Van der Rohe and Johnson?'" he asked.[14] In that moment, Johnson gained the role of co-architect, a suitable reward for his quarter century of advocacy on behalf of Miës. Johnson's eyes grew wet with tears.[15]

On October 28, 1954, the parties executed a Memorandum of Agreement to design the building. The large and well-established New York firm of Kahn & Jacobs was retained as associate architect to execute construction drawings. By December 1, Philip Johnson had reestablished a New York office. The new firm took space on Manhattan's East Forty-Fourth Street, a short walk from the Chrysler Building and the Seagram offices. Surrounding a large central design space were a conference room and three offices, one each for Miës, Johnson, and Seagram's newly appointed director of planning, Phyllis Lambert.

———

ONE SATURDAY EVENING that autumn, Johnson welcomed Miës van der Rohe and Phyllis Lambert to the Glass House. Although theirs was a working session, alcohol was consumed in quantity and the conversation ranged widely. As Lambert remembered it, Miës was unhappy at Johnson's misreading of Miës's steel details at the Glass House (according to a Miës associate, Johnson had copied them onto little index cards from a drawing he saw on visiting Miës's Chicago office).[16] A simmering resentment—Miës had visited the Glass House numerous times before—was fueled by what he saw as the dishonesty of Johnson's use of wood-frame ceiling joists in a glass and steel house. "He thought I should have understood his work better," Johnson later explained.[17] "I just think he felt that my bad copy of his work was extremely unpleasant."[18]

The voices grew louder after Lambert departed, and at two o'clock in the morning, the row reached an angry conclusion when Miës exploded, "Philip, take me somewhere else to sleep."

Johnson thought Miës was joking, but he was not.

When Johnson realized he had no choice but to oblige, he telephoned Bob Wiley, a friend and neighbor, asking whether he might accommodate Johnson's guest even though it was the middle of the night. Wiley, who lived in a house Johnson had designed, agreed to take him in, and the angry Miës was duly delivered. "He never came back," Johnson remembered. "He never would come near this house."[19]

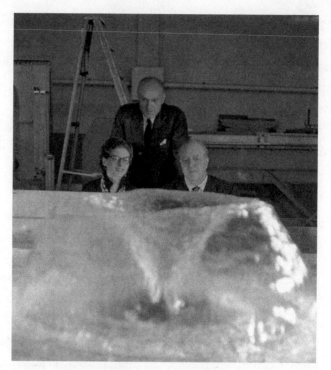

*In 1956, collaborators Philip Johnson (rear), Phyllis Lambert, and Miës muse on a
test at MIT of a model fountain for the Seagram Building plaza.* (Frank
Scherschel/The LIFE Picture Collection/Getty Images)

Their collaboration at 375 Park Avenue, a New York marriage of
convenience, proved more amenable, and the two men settled into their
new partnership.

III.

*1954–55 . . . 219 East Forty-Fourth Street . . . Van der Rohe and Johnson,
Architects*

IN DECEMBER 1954, the junior associates at van der Rohe and
Johnson constructed a cardboard model that represented the dozen

blocks north and south of 375 Park Avenue. Set on a high table in the architects' studio, the model permitted Miës, a man renowned for his silences, to sit in a nearby chair, cigar in hand, and spend hours wordlessly examining the scaled-down avenue as if from sidewalk level. When inspiration struck, Miës would order the fabrication of a new configuration of the Seagram tower; its built-to-scale mass would then be slotted into the miniature streetscape, and Miës could resume his musings.[20]

Tall buildings had been rising all over Manhattan in the fifties, as New York enjoyed the biggest building boom since the pre-Depression twenties. The city's widest boulevard was a desirable location, particularly between Fiftieth and Fifty-Seventh streets, a longtime residential section rezoned for commercial development.

City regulations meant that a typical new building resembled a wedding cake. The goal was to prevent the new skyscrapers from blocking sunlight from reaching the street. The radical 1916 zoning code had meant that owners could build out to the entire lot size only if their tall structures setback at specified heights. That meant that by the 1950s, when Miës, Johnson, and Lambert eyed the mock-ups of the facing masonry-clad buildings, most of the structures they saw stepped back from the façade line at ten stories and above, thereby both reducing the mass of the structures and keeping the street from being plunged into darkness.

One notable exception to the new normal sat one block north and across the avenue from the site of the proposed Seagram Building. The zoning regulations also specified that no setbacks were required for a tower that occupied only a quarter of its lot, and the green-tinted Lever House met that standard. Completed in 1952, the city's first glass tower consisted of a vertical slab, its rectangular footprint perpendicular to the avenue. A contrasting one-story horizontal slab occupied the balance of the site, raised on columns to leave a courtyard below. The work of Gordon Bunshaft and Natalie de Blois, it was unmistakably in the mode of Miës and the International Style.

The three principals lunched together often at an Italian restaurant near their office. There Johnson and Miës, Lambert reported, usually downed two martinis each. Early on, zoning limitations figured into their discussions. The agreed-upon preference was a Lever-like tower, but using the 25 percent multiplier, the calculation yielded a maximum footprint that was too small to be economical.

Once again, builder Lou Crandall helped devise a solution. Seagram owned two adjacent properties, one facing Fifty-Third, the other facing Fifty-Second Street. At a meeting in Crandall's office, it was agreed that, by pulling down the two existing buildings on those plots, the project would be viable, since the added land meant added building volume.

The terms of Miës's contract with Seagram's required that he reside in New York. Leaving his rooms at the Barclay Hotel each morning, he walked the five blocks to the future building site, examining the surrounding buildings, considering the context as well as the restrictions imposed by the building code and zoning. With surprising speed, the contemplative Miës, a man more likely to think his way to a solution than to sketch it—his arthritis grew more debilitating by the year—was soon ready to commission a model of the building that he, likely with a minimum of input from his junior colleagues, envisioned. Begun early in 1955, the model was completed by mid-February.

Just twenty-six inches tall, it was fabricated of bronze plates. Though inadvertently, Samuel Bronfman himself had suggested the bronze. "What's that material?" he had asked Lambert and Johnson as they strode past the Daily News Building. "I like it," he said, indicating the bronze rim on the doors. "Why can't we have a building in that?"[21] Miës thought the material a good choice; he regarded bronze as "a very noble material [that] lasts forever if used in the right way."[22]

Precision milling meant the model's three-dimensional surface replicated Miës's innovative window mullions, which consisted of vertical I beams mounted to project beyond the steel-and-glass plane of the curtain wall. Precisely cut self-adhesive pieces of a plastic membrane indicated the glass. In contrast to the large drawings that Miës usually had prepared for his clients, the little model that the team readied for Samuel Bronfman was, in Lambert's words, "a jewellike presentation."[23]

Perhaps more surprising than either its surface or size was the model's position. Mounted on a two-by-three-foot base that represented the two-hundred-by-three-hundred-foot building site, the Park Avenue façade of the Seagram tower as represented would not align with the existing street wall. Like a single soldier trailing a stride behind his brethren in parade rank, the tower was to stand well back from and parallel to the sidewalk, forming a plaza a full ninety feet deep and extending the entire north-south width of the block. It was, Lambert confided in a friend, "almost Baroque . . . with a magnificent plaza and the building not zooming up in front of your nose so that you can't see it, only to be oppressed by it and have to cross the street to really look at it, *but a magnificent* entrance to a *magnificent* building all in front of you."[24] Even at its small scale, the precisely articulated tower façade and the way it broke the canyon wall were entirely unexpected.

In early March, the triumvirate of Director of Planning Lambert and architects Miës and Johnson, pleased with their progress, scheduled a presentation. No budget or building schedule were proffered to Samuel Bronfman and his corporate advisers. The beautiful bronze model was on its own.

It met with a stony silence, leaving the three "desolate."[25]

A fortnight later, however, word came down that Samuel Bronfman had not only approved the design but, as Lambert reported, "My father is in thralls of delight—a minor miracle."[26]

Much remained to be resolved, including how to extrude the bronze I beams for the exterior, the choice of glass for the floor-to-ceiling windows, and the challenge of integrating climate control into the revolutionary building, with its applied bronze-and-glass skin and concrete-covered steel skeleton. The rear, east-facing section of the building would evolve, with rigid, sheer walls added to stiffen the thirty-eight-story building.

With the essentials agreed upon, the Joseph E. Seagram and Sons corporation advanced like a tank on the battlefield, and in barely three years, the tabletop bronze model became a habitable 515-foot tower, with company executives occupying their offices by December 1957. But 375 Park Avenue wasn't the only construction site in town.

IV.

The Mid-Fifties . . . Manhattan Island . . . Getting a Permit

IN CONTRAST TO the unstoppable momentum at Seagram, the Guggenheim Foundation floundered. After Solomon Guggenheim's death, on November 3, 1949, the Fifth Avenue museum-to-be landed in limbo, and with their sponsor gone, Wright and Hilla Rebay faced an uncertain future.

In his will, Guggenheim earmarked $2 million for the construction of the museum, but to Wright's consternation, the dying man failed to specify who was to be the architect. During the year it took for the will to be probated, Wright went about leveraging his relationship with his dead benefactor into a new commitment on the part of the heirs.

A few weeks after Guggenheim's funeral, he wrote to one trustee, "Were it not for my promise to Mr. Guggenheim several weeks before he died that I would be building this building for him . . . I would be quite content to withdraw and leave the matter to the trustees. But I do have a conscience in this matter . . . [and] I am ready to keep my promise."[27] He sent a warm remembrance to nephew Harry Guggenheim, the new president of the foundation, and looked to make an ally of the Seventh Earl Castle Stewart, an Anglo-Irish peer, husband of Solomon's daughter Eleanor May Guggenheim, and soon-to-be foundation chairman.

At an early meeting of the reconstituted trustees, Wright made it his business to get himself onto the agenda. As Lord Stewart remembered the afternoon, "[Wright] handled the situation so admirably that we were all deeply impressed listening to him present his ideas in a clear, simple and direct way." Afterward the earl graciously made a point of saying as much to Wright, expressing admiration for the way he handled a roomful of businessmen.

Seeing an opening, Wright did not just accept the compliment. Instead, he smiled and inverted Stewart's sentiments into a challenge: "It was just an expression of my belief that your father-in-law's dream will come true, my boy—that is all."[28]

By April 1951, Wright's influence over the Guggenheim heirs was such that the foundation purchased another key piece of real estate. On a visit to England, Wright had convinced Eleanor Castle Stewart to support the acquisition of the "old hang nail at the corner,"[29] as Wright called it, and the acquisition of 1070 Fifth Avenue meant the museum's footprint could expand to fill the entire Fifth Avenue block-front. The two existing buildings at 1070 and 1071 Fifth Avenue would have to come down, permitting the redesigned museum to occupy a site that measured 201.5 feet north to south, 127.8 feet east to west. Wright and his apprentices raced to revise the design to suit the site. In February 1952, the trustees approved Wright's noticeably more horizontal version.

Where Wright succeeded, Rebay failed. Without the protective presence of Solomon Guggenheim, negative press coverage put the baroness's directorship in jeopardy. *New York Times* art critic Aline Louchheim criticized Rebay's "immodest" exhibition of her own work and that of "her once close friend" Rudolf Bauer. Citing Rebay's "mystic-double-talk" and her "evasiveness" regarding the pending construction of Wright's "imaginative building," Louchheim suggested the foundation might consider folding its holdings into those of another museum.[30]

The board reacted, pressuring Hilla Rebay to resign as director. As a consolation, she was appointed director emerita and given a seat on the board, but her influence waned rapidly, especially after Harry Guggenheim announced at a news conference that May that the onetime Museum of

Non-Objective Art would thereafter be known as the Solomon R. Guggenheim Memorial Museum. The new name, a broader collection policy, and a new director (James Johnson Sweeney was named to the post that autumn) rendered Rebay irrelevant.

Meanwhile Wright, with revised drawings completed, recognized the need for allies in facing down powerful forces in a strange city. Before Solomon Guggenheim's death, Wright had enlisted New York architect Arthur Cort Holden to facilitate the permitting; with matters in motion once again, Wright drew upon Holden's three decades of experience with the New York bureaucracy. Holden became the architect of record and informally approached the Department of Building and Housing prior to filing for a building permit for the unusual building. Holden's goodwill gained him the cooperation of both the Manhattan superintendent of buildings and a staff engineer, Isidore Cohen, whom the building commissioner regarded as one of the ablest men in the department.

All parties understood that the building department was charged with enforcing a building code written for traditional buildings—and, as Holden reminded Wright, "the design for the Guggenheim Museum is unique in the City's construction experience."[31] But Cohen agreed to try to identify ways to obtain approval for elements that didn't conform. His subsequent report revealed how significant the discrepancies were, as he enumerated thirty-two areas in which the design transgressed the code.

Some were minor and easily remedied, but major concerns involved technical matters such as floor loads and the fire resistance of glass and plastic. Wright's son-in-law Wesley Peters, the Taliesin project manager, produced an elaborate structural analysis to gain Cohen's approval. Some variances were obtained, the stairways widened, and the dome redesigned, and fire exits added to satisfy the fire safety code. But hurdles remained.

———

AS GETTING THE approvals dragged on, the museum demonstrated its commitment to Wright's vision, commissioning what became the largest exhibition ever devoted to his work. He devised a pavilion for the installation that occupied the parking lot at the Eighty-Ninth Street corner of the foundation's Fifth Avenue property. Of the hundreds of drawings, models, and other objects, one dominated: Wright designed a full-scale Usonian house and oversaw its construction at the Guggenheim site.

The 1,700-square-foot, two-bedroom dwelling offered a fresh take on what Wright saw as "democratic," middle-class housing. "I think this has the old Colonial on the run," Wright told the press.[32] Most members of a public curious to see a suburban house at 1070 Fifth Avenue walked into an open plan for the first time; the layout meant, Wright explained, "[the housewife] was now more hostess . . . instead of being a kitchen-mechanic behind closed doors."[33] Visitors came in droves to view *Sixty Years of Living Architecture: The Work of Frank Lloyd Wright*. In response to public interest, the exhibition remained open seven days a week and until ten P.M. on Wednesday through Saturday nights.

Wright delighted in the attention of the great crowds of New Yorkers. "Go on up to Fifth Avenue and see the show," he instructed one young apprentice. "It's the only instance of the third dimension in this entire town."[34] But he didn't limit his braggadocio to the ears of his youthful admirers, as Lewis Mumford discovered when Wright gave him a guided tour of the Guggenheim exhibition. Though he had become a Wright booster many years before, Mumford had distanced himself from Wright during World War II (Wright had done all he could to oppose the war; Mumford mourned his only son, dead in battle). But their former intimacy was tainted further by their time together in 1953, with Mumford noting, "I realized as never before how the insolence of his genius sometimes repelled me."[35]

Yet Wright's longevity served him well, as did his growing association with New York, New York. In his mid-eighties, he emerged as a true celebrity.

For decades, Wright had disparaged the city, citing its congestion, polluted air, and the squalor in which some of the inhabitants lived. He described New York as a "medieval hangover."[36] He disliked its architecture; the buildings were, among other things, simply too vertical for his taste. Nevertheless, he had visited often over the years, frequenting Broadway theaters and enjoying the city's restaurants, walking its streets, cultivating friends and contacts.

With the ongoing Guggenheim association, Wright's visits to Gotham grew longer and more frequent. The installation of the Guggenheim show and the Usonian house required many trips to New York and gained him new visibility. Arthur Holden, the architect hired to facilitate the building permit for the Guggenheim, described a taxi trip downtown to the Building Department: "The taximan . . . knew Mr. Wright's name and lost an ear all the way down listening to Mr. Wright's comments."[37]

The editor of *House Beautiful*, Elizabeth Gordon, added to his renown. She held Wright in high esteem, publishing Wright interviews and features, devoting an entire issue to him in 1955, and issuing her like-minded dismissal of the International Style. "The Threat to the Next America" characterized the Tugendhat House and Le Corbusier's Villa Savoye as evidence that "something is rotten in the state of design."[38] Wright had the answers, she told readers, and the Europeans did not.

A city of celebrities welcomed a new one, and Wright's clients soon included Elizabeth Taylor and Marilyn Monroe. Although his notions for the actresses' houses were never executed, it was perhaps inevitable that, when the plans for the Guggenheim Memorial at last neared approval, Wright decided he needed a place to call his own in Manhattan.

More and more of his attention would be required, he reasoned, to be sure the building rose as he wished. He would need to be near the job site. As a man of many certainties, he knew precisely where he wished to stay.

On escaping Oak Park and his marriage, in 1909, he and Mamah Borthwick Cheney had taken rooms at the Plaza prior to sailing for Europe. He had entertained Mumford, Alexander Woollcott, and others in the hotel's dining rooms; in the 1940s, Solomon and Irene Guggenheim repeatedly welcomed Wright and Olgivanna to their art-filled apartment in the Plaza.

After inspecting the available rooms, Wright rented suite 223–225. Entered via a private vestibule, each of its two principal rooms had thirteen-foot-tall ceilings, a fireplace, and arch-topped windows. The corner sitting room overlooked Central Park and Fifth Avenue, while the bedroom looked down upon Grand Army Plaza. The suite included a kitchen, maid's room, and other support spaces.

Like several previous occupants—the list included famed financier "Diamond" Jim Brady, French couturier Christian Dior, and film producer David O. Selznick—Wright redecorated the space. He chose Japanese rice paper flecked with gold leaf to cover the wall panels and specified a rosy hue for the trim. He designed elaborate window treatments that featured deep red velvet drapes and roundel mirrors. Peach carpets covered the floor. The mix of new furniture included chairs from the Usonian exhibition house, a Steinway grand piano, and a vanload of pieces from Wisconsin that Wright designed specifically for the Plaza, fabricated and delivered by Taliesin apprentices. The corner room remained a sitting room, and the other main room became both bedroom and office, with a louvered screen to separate the sleeping quarters from Wright's desk. To visitors, the place clearly conveyed something of the Wright vernacular, and the editor of *Architectural Forum* soon dubbed it "Taliesin the Third."

The high-toned setting suited Wright's style. Each day he rode the elevator to the basement barbershop for his morning shave. The chairs in his vestibule were frequently occupied by newspapermen, as well as clients, awaiting their time with Wright. The suite's three phones rang often, and Taliesin retainers bustled in and out, working at type-writers and at drafting boards with their T squares and triangles. As the apprentice who worked as Olgivanna's secretary put it, the place was "pandemonium . . . almost all the time."[39]

Wright's notoriety grew by another order of magnitude thanks to TV crews, who arrived to take over the suite's sitting room. New York emerged as the nation's television capital in the 1950s, and Wright mastered his self-appointed role as American architecture's chief spokesman. Asked by Hugh Downs about his seemingly boundless self-confidence, Wright told the audience for NBC's *Conversations with Elder Wise Men*, "Early in life I had to choose between honest arrogance and hypocritical humility. I chose honest arrogance."[40] He was a guest on a new morning broadcast called the *Today* show and taped two segments on *The Mike Wallace Interview*. In some two dozen television interviews, in a city with thirty daily newspapers, Wright reveled in offering his provocative opinions, preaching his architectural gospel to viewers and readers.

His visibility took another boost in March 1956 when, finally, almost thirteen years after Hilla Rebay's letter of inquiry, a building permit was issued for construction of the Guggenheim Museum.

v.

1956–57 . . . Fifth Avenue . . . Wright's Pantheon

As CONSTRUCTION APPROACHED, Wright decided the museum needed a new name. He came up with *archeseum*, a contraction of the words *architecture* and *museum*. The title "Archeseum" appeared on Taliesin plans and specification sheets until Harry Guggenheim, realizing Wright's neologism might become the name by which the museum was publicly known, wrote to Wright from the Guggenheim Foundation offices at 120 Broadway. "Please lay off for all time this 'archeseum' stuff," he instructed. "The family do not want it. They want to honor my uncle."[41]

The timing of Harry Guggenheim's letter was not accidental. With official groundbreaking to take place a few weeks later, on August 14, 1956, the man on the street was quite literally beginning to take notice of what was happening. The two buildings that had once stood on the Guggenheim property had been demolished. Soon enough a great hole would be dug, a jungle of wooden forms constructed, and traffic slowed by the coming and going of men, equipment, supplies, and convoys of cement trucks.

In the dozen years since the approval of the initial design, eight complete sets of drawings had been executed incorporating uncountable changes to the plans.[42] The enlargement in the site had required many adjustments, and uncharacteristically, Wright had over time compromised on many points in an effort to get his building built. The marble facing he favored was gone, as was the roof garden and the director's apartment. Neither the glass elevators nor the tubular glass in the dome survived. A proposed eleven-story apartment tower behind the museum was rejected.

Despite the many aspects that changed, the basic conceit did not. The spiral, standing a bit over one hundred feet in height, would enclose a ramp (length: roughly three quarters of a mile) that was pitched to drop three and a half inches per twenty feet. The central well would expand some twenty-four feet from grade to the building's crown. As the building rose, the galleries along the ramp remained the same height but grew wider. If the raiment Mr. Wright had tailored for Mr. Guggenheim differed in countless particulars, the torso within remained recognizable.

By September 1957, the lower section of the coil of reinforced concrete became visible, taller than the wooden construction fence at the perimeter of the site. People noticed, and such significant progress amounted to news. The *New York Times* dispatched a staff art critic to take a look at the building that Wright, on returning from a recent trip to Rome, had taken to calling "my pantheon." Mr. Wright acted as tour guide and chief explainer.

Although he liked to dismiss Philip Johnson and others as "propagandists," Wright took pains to shape the perception of his building and how it embodied his philosophy. "This is the only organic building in New York," he assured Aline B. Saarinen, "the only twentieth-century architecture; the only permanent building."[43] She listened attentively, taking copious notes.

Wright liked handsome women, and Saarinen was beautiful, self-assured, and well connected; she was also more than a *Times* staffer, as she was the niece of E. J. Kaufmann and the wife of a respected colleague, Eero Saarinen, whom Wright couldn't resist calling "your architect." (Husband and wife had met for the first time several years earlier, when she had profiled Saarinen for the *Times*.) A striking blonde, often photographed with a cigarette in hand and usually smiling, she understood architecture, having earned a master's in architectural history from NYU's prestigious Institute of Fine Arts. She had visited Wright at Taliesin in 1954; she was a veteran reporter, her first book at the printers. Indeed, her critique of Hilla Rebay's "doctrinaire attitude" in the pages of the *Times* had precipitated Rebay's departure.

Aline Saarinen needed to be persuaded, and Wright was at his cordial best. As Saarinen would soon tell her readers, "For years Mr. Wright has been belligerent in interviews, contentious and rebellious in his opinions. But now his words are mellow with good humor."[44]

He took her on a "walkie-talkie tour," she reported, climbing the spiral that by then rose a level and a half. She thought him surprisingly youthful, his "handsome face seem[ing] more weathered than wrinkled." He stepped easily around the work-site obstacles, wielding a "cane that is patently more necessary as a theatrical prop than as an old man's crutch."

He dismissed the city's steel-and-glass skyscrapers, among them "the whiskey building." He called them "cages . . . rusting at the joints. They have arthritis. They have limited lives." In contrast, he pointed to a bundle of steel reinforcement rods. "We can . . . build as in nature because we can use steel this way now. Just these thin rods. They are the tendons and muscles of the building; the concrete is the fatty tissue and the flesh; the rubberized, waterproof paint is the skin. Reinforced concrete makes all this possible."

Wright was expansive. "Here, for the first time you will see twentieth-century art and architecture in their true relation . . . Architecture is the mother of art. You will really feel like looking at pictures here and you will see them well in their proper atmosphere."

"When will the building be completed?" he was asked on that clear September morning in 1957.

"Probably by late spring," he replied. And the conversation went on as Wright confided and cajoled, obviously enjoying his time with the astute and appealing reporter.

In a way that he rarely did, he even acknowledged, at least by implication, his own mortality: "This eleventh-hour building is a thoroughbred."

VI.

1957 and After . . . A Very Public Debate . . . Installing the Art

THE LETTER ARRIVED like a warning shot fired across a warship's bow. The undated, typed sheet landed on James Johnson Sweeney's desk. Addressed to both Director Sweeney and the Guggenheim Museum trustees, it bore the individual signatures of twenty-one artists, among them Willem de Kooning, Robert Motherwell, Sally Michel, and Milton Avery.

The signers had agreed, "The interior design of the building is not suitable for a sympathetic display of painting and sculpture."[45] The letter, subsequently published for public consumption, continued, "The basic concept of curvilinear slope for the presentation of painting and sculpture indicates a callous disregard for the fundamental rectilinear frame of reference necessary for the adequate visual contemplation of works of art."

An angry Wright immediately concluded Sweeney was behind the letter. The two men openly disliked each other, with Wright describing the former MoMA curator at various times as a "fool" and a "showman." Wright had not wooed Sweeney after Rebay's departure, as he had done with the board following Solomon Guggenheim's death. The two men had become "irreconcilable opposites," as one apprentice saw it. "It's too bad that Mr. Wright never decided to 'Sell' Sweeney. I'm sure that he could have with a little soft soaping and flattery. But he simply wouldn't be bothered."[46]

Harry Guggenheim did his best to referee, but the debate continued as Sweeney added to the demands. He might as well have been a stand-in for Philip Johnson, sharing a taste for white walls (Wright preferred a cream color consistent with the exterior) and harsh but constant fluorescent lighting. Trying to get out of the cross fire, Guggenheim asked that Wright prepare perspective drawings to demonstrate how, in the architect's view, art should be exhibited in the museum. Wright agreed to make a presentation.

Drawn by apprentices, the four large sketches amounted to vignettes. In the pencil drawings, museum visitors were portrayed looking at artworks within the curve of the Guggenheim's ramp. One image portrayed watercolors installed on easel-like stands, two others pieces of art in museum alcoves. When he walked into the drafting room at Taliesin to review progress on a Sunday morning in 1958, Wright was drawn to the fourth.

It bore the title "The Masterpiece." In silhouette, a dozen visitors to the museum were pictured, most of them sitting or standing before a large non-objective painting—a "masterpiece," worthy of a Kandinsky. Finished in colored pencils, the canvas was brightly colored compared to the muted hues elsewhere on the sheet.

The renderer, Ling Po, had cleverly added a thirteenth figure, a school-age girl whose attention had evidently wandered from the artwork on the museum's perimeter wall. She leaned on the ramp's interior parapet.

Wright looked at the drawing, still on the drafting table, preparing to affix his initials in the block provided beneath the title. Instead, he sat down in Ling's chair and picked up a pencil. With practiced ease, he added a line that extended a short distance downward from the girl's left hand. The line became a string when Wright sketched at its end a circle, and inside that an arc. In a second or two, Wright had dangled a yo-yo, giving unexpected life to an imagined moment, subtly reminding the viewer the big Kandinsky painting wasn't the only work of art on view. Architecture was to be seen, too, with a spiraling balcony that enveloped a seven-story-tall central rotunda that even the most innocent minds might enjoy (see Fig. XVI).

"Boys," he said to the attentive apprentices looking on, "in all this endeavor we must never lose sight of a sense of humor." Only then did he sign the drawing.[47]

VII.

1958–59 . . . Seasons of Change

PHILIP JOHNSON WAS a supporting actor at 375 Park Avenue. How much influence he had in shaping the concept isn't clear, although the preceding towers that Miës had designed for Chicago's Lake Shore Drive, built between 1949 and 1952, were asymmetrical and dynamic while the Seagram Building is symmetrical, even classical, a taste to which Johnson was more inclined than Miës. Whatever Johnson's contribution to the overall look, his work, particularly on the inside, clearly elevated him to the A-list of New York architects.

As Miës had promised, the completion of the drawings for the Seagram Building required eighteen months, the construction another year and a half. Phyllis Lambert fought to build the tower as it had been designed when the Building Committee, consisting of Seagram's executives, threatened at regular intervals to alter it. "There was no hanky-panky, nobody cut corners," said Johnson later. "It wasn't that she knew anything about buildings, but it was like having the crown prince present."[48]

Johnson began as Miës's junior and Lambert's confidant, but his status rose rapidly when Miës, caught in a bizarre bureaucratic cul-de-sac, was refused a New York architect license. According to the New York Department of Education, the man who had been building widely admired buildings for more than forty years wasn't technically qualified to practice in the state of New York because he lacked a high school equivalency. The angry Miës abruptly returned to Chicago, and as of December 12, 1955, Philip Johnson became the building's architect-of-record in the eyes of the law.

The change was more than nominal, as it meant Johnson took charge of the office well before construction began. He managed the entire process until February 1957, when the collective clout of the Bronfmans finally got Miës's New York license granted. Yet even with Miës's reinstatement, Johnson never fully relinquished the influence his mentor's absence had given him. Johnson was on-site; Miës and Lambert trusted him. Perhaps more important, Miës's primary preoccupation was with the expression of the structure, the articulation of the building's form and its bronze and glass curtain wall. He focused on devising a radically new air-conditioning system that made floor-to-ceiling glass walls practical for the first time. But Miës found many of the building's other details uninteresting.

That meant Johnson exercised almost complete control over the revolutionary lighting plan that would make the building a beacon. He also designed the main lobby and the Seagram offices. He devised a new (and soon to be commonplace) look for the elevator cabs (a finish of woven wire), and he conceived the glass canopies for the side entries from Fifty-Second and Fifty-Third streets. He detailed the interiors, from water faucets to mail chutes, door handles, and fire alarms.

Johnson's manner was a precise minimalism worthy of Miës; as Johnson's old compatriot Henry-Russell Hitchcock quipped to a reporter from *Time* as the building neared completion, "I've never seen more of less."[49] The generous Seagram budget, roughly twice the norm for the neighborhood and four times the per-square-foot cost Miës had been allotted for his Lake Shore Drive buildings, meant that Johnson could improve upon many standard industrial design elements.

Nowhere was Johnson's sensibility more in evidence than in the restaurant that became the Four Seasons.

The tower was well under way before a decision was made about what the building's low east wing should contain. Inspired by Wright's new Hoffman Auto showroom a few blocks north at 430 Park Avenue, Seagram executives initially thought the two grand sixty-foot-square spaces would be well adapted for automobile showrooms. Later Bronfman summoned Johnson ("Don't tell Phyllis," Bronfman ordered) and asked what Johnson thought of renting the twenty-foot-tall first-floor spaces to a bank. Johnson told him it would ruin the building.

The eventual solution was a restaurant. Its northern room featured a walled pool surrounded with tables and chairs of chrome and black leather, based on Miës's design for the Tugendhat House. The simpler southern room contained a square bar. Johnson's several collaborators included Restaurant Associates, the firm that had leased the space and would operate the restaurant; lighting designer Richard Kelly, who had helped Johnson solve reflective issues at the Glass House; interior designer William Pahlmann; and a landscape designer, Karl Linn, who added seventeen-foot trees and other vegetation to the interiors. Johnson blended fine materials (travertine and French walnut) with carefully selected artworks, including a tubular bronze sculpture over the bar.

Alfred Barr pointed the way to what would become a decorative centerpiece, a stage curtain painted by Pablo Picasso. In March 1956, Barr advised Johnson that the immense canvas was for sale. Painted for Sergei Diaghilev and the Paris premiere of the ballet *Le Tricorne* (*The Three-Cornered Hat*) in 1919, the great canvas featured a procession of spectators in the foreground as a bullfight, framed by an arcade, unfolded to the rear. Nearly a year would be required to complete the transatlantic transaction, but a persistent Phyllis Lambert managed to acquire the work. Hung in an imposing linking hall between the two principal rooms, the roughly twenty-foot-square painting was visible from the Park Avenue entrance to the building.[50]

A memorable decoration solution that almost went wrong involved the curtains for the restaurant's immense windows. The specified treatments consisted of swagged chains of anodized aluminum. But Johnson got a panicked summons when, on installation, there appeared to be a problem.

The laboriously fabricated draperies had been hung by the time he arrived to have a look. Johnson saw that the great curving metal swags unexpectedly swayed in the column of air at the window wall. He wondered at first whether diners might be at risk of motion sickness; obviously, that would be a disaster. But the more the team looked at the reflective, shimming screen, the better they liked it. It seemed to add an atmosphere of elegance, a judgment soon affirmed by customers and the press.

"There's always a certain amount of luck," observed Johnson.[51]

———

JOHNSON'S DESIGN FOR the Four Seasons unexpectedly articulated one of the major preoccupations of his later work and, not coincidentally, revealed how his evolving architectural theories had benefited from the unasked-for influence of Frank Lloyd Wright.

Despite having been both curator and critic, Johnson never felt obligated to remain entirely impartial. An admitted acolyte of Miës's, he saw Wright and Miës as representatives of different, even opposing historical tides. But during the construction of the Seagram Building, he came to accept—and even embrace—the notion that Wright's ideas weren't antediluvian. It was as if, having stood on one side of the estuary, he found himself irresistibly drawn to the other shore.

He went public with his change of heart to a group of architects. The evening was a centennial celebration of the founding of a local chapter of the American Institute of Architects. No doubt conscious of the long-established tradition that one AIA member was not to criticize another's work, Johnson cautiously observed, "I'm annoyed by Mr. Wright's talking a good deal." Then he summarized the experience of arriving at Wright's encampment in Arizona.

He disparaged the approach to Wright's community in the Arizona desert, Taliesin West, describing the "dusty, nasty, and ill-kept" access road that led to a "meaningless group of buildings." But as the teller warmed to his story, he offered a significant admission. "[Wright] has developed one thing which I will defy any of us to equal, the arrangements of secrets of space."[52]

Johnson described how, in negotiating the pathways of Wright's built landscape in Scottsdale, he encountered changes in level and shifts in direction. Just as important, said Johnson, "[Wright] takes your eyes and makes them follow."

The terrain rises to a "prow," Johnson explained, with a panoramic view of the mountains. Then, walking on, the visitor follows an unpredictable path to "a little private secret garden" and, incongruously, comes to a New England lawn. Finally, Johnson (and his audience) arrived at Wright's sanctum, with its paradoxical wall of plants and great fireplace (see Fig. VII and VIII).

"My friends," Johnson confided in his audience, "that is the essence of architecture."

A year later, in 1958, he would offer an admiring aside in the same vein, this time to an audience of architecture students: "Take no more courses in architecture but go to Taliesin West in Arizona . . . where he lives and where he has built space to suit nobody but himself."[53]

The scholar in Johnson yearned to name the experience, and the label he chose was "the processional element in architecture." He had referred to it before—in an early lecture at Yale, in 1950, he spoke of "ceremonial, of hieratic space" and cited Taliesin West as a case in point.[54] He had come to believe that "architecture exists only in time."[55] He resisted what he called the "modern perversion of photography." It was illusion, he said, to think of architecture in two dimensions or even three. Time added a fourth dimension, and the coming and going, Johnson believed, was critical. Or, as he euphoniously put it, the "whence and the whither."

As for Wright, he was not persuaded by Johnson's thinking. He told a visitor in 1956, "[Philip Johnson] is a highbrow. A highbrow is a man educated beyond his capacity." Wright added, "Philip is not to be trusted."[56]

Whatever Wright's opinion of him, Johnson had internalized the other man's thinking as he considered the immense space that would become the Four Seasons Restaurant. Its twenty-foot-tall ceilings alone meant it could be no intimate, table-in-the-corner sort of place. Three levels also had to be negotiated—and staircases were traditionally regarded as a restaurant no-no. But Johnson turned the challenges into processional possibilities.

To rise from the low-ceilinged lower level, he created a stone staircase in a Miësian manner that offered with each step a slow reveal of the large volumes above. He introduced the illusion of a more human scale in the Grill Room by introducing the sculpture of suspended bronze rods over the bar that, in effect, lowered the ceiling and thereby created a sense of intimacy. Plants brought nature inside, and the sounds of the pool, with its Carrara-marble surround, added to the sense of natural drama in the Pool Room. Specially designed lighting washed the walls. The metallic draperies screened the sun, reflected light, and added a sensuous sense of motion. The Picasso backdrop in the hall invited and dwarfed the visitor.

In July 1959, with the restaurant ready to open to the public, Johnson himself walked the procession. He entered from Fifty-Second Street and ascended the broad stairs. Arriving in the Grill Room, he noted the swaying "Venetian" curtains, then strode back through "Picasso Alley" to the Pool Room. Not yet filled with the buzz of diners, the room's only audible sound was the bubbling that came from the blue-green water in the pool.

A contemplative Johnson took in what had become the most expensive restaurant installation of its time: the total cost approached

$4.5 million. He shook his head and sighed, "Isn't it beautiful," he remarked. "It's a shame to spoil it with people."[57]

The press liked the place inhabited and not, as the Four Seasons met with widespread acclaim. The commentary in *Interiors* magazine was typical, expressing admiration for the "exquisite refinement" of the Four Seasons, adding, "In a period when so many restaurants are designed to look like boudoirs or bawdy houses," Johnson and company had achieved the opposite, with "understated strength and masculine nobility."[58]

Johnson himself became one of the actors on the busy Four Seasons stage. He dined there nearly every day for decades to come, seated at table thirty-two in the Grill Room.[59]

––––––

AS THE NEW decade approached, Wright was noticeably failing. In November 1958, one apprentice confided in William Short, the New York architect acting as Wright's clerk-of-the-works, "I think [Mr. Wright] is so tired or weary of the fight that he is not very convincing about details and decisions. I also get somewhat discouraged at the mistakes that are made in checking shop drawings in Taliesin, which are terribly hard to rectify later."[60] The nonagenarian Wright—he had turned ninety-one the previous June—visited the Guggenheim construction site for the last time in January 1959.

At home, in Arizona, he thought aloud about his mortality in a February interview with a *Time* magazine editor: "If I can just stay aboveground for, well, three more years, we can bring in three million dollars in fees. There has never been so much work."[61]

His wish would not be granted. After years of apparent indestructibility and robust health, Wright, hospitalized after complaining of abdominal pains on April 4, 1959, underwent surgery for an intestinal blockage. At first, he impressed the staff at Saint Joseph's Hospital in Phoenix with his recuperative powers. Then, shortly after a nurse had checked his vitals early on the morning of April 9, a blood clot in his heart ended in his life. According to widely published reports, "He just sighed and died."

A caravan of vehicles escorted the panel truck carrying his remains on its nearly two-thousand-mile journey to Spring Green; there a second cavalcade, this one consisting of a horse-drawn farm wagon followed by some two hundred mourners, returned Wright to the Unity Temple. Seven decades earlier, his architectural life had begun there with early drawings and an introduction to his first mentor, Joseph Lyman Silsbee.

Back in New York, in the absence of Wright to defend the castle, Sweeney would have his way, and when the museum opened in September, the walls were painted white, brackets had been added to plumb the paintings, and fluorescent lighting provided the illumination. Yet Wright, stealthy and stubborn, had left a building that competed with the art on its own terms—nonrepresentational, geometric, abstract. As Mumford observed later that year in the *New Yorker*, "You may go to this building to see Kandinsky or Jackson Pollock; you remain to see Frank Lloyd Wright."[62]

———

THE LUSTER OF Miës's design for the Seagram Building rubbed off on his junior partner. As the first tenant, Johnson enjoyed a panoramic view of the East River and Long Island from new architectural offices on the thirty-seventh floor of the bronze landmark he helped design; fittingly, he would greet significant new clients there for more than a quarter century. Some said Johnson had been "a damn fool to be under a big man, that that was a hell of a lousy way to start to be an architect." But Johnson had his own view: "I got my foot in the door working with Miës."[63]

He managed not to be overshadowed and, in practical ways, gained greatly from the circumstances. The staff required to complete the Seagram Building gave him the manpower to embark on other jobs of his own, larger ones than before. His right-hand man, Richard Foster, charged with running the Seagram project in the van der Rohe and

Johnson office, subsequently became Johnson's partner, one of the series of men, such as Landis Gores before and, later, John Burgee, who brought practical skill sets complementary to Johnson's.

The publicity surrounding the Seagram project certainly drew attention to Johnson, but his new clients also saw his capacity as an independent man. By 1955 he had been commissioned to design a museum space for the Munson-Williams-Proctor Institute in Utica, New York (completed 1960). He was soon building an eccentric roofless church in New Harmony, Indiana (1960), and another museum in Fort Worth, the Amon Carter (1958–61). His reputation rose as his building on Park Avenue did. By 1958, Aline Saarinen remarked in her book about collectors that the "fleet, sophisticated" Johnson was becoming "a go-to designer for the wealthy looking to create exhibition spaces, thanks to his architectural marks [of] elegance and dignity."[64]

Ironically, Johnson's partnership with Miës, which began and ended with the Seagram project, coincided with Johnson's shift away from the rigor and austerity Miës favored. Perhaps their disagreement at the Glass House had been inevitable as Johnson, beginning to think for himself, looked to create a separation. The work he began independently of van der Rohe and Johnson signaled his divorce from a Miës-like concentration on the tectonic; Johnson became less preoccupied with structure for its own sake and more engaged with the evocative and the sensuous. His early hallmarks included lighting effects that glowed, spaces that revealed themselves dramatically, and the use of rich materials that conveyed a mood or even emotions. The rigor and coldness of Miës was gaining a warmer, moodier, and wittier Johnsonian character.

Johnson could have been overshadowed by Miës; instead, the Seagram association signaled to the world that Johnson had arrived as a major architect, one deserving of corporate, institutional, and other highly visible commissions, many of them large in scale, larger than most that Wright did. When Wright had gone to his grave in Spring Green, Johnson was positioned to assume—in time, over a period of years—the mantle as America's chief architectural entertainer. Ironically, Johnson became the man to whom the press and the hoi polloi often looked for insights into the legacy and influence of the Master of Taliesin.

Johnson's opinion suddenly mattered more than it ever had. His work at the MoMA had given him status in the museum world, but with his emergence on the scene as an architect of genuine stature, his influence reached well beyond that.

People wanted his opinion. When the Guggenheim opened in September 1959, the *New York Times* asked him what he thought. Johnson the wordsmith put it boldly: "Frank Lloyd Wright's greatest building" and "New York's greatest building." He added that its central space was "one of the greatest rooms created in the twentieth century."[65]

Museum News solicited Johnson's thoughts. "In that room," Johnson told its editors, "museum fatigue is abolished, circulation obvious, simple, direct. It is an exciting room to be in." Indulging in his fondness for irony, Johnson added, "For the fact that it does not work as an art gallery, my profuse apologies."[66] These were themes Johnson would return to over the years: "Can you imagine looking at [pictures] as you descend that interminable ramp on your roller skates? Why should Frankie care? He hates modern art." And: "He love[d] that building because it is magnificently round in a city that is square, and has no façade where façades frown on you from morning to night." And: "Of course it's an incomparable building. It's art defying architecture!"[67] Later: "Never use the elevator! It murders Wright's great space."[68]

Not everyone was as respectful in offering commentary about Wright's museum. According to *Life*, one jokester likened the Guggenheim to a marshmallow; another opted for "washing machine." A headline in *Newsweek* inquired MUSEUM OR A CUPCAKE? *Time* reported comparisons to a snail and an "indigestible hotcross bun." Ada Louise Huxtable, a former curatorial assistant to Philip Johnson and a freelance contributor to the *New York Times* (she would become its architecture critic in 1963), wondered at the building's "belligerent strangeness."[69] An ambiguous

New York Mirror called it a "joyous monstrosity."[70] Robert Moses opted for "an inverted cup and saucer with a silo added for good luck."[71]

Yet none of the nicknames adhered. Wright had transformed a mathematical figure into a unique architectural accomplishment. "The Guggenheim," bearing its own name, attained an entirely independent standing of its own.

What Wright wrought was more than a sculptural building; it was a museum, a public place for the viewing of art, one entirely unlike any other. Its great, long ramp was unprecedented. The gentle pitch of the floor and the outward tilt of the walls of the gallery shifted the optics and the psychology of the traditional museum.

In a subtler way, the new House of Seagram shifted the paradigm for the commercial tower; if the Guggenheim was inimitable, the Seagram was easy to copy—and too easy to copy badly. Perhaps the best of its kind ever built, the structure of bronze and amber glass, with its unified deep hue of an aged whiskey was, Lewis Mumford wrote, an embodiment of what Wright's mentor Louis Sullivan had called a "proud and soaring thing." Mumford saw its setting—the plaza as podium—as worthy of comparison to Palladio's San Giorgio Maggiore for its "quality of mind and expression." In sum, he thought it "sombre, unsmiling, yet not grim . . . a muted masterpiece—but a masterpiece."[72]

Although Wright never got to dine at the Four Seasons, his widow, Olgivanna, reported in her memoir *The Shining Brow* (1960) that Wright had remarked upon the Seagram Building shortly before his death. As if to echo Johnson's dismissal of him as a relic of the previous century, Wright reportedly observed, "Although this building should be dated nineteenth century, it is the best the Internationalists have produced. Miës van der Rohe has come closest to the ideal of negation as a cliché."[73] With Mrs. Wright's help, the Master returned from the dead, firing a pointed bon mot that Philip Johnson knew perfectly well was aimed in his direction.

A Friendly Wrangle

Come out to Taliesin West sometime this winter—bring a friend—why not Philip?—for a friendly wrangle over consequences.
—Frank Lloyd Wright

A glass box may be of our time, but it has no history.
—Philip Johnson

I.

1958 . . . New York City . . . Closing Conversations

BEFORE HE DIED, Wright had experienced intimations of his mortality. In the autumn of 1957, he frightened everyone around him at Taliesin when he took a tumble. Wright read the fall as a warning. A spirit like the one that had permitted him to soften his style with Aline Saarinen left him thinking aloud about his legacy.

In February 1958, Wright, long a rider of trains, chose to fly to New York from his winter quarters in Arizona. On the way to check construction progress at the Guggenheim Museum, he had arrived at New York International Airport, the site of Eero Saarinen's new TWA terminal, a building that, like the Guggenheim, featured organic curves. Soon that structure would be likened by critics to bird wings and clamshells.[1]

The clerk-of-the-works at the Guggenheim, New York architect

William Short, picked him up at the airport. Speaking of the spill he had taken, Wright told Short, "I thought that was the end and I am chastened. It made me think that enmity is a very petty thing and I do not want to die with any enemies, so I am going to call up Philly Johnson, [Guggenheim director] Sweeney, Miës and Henry-Russell Hitchcock and have them all in for dinner."[2]

Wright had indeed called Philip Johnson and Hitchcock: "Philip, I am getting too old to have any more of these fights and have enemies, I can't stand it, let's have dinner together." When they met—Hitchcock, due to a bout of the grippe, was unable to attend—Johnson found Wright "mellowed," less his usual "temperamental and peppery self."[3]

At the time of their dinner, Johnson was filling in at Yale for Professor Vincent Scully, off on sabbatical. Co-teaching a survey course with Hitchcock and John McAndrew, Johnson focused on his allotted portion of the syllabus, twentieth-century architecture.[4] He talked of Miës and Le Corbusier, but one May evening he wandered off his prepared text. He mused aloud with the students about his meal and conversation with Frank Lloyd Wright, which had transpired a few days before.

"My unfortunate remark about his being the greatest architect of the nineteenth century," Johnson began, "is like all such silly statements full of inaccuracy."

Johnson flashed slides of the Robie House and the Johnson Wax tower. When the model of the St. Mark's Church-in-the-Bouwerie Towers appeared on the screen, he expressed surprise. "I used to dislike this building extremely . . . because it's so against anything that I would do. But who is right here, you see? It's just fairly possible that Mr. Wright is further ahead than any of us. It's perfectly possible that this building may represent the relief from the blandness of the past twenty years."[5]

Having spent decades jabbing Wright with his sharp elbows while defending the austerity of Modernism, Johnson offered the man—in absentia—a pat on the back.

A few months later, shortly before his death, Wright called Johnson again from his suite at the Plaza. Johnson remembered the conversation this way:

"He called me one day without announcing who he was; the voice sounded familiar. He said, 'Who's this, do you think?'"

"If I didn't know better," Johnson remembers replying, "I'd say it was Frank Lloyd Wright."

Wright again extended a dinner invitation, and Johnson agreed.

"We had a stroll," Johnson recalled. "I brought Phyllis Lambert along. I thought it was good for her education. Most charming man in the world."

Perhaps Wright was making amends, but Johnson couldn't be sure. "I think . . . that's why he called me that night. I think he wanted company . . . He didn't like me particularly, but I stirred him up, anyhow. So he just called."[6]

That would be their last conversation.

"We'd made all the battles we were going to have," Johnson remembered.[7] That said, Philip Johnson, age fifty-two, would find he still had to wrestle with Wright's cantankerous spirit for more than four decades.

II.

The Glass House . . . The Diary of an Eccentric Architect

FRANK LLOYD WRIGHT's death aligned with a change in Philip Johnson's practice. Commissions had been running roughly four to one in favor of domestic clients, but after 1959, the balance shifted with the arrival of more university, museum, theater, library, and other public work.[8]

Johnson's designs changed, too. "I have always been delighted to be called Miës van der Johnson," he announced at Yale a few weeks before Wright died. "It has always seemed proper in the history of architecture for a young man to understand, even to imitate, the great genius of an older generation." But, Johnson announced, he was ready to move on. "I grow old. And bored."

He offered one hint concerning his new orientation: "I try to pick up what I like throughout history." Then he added another clue, a phrase that would echo through the years: "We cannot not know history."[9]

At the time, his words sounded cryptic, but Johnson was distancing himself from strict Modernism. His new and evolving mode (he called it "eclectic traditionalism") was in part a reaction against rigorous functionalism. He was working his way backward, as he told a lecture-hall audience at the Metropolitan Museum in 1961. "We find ourselves now all wrapped up in reminiscence . . . It's a stimulating and new feeling of freedom . . . We have no wish to revolt against the past; . . . we can be freer."[10]

Three years after Wright's death, Philip Johnson would add a new and largely decorative structure at his Glass House property. He called it

Philip Johnson, ca. 1963. (Carl Van Vechten, Library of Congress/Prints and Photographs)

a folly, alluding to the landscape gardens of Enlightenment England with their collections of little teahouses, faux ruins, and classical temples. The little temple he built on his Ponus Ridge Road property would be one of the first blooms in what would be the second flowering of his architectural career. Like Wright's Taliesins, Johnson's New Canaan acreage would become—as he himself put it—"a clearinghouse of ideas which can filter down later, through my work or that of others."[11]

———

RECALLING THAT HIS mother once did the same thing in Ohio, Johnson dammed the little stream that meandered through his New Canaan property. A fountain plumbed beneath the new man-made pond shot a narrow jet of water more than a hundred feet into the air. Just out of reach of the spray that fell back to earth, Johnson installed his garden temple of precast concrete.

He called it his Pavilion. Built on a plan Johnson likened to a Mondrian grid, the little structure was flat roofed, its walls consisting of open arcades. The flattened arch occupied his professional attention at the time, as he experimented with façade designs for the Amon Carter Museum in Fort Worth, Texas, and the Sheldon Memorial Art Gallery (1963), in Lincoln, Nebraska.

Yet the picnic Pavilion wasn't quite what it seemed. The little belvedere was, in fact, an exercise in trompe l'oeil. Built just under human scale, its size gave it the appearance of being farther from the Glass House than it actually was. The oddity of its proportions became abundantly clear on approach, since guests six foot and over had to stoop to enter.

"My pavilion is full scale false scale," Johnson explained to readers of *Show* magazine, "big enough to sit in, to have tea in, but really 'right' only for four-foot-high people."[12] The New Canaan temple, which appeared to be sitting upon the water, represented a venture into the classical past, a hint of immensely larger experiments in Johnson's historicist future.

Johnson's picnic place, built in what he called "full scale false scale."
The pavilion is bigger than a dollhouse, but with arches that are just under
six feet tall, Johnson had to duck his head to enter. The folly is very much
in the viewscape of the Glass House, seen here at the horizon line.
(Carol Highsmith, Library of Congress/Prints and Photographs)

With the appearance of David Whitney, Johnson's personal life also changed in a significant way. A student at the Rhode Island School of Design, Whitney attended a Johnson lecture, in 1960, at nearby Brown University. He approached Johnson afterward, asking for a tour of the Glass House; his arrival the following weekend in New Canaan precipitated their long relationship. Despite being thirty-three years younger, Whitney helped Johnson to a new constancy in his private affairs, and they remained a couple at Johnson's death more than four decades later. In the interim, as a some-time MoMA curator and, later, a gallery operator, Whitney also disciplined Johnson's art collecting. "David is my contemporary art," Johnson once told the *New York Times*. "I don't have an original eye."[13]

A rapid growth in Johnson's art holdings was soon reflected in the construction of two more buildings on his property in New Canaan. The Painting Gallery came first, in 1965, a building with a cloverleaf plan, a showcase almost as unexpected as Wright's Guggenheim. Each of its four "leaves" featured a central post around which movable gallery walls pivoted like spokes on a wheel, displaying works by Jasper Johns, Frank Stella, Robert Rauschenberg, Andy Warhol, and other contemporary artists. Dug into the slope just north of the Glass House, the gallery was buried beneath a mound of earth like a Neolithic barrow. Later the Sculpture Gallery, built in 1970, enclosed a central court—really an outsize brick stairway that descended five levels from grade—beneath a glass-and-steel roof that cast linear shadows on the sculpture displayed. In Johnson's public life, too, he was very much an art-gallery man in these years; in addition to the Amon Carter and Sheldon museums, he designed the elegant set of nine glass cylinders for the Museum of Pre-Columbian Art at Dumbarton Oaks (1963), in Washington, D.C., as well as the MoMA's East Wing (1964).

In 1980 Johnson built himself a freestanding studio and library in New Canaan. "A monk's cell by intent," Johnson said, it was an experiment in pure geometry, a conjoined cube and cylinder capped by a truncated cone that resembles a chimney but houses a skylight. In 1984 a kennel-like construction of chain-link fencing in the shape of a simple gable-roof house was constructed. Called the Ghost House, this homage to Johnson's friend Frank Gehry was built atop an old barn foundation.

Numerous other buildings were added to the property over the years. The last of them, which Johnson called Da Monsta, was intended to accommodate visitors after Johnson's death. Looking to secure his legacy, Johnson conveyed the New Canaan property to the National Trust for Historic Preservation, whose roster of sites already included Frank Lloyd Wright's Home and Studio in Oak Park, Illinois. The undulating lines of the visitor center reflected a late reprise of Johnson's MoMA connection, namely the 1988 exhibition *Deconstructivist Architecture*. As co-curator,

Johnson arranged for the participation of such notable end-of-the-century architects as Gehry, Peter Eisenman, Zaha Hadid, Rem Koolhaas, Daniel Libeskind, and Bernard Tschumi. When Johnson designed Da Monsta, he incorporated echoes—whether consciously or not—of the sinuous surfaces, unlikely fenestration, and obscured entrance of Wright's Guggenheim. That building had become an undeniable presence in the mental slide tray of every museum architect.

Johnson's Painting Gallery has been said to be a descendant of another late Wright design, but Wright's influence on Johnson's relationship with his landscape is more apparent.[14] In creating the Pavilion and the dozen-odd other follies, Johnson extended his reach into his setting. As his holdings increased over the years (eventually, he would own almost fifty acres), so did his deep debt to the Taliesins. As his sometime Yale colleague Vincent Scully would observe, "His place now joins . . . Taliesin . . . as a major memorial to the complicated love affair Americans have with their land."[15]

Wright had revealed to Johnson how integral landscape is to architecture. That knowledge informed Johnson's siting of his buildings in the context of rural Connecticut's stone walls, rolling and sloping terrain, and trees ("Trees are the basic building blocks of the place," offered Johnson).[16] Johnson incorporated water, just as he had done earlier in designing the Abby Aldrich Rockefeller Sculpture Garden at the MoMA (1953), where he employed trees and "canals," as he called them, to interrupt museumgoers' progress, explaining the effect he wanted was "always the sense of turning to see something." He linked his inspiration to Wright: "By cutting down space, you create space. Frank Lloyd Wright understood that, but Miës didn't. Miës would probably have designed it symmetrically."[17]

Their objectives for their homes differed. Wright ran a school, and the unique campuses he created in Wisconsin and Arizona doubled as architectural laboratories. Johnson's New Canaan property was more personal; in his own words, it amounted to the "diary of an eccentric architect."[18] To visit the Glass House estate was to walk the backbone of

Johnson's architectural career, starting with its most essential datum, the Glass House itself. The house hadn't leapt out of his forehead all in a moment—recall his trial run at 9 Ash Street and his debt to Miës—but it represented the unexpected emergence of the understudy as a star.

For both Wright and Johnson, their homes became their testing grounds, places where they built structures that encompassed many of the themes of their architectural careers. Two of the most eccentric structures—one at Spring Green, the other at New Canaan—contrast with undeniable clarity the workings of the two men's architectural imaginations.

Early in his career (then, in 1896–97, Wright actually was a nineteenth-century architect), he built the Romeo and Juliet Windmill (see Fig. XXIII). Aunts Nell and Jane Lloyd Jones needed a reliable supply of water for their school, and a commonplace windmill of steel trusses purchased out of an agricultural catalog would have done the job of pumping it from a deep artesian well to the hilltop reservoir. But nephew Frank chose to make a statement in designing a fifty-six-foot-tall tower with a fourteen-foot wheel.

He designed the structure on an octagonal footprint, but one into which a diamond had been driven like a dagger. The diamond-shaped prow that resulted pointed southwest, into the prevailing winds, slicing through them to diminish their force on the tall building. Covered with board-and-batten siding, the wooden superstructure was stiffened and secured to its base of stone with iron rods. It gained its name from the manner in which the octagon embraces (and is penetrated by) the diamond. Situated on a Taliesin hilltop, the Romeo and Juliet Windmill surveys the Wright demesne.

In contrast, Johnson's Kirstein Tower, constructed in 1985, had no utilitarian purpose; it's very much an eye-catcher in the spirit of the eighteenth-century landscape garden. Built of concrete block, it's named for Johnson's enduring friend and confidant Lincoln Kirstein, a poet and cofounder of the New York City Ballet, for whom Johnson built the New York State Theater (1964) in Manhattan's Lincoln Center. An orderly and immense stack of eighteen-inch-square blocks, the Kirstein Tower in New Canaan looks like an idle doodle on a notepad come to life—but on examination, its pure geometry resolves into a stair rising to nowhere. It is monumental and cantilevered, with intimidating tall treads and no rail.

Set into the hillside overlooking the pond and the temple, it is, according to Johnson, "a study in staircases." Perhaps it references Kirstein's preoccupation with dance. It's rectilinear, but the "treads" encircle (and are) the structure. It's ambiguous—"I suppose it's architecture," commented Johnson, "or is it sculpture?"[19]

The Kirstein Tower and the Romeo and Juliet Windmill reflect their creators' differing inspirations. Wright built something elemental, at once decorative yet inseparable from the earth, wind, and water. Johnson employed wit and whimsy. Both produced biographical vignettes.

III.

New York City . . . Skyscraper Days

I N 1 9 7 9 , *Time* magazine made the arrival of Post-Modernism official. The style's papal presence, Philip Johnson, adorned the cover of the January 8 issue. He held a three-foot-tall model of his new project, the AT&T Building (now the Sony Plaza), as if it were one of Moses's tablets. With his coat draped over his shoulders like a cape, Johnson was eerily reminiscent of the man whose influence he so often disowned but grudgingly loved.

The AT&T Building came to be called the Chippendale Skyscraper because its form resembled that of high-style, eighteenth-century case furniture. Though the building on Madison Avenue was not completed until 1984, the publicity surrounding it anticipated an embrace of architectural history by the American corporation, partly in reaction to stripped-down, steel-and-glass Modernism, which, after the Seagram Building, has become the de facto urban style. It contained echoes of the brilliant Louis Sullivan, Wright's long-dead mentor. Almost a century later, Sullivan's 1896 essay "The Tall Office Building Artistically Considered" was rediscovered by a generation bored with glass boxes. Johnson and others adopted his notion of the skyscraper as consisting of three parts: in effect, a plinth of several stories at the base; a shaft ("tiers of typical offices"); and a capital (Sullivan called it an "attic") that offered the building's "conclusiveness of outward expression."[20]

In partnership with John Burgee ("I've always had a John Burgee," Johnson would explain, "to keep things on the straight and narrow"), Johnson exercised his gift for salesmanship as well as his eclecticism ("I had the ideas and the flair").[21] He demonstrated a penchant for geometric experimentation in Minneapolis with the faceted-glass atrium of the IDS Center (1973); in Houston with Pennzoil Place (1976), which consisted of twin, trapezoidal-topped towers; and, later, with the elliptical "Lipstick Building" (1986) at 885 Third Avenue in New York. His historicist experiments extended to Gothic pinnacles for PPG Place (1984) in Pittsburgh; an Empire State Building wannabe (the Transco Tower in Houston, 1983); and a nearly straight lift of an unbuilt ca. 1800 school design by French neoclassicist Claude Nicolas Ledoux, which became the University of Houston Architecture Building (1985). As a young man, Johnson had established himself as an architectural historian; as an aging one, he explored his intellectual attic, employing ideas from what Scully admiringly termed Johnson's "stored mind."[22]

Johnson won the first-ever Pritzker Architecture Prize, in 1979, an instantly prestigious honor given only to living architects. From his corner table in the Grill Room at the Four Seasons, he moderated an ongoing seminar and power chat devoted to American architecture. He dined with fellow Post-Modernists, two of whom, Michael Graves and Robert A. M. Stern, he credited with helping brainstorm his highboy tower for

AT&T. Johnson would also welcome to his table the Deconstructivists and numerous others who benefited from his patronage. By the time Johnson's first full-scale biography appeared in 1994, written by Franz Schulze (who had written an admiring and admired life of Miës van der Rohe), the *New York Times* (in the person of architecture critic Paul Goldberger) could fairly term Johnson "the greatest architectural presence of our time." Often referred to as the "Dean of American Architecture," Johnson had become the most celebrated American architect of his generation. His name amounted to a designer label for big-ticket projects; his face had become well-known to television audiences and appeared on the covers of glossy magazines.

Johnson continued to build museum, ecclesiastical, and domestic structures, but in a way that Wright could never have done, he designed the skins for corporate towers, commissions that typically arrived with predetermined volumes that he was permitted to decorate (among them the Transco Tower in Houston and International Place in Boston). A proud citizen of the city, Johnson adapted his works to their urban environs. He merged his buildings with the pattern of the places—unlike Wright, who, denying the weft and warp of a rectilinear place, had spun spiral in his only two permanent New York structures. Johnson's buildings were diverse, dispersed around the country and the world, and were rarely executed in anything resembling a Wright vernacular.

Yet Wright remained a presence in Johnson's thinking. "I'm not a form giver," Johnson told *Vanity Fair* in 1993. "I'm no Miës. I'm not Wright. I wish I were."[23]

IV.

The Form Giver and the Aesthete

IN LIFE, WRIGHT enjoyed tweaking Philip Johnson, but over the years, his manner had softened.

Both Wright and Johnson pushed boundaries, and their designs were known to test (and sometimes exceed) the technological limits of their times. Late in the evening of their memorable 1955 encounter at Yale ("Philip! I thought you were dead!"), Wright had also remarked to Johnson's face, "Little Phil, all grown up, an architect, and actually building his houses out in the rain." In an unexpected way, the latter remark can be seen as almost comradely.

Its origin, twenty-five years before, was an observation made by Mrs. Richard Lloyd Jones. Her husband, a cousin of Wright's, had commissioned him to build a house during Wright's quietest years. When a prospective client, Herbert "Hib" Johnson, came to scout Westhope (1929) in Tulsa, Oklahoma, he arrived in a driving rain. On entering the home, he saw a number of strategically placed containers, each located to catch the copious drips that fell from the leaky roof. Seeing Johnson's quizzical look, Mrs. Lloyd Jones explained, "This is what happens when you leave a work of art out in the rain."

To Wright's good fortune, however, Hib Johnson had been undeterred (he would commission Wright to design him a home and the landmark Johnson Wax Administration Building with its unforgettable mushroom columns and the memorable Pyrex-tubing roof, which also leaked volumes of water). Wright's reuse of the out-in-the-rain drollery to apply to Johnson's Glass House could well have been a backhanded, welcome-to-the-club commentary, one catty architect to another.

The old master, whom Johnson had dismissed in early manhood, gradually became a touchstone as Johnson himself aged. In 1975, he gave a lecture he titled "What Makes Me Tick." He told the assembled students at Columbia University, "In modern times, at Taliesin West, Frank Lloyd Wright made the most intriguingly complex series of turns, twists, low tunnels, surprise views, framed landscapes, that human imagination could achieve."[24] In critiquing one of his own buildings, in 1985, Johnson found the Bobst Library at New York University (1973) "strangely unsatisfactory," since, Johnson explained, "the third dimension—I mean

Frank Lloyd Wright's great passion—was lacking."[25] In 1977 he told Calvin Tomkins of the *New Yorker*, "We didn't know how good Wright was then."[26]

Later still—by then he was well into his eighties—Johnson told an interviewer, "There isn't a day that doesn't go by without my thinking of Mr. Wright; there isn't a day that I don't feel—when I have a pencil in my hand anyhow—that the man isn't looking over my shoulder."[27]

Over the years, it became second nature for Johnson to call Wright "the greatest architect of our time." Once, when asked to explain his change of heart, Johnson didn't hesitate: "No, I don't have any ambivalence. I was wrong about Wright in the thirties." Johnson added, "Don't forget I knew him before his great masterpieces were built—Fallingwater and Johnson Wax. Those two buildings alone could put an architect at the head of the century."[28]

Johnson's recollections softened personally as well as professionally. "Wright was a very protean type. I mean he was in the middle of writing these awful letters [their ca. 1932 MoMA correspondence], and we'd get together and joke ... Wright was a very genial, loving man—very forgiving. I mean I wouldn't have forgiven that little snot Philip Johnson. Why would he? Because I was always, as you know, indiscreet and yappy. He was a very great man."[29]

In a way, the Wright connection was, for Johnson, lifelong: Louise Johnson had talked about hiring Wright to build her house before she became a mother. That isn't to say that her son didn't work to resist Wright's influence; as he recalled in a 1994 interview, he had thought of Wright when he sited the Glass House: "[Wright] said never, never build on top of a hill. I chose the site because of the famous Japanese idea: Always put your house on a shelf, because the good spirits will be caught by the hill that's behind the house; the evil spirits will be unable to climb the hill below the house."[30] But he didn't mind when Wright complimented him. "I remember his telling me that's the only thing he liked about my house, that I had sense enough to build it on a shelf ... The shelf idea? I think I might have got it from Wright."³¹ They did have their commonalities, and Johnson felt them. "Nature to Frank Lloyd Wright was fields, wetlands, and wild bushes . . . And my house is a house in the field . . . I was brought up in the same kind of culture he was."³²

Johnson made a similar admission to Robert A. M. Stern. When Johnson launched himself as an architect in the forties, he later told Stern, "I was still a total believer in the modern movement . . . But I also had a tinge of this other Wrightian, hovering-house feeling."³³ Yet in interviews, questions about Wright often made Johnson cranky, too, as if Wright were a family member. With blood relatives, you can't very well disown them—but that doesn't mean you can't both love and deride them.

———

DID JOHNSON INFLUENCE Wright? Wright was nothing if not adaptable. Just a few years after the 1932 MoMA exhibition, he had clearly taken aboard the European experiments he had earlier rejected and designed what many regard as the most memorable house ever constructed in the International Style. Very much later, Johnson put it succinctly: "Wright really built the Edgar Kaufmann house, Fallingwater, as an answer to our 1932 show at the museum—as though he were saying, 'All right, if you want a flat roof, I'll show you how to really build a flat roof.'" Wright rejected the suggestion the Kaufmann house was Internationalist, but Johnson, like a proud uncle, just smiled, observing, "It was a wonderful answer."³⁴ In the same vein, the Guggenheim is surely closer to the spirit of Modernism than to Wright's pre-1932 work.

Two decades after Wright's death, Johnson recalled Wright's periodic visits to the Glass House. Johnson was half-annoyed that "Wright joked about my house" and half-admiring that the eightysomething Mr. Wright kept coming back. "His eyes stayed open."³⁵

By the time Philip Johnson died, in a hospital bed installed in the Glass House, in January 2005, it was clear that he and Wright had shared a rare gift: Both possessed the capacity for personal reinvention—and both exercised it over their long lives. The great works of Wright's early, middle, and late life could easily have come from the drafting tables of three different men. The young Johnson was an idealistic curator; he became in midlife an architect in the Modernist vanguard; in his closing decades, he was an architectural polygamist who dallied with Post-Modernism and Deconstructivism but, through it all, never severed his ties to classicism.

Johnson has been called an ironist—he was happy to describe his glass-walled house as "my place to hide."[36] He called himself a *pasticheur*. Termed by various critics an impostor and a joker, Johnson was capable of shocking cynicism in his own defense. He told a roomful of internationally recognized architects, in 1983, "I do not believe in principles, in case you haven't noticed." Then he added, "I am a whore, but I am paid very well for building high-rise buildings."[37]

The word that his authorized biographer, Franz Schulze, chose to describe his elusive subject was Harlequin, the stock theatrical character that emerged from commedia dell'arte. Johnson was indeed a nimble trickster, characterized by his sly, mischievous, and changeable nature.

In contrast, the character of Wright's work was notably constant. Certainly his forms varied. His architectonic preoccupations ranged from great sweeping Robie roofs to the cyclone on Fifth Avenue, from rectilinear to hemicycle, from Gilded Age mansion to Depression Era Usonian. Yet his organic creed was more than a rhetorical claim, and his adherence to organic principles remained fixed throughout his career. In 1896, he stated, "I have a mind to control the shaping of artificial things and to learn from Nature her simple truths of form, function, and grace of line."[38] By remaining faithful to the deceptively simple, though open-ended, principle of organic unity, he permitted his imagination to range freely. Paradoxically, that unity came to represent a creative freedom to explore diverse forms.[39]

Johnson never pretended to possess any gift whatever as a draftsman, but always had capable men at hand, starting with Landis Gores. Wright was an artist in the traditional sense, a master of the line who proudly recalled his role as head draftsman at Adler and Sullivan. He, too, hired talented draftsmen in his offices, ranging from Marion Mahony in the Oak Park days, who executed many of the most memorable drawings that emerged from Wright's studio on Chicago Avenue, to John "Jack" Howe, head draftsmen at Taliesin for more than twenty-five years. But it was more than a matter of good drawing for Wright. As Lewis Mumford wrote a few months after Wright's death, "The finished presentation drawings of his buildings are works of art in their own right . . . The drawings show—sometimes more clearly than even the actual buildings—the combination of formal discipline and effulgent feeling . . . the union of the mechanical . . . and the highly individualized arts, that were the man himself."[40]

Johnson's corporate clients understood they were getting a name-brand architect but one whose engagement would rapidly fade once the essential shape was agreed upon and the parti developed. Wright hungered for control all the way. Johnson never claimed an enduring philosophical underpinning; for Wright the philosophical almost rivaled the architectural.

If Wright found in his organic unity a means by which to explore diverse forms, Johnson's unbridled approach was to pursue architecture for its own sake. He was an aesthete, not an artist; it is revealing that the Glass House, for which he is best known is, at least among architecture professionals, admired as much for the treatise he published in 1950 about it as for the building itself; it anticipated such next-generation architect-theorists as Robert Venturi, Rem Koolhaas, and Peter Eisenman, each of whom would routinely issue theoretical texts they wished to have attached to their designs.

Johnson began as a student of the classical past; for him, as a student of art committed to beauty first, architecture was all about style. He built one great house—his own, of glass—and contributed to one great urban building, a monument to whiskey. With the able assistance of men like Burgee, he made other intriguing buildings and influenced the corporate culture of his time and the look of the new city. He would remain true to his 1954 statement that "the aim of architecture is the creation of beautiful spaces."[41]

Wright's aspiration differed. He harbored loftier ideals, invoking democracy, truth, and the common man. He found his inspiration in Nature; he regularly disclaimed the influence of any and all other architects. He claimed to be original—as Johnson would widely be quoted as describing him, "the type of genius that comes along only every three or four hundred years."

Johnson was content to mirror the work of the others, explore and expand upon tradition. While Johnson was a great looker, Wright was a seeker. Wright sought truth, while Johnson looked for something that pleased him. To tour a typical Johnson house is to engage a fine mind and sensibility at work; to explore a Wright house is to have an architectural experience.

One way to think about Johnson and Wright is to personify their signature buildings, to read Fallingwater and the Glass House as the men themselves.[42] Fallingwater reaches out: It isn't a bridge that straddles a stream; like the palm of a giant hand extended as a platform, it offers a suspended moment over the stream. The Glass House is a look-at-me place if ever there was one. Visitors are surprised at its substance—it is much more than an ephemeral moment to be summed up in an after-dinner anecdote. It conjures questions about place and home; its pristine, uncluttered character conveys a sense of clarity about the relationship between dwelling and place.

Fallingwater may be the most admired house of the twentieth century, but the *most-remarked-upon* superlative surely falls to the Glass House. It's loved by many, it has intrigued countless visitors—but if words were stones, the house would long ago have become a steel frame surrounded by shattered plate glass. Instead, it survives, along with Fallingwater, two country houses that together lure roughly half a million people a year through their doors. One may be, to borrow a phrase from a nineteenth-century travel writer, an "incident in the landscape,"[43] but the other must be seen as an "episode in the history of twentieth-century architecture."[44]

Johnson wrote few melodies but he was a great orchestrator. Well before Johnson became as well-known for his bons mots as for his buildings, his work was described as having an "epigrammatic quality," one that suggested the "application of a critical and evaluative intelligence rather than the inventions of an inductive creative imagination."[45] But Johnson made himself a powerful cultural tastemaker: When he arrived on the architectural scene, the steel-and-glass towers that today define the modern city did not exist. Johnson was Modernism's midwife and the man who introduced Miës to America.

Rather against his will, Johnson evolved into one of Frank Lloyd Wright's most important public admirers. As a man who worshipped the

(John Dolan)

zeitgeist, he found that his old nemesis's ideas retained remarkable vibrancy. As he came to recognize the importance and the value of their odd alliance, he also grasped that Wright's work transcended style and even time. Though it rendered his work inimitable, Wright's genius was, quite simply, of a greater magnitude than Johnson's.

Today, more than half a century after his death, Wright remains America's best-known and most admired architect. By the time Johnson died, barely a decade ago, he had become what he himself disparagingly called "the famous architect."[46] With his death, his fame began to recede; inversely, Wright's clearly grows. Yet their connection, in death as in life, enriches our understanding of both grand men of American architecture.

ACKNOWLEDGMENTS

As the long list of names that follow indicates, many people proved invaluable in researching and writing this book. As always, I relied upon a matrix of architecturally inclined friends, near and far, to offer counsel as this book took shape over the years. Among those whose thoughts and guidance proved valuable were Susan Anderson; Bruce Boucher; the late Don Carpentier; Christina Corsiglia and Michael Koortbojian, Princeton pals; Heather Dean; James Dixon; Edward Douglas; Charles Duell (whose father published numerous Wright books and who himself was acquainted with Philip Johnson); Joe Grills; Kinney Frelinghuysen at the Frelinghuysen Morris House and Studio; Jerry Grant; Marilyn Kaplan; Sharon Koomler; Erin Kuykendall; Travis McDonald; John I Mesick and Jeff Baker at the firm of Mesick Cohen Wilson Baker; Ron Miller; Richard Moe; Brian Pfeiffer; Abraham Thomas; Marc Truant of Marc Truant & Associates; Catherine Truman; Richard Guy Wilson; and Kathy Woodrell at the Library of Congress. My special thanks to photographer and friend Roger Straus III, my frequent collaborator, who seems always to see aspects of a building my eyes do not (evidence of that is apparent indeed in the several images of Roger's that grace this book's color insert). My appreciation, as well, to John Dolan for his two stunning black-and-white shots of the aging

Philip Johnson. And to Donald Gellert for his photograph of the Tugendhat House in Brno.

The words of numerous old Wright acquaintances from earlier projects still inform my thinking; I acknowledge my debt, then, to Taliesin Fellows Bruce Brooks Pfeiffer, Cornelia Brierly, Tom Casey, Susan Jacobs Lockhart, and Frances Nemtin, as well as Donald Hallmark and John O'Hern. My apologies to the other helpful friends and acquaintances whom I've forgotten to cite but whose insights are reflected in these pages.

As for the business of publishing, my thanks first to George Gibson, publishing director at Bloomsbury USA, who brought both high enthusiasm and his fine editorial eye to *Architecture's Odd Couple*. My appreciation, too, to Peter Ginna, who was present at conception, and to Callie Garnett, for her resourcefulness and enthusiasm as we went about selecting the pictures for this book and for tending to a thousand details along the way. My thanks as well to Gleni Bartels, production editor, for her good labors in preparing this book for the press; to copyeditor Steven Henry Boldt, whose careful attentions saved me from numerous missteps; to Katya Mezhibovskaya for her clever conflation in designing the jacket; and to Sara Mercurio for her invaluable efforts to let the world know this book exists. As always, my heartfelt thanks to Gail Hochman—invaluable friend and sage adviser.

I spent many, many hours in more archives and libraries than I can list. My thanks, then, to Marisa Bourgoin and Richard Manoogian at the Archives of American Art; Karen Bucky at the Sterling & Francine Clark Art Institute; Jason Escalante and Nicole Richard at Avery Drawings & Archives, Columbia University, and Erica Fugger and Andrea Dixon at Columbia's Oral History Project; Linda Waggoner at Fallingwater; Sally McKay at the Getty Research Institute; Irene Allen at the Glass House; Sarah Haug at the Solomon R. Guggenheim Museum; Megan Schwenke at the Harvard Art Museums Archives; Houghton Library; the staff members who helped me on my many visits to MoMA, among them archivists Naomi Kuromiya, Michelle Harvey, and Elisabeth Thomas, as well as Jennifer Tobias, librarian, and Paul Galloway and Pamela Popeson, both of the Department of Architecture and Design. My appreciation to Jenn Milani at the New Canaan Historical Society; old friend Susan K. Anderson, the Martha Hamilton Morris Archivist, Philadelphia Museum of Art; the staff at Rare Books and Special Collections, Firestone Library, and at the Seeley G. Mudd Manuscript Library, Princeton University; and Christopher Wilk and Stephanie Wood at the Victoria and Albert Museum. At my most essential resource destination, Williams College, I thank Wayne G. Hammond at Chapin Library; alumnus Robert Penn Fordyce '56, donor of the library's considerable collection of Wright-related materials; and David Pilachowski, Rebecca Ohm, Kurt Kimball, Christine Ménard, Alison Roe O'Grady, Linda McGraw, and Jean Caprari. I've asked pestering questions and found valuable materials at many other libraries, including those at the New-York Historical Society Library, the University of Virginia Alderman Library, and the Chatham (New York) Public Library. I have regularly drawn upon the collective resources of both the Mid-Hudson Library System and C/W MARS, the central and western Massachusetts library system. My library of last resort, one that rarely fails me even when all the others have, is the New York Public Library.

NOTES

PROLOGUE: *The Master and the Maestro*

1. Johnson had uttered the dismissal before, but, for the record, he used the phrase in an informal talk at the School of Architectural Design, on December 7, 1954. See "The Seven Crutches of Modern Architecture" (1955), reprinted in Johnson, *Philip Johnson* (1979), 140.

2. James Reese Pratt, quoted in Welch, *Philip Johnson & Texas* (2000), 32.

3. *Holiday*, August 1952, quoted in Earls, *Harvard Five* (2006), 137.

4. Stern, "Encounters with Philip Johnson: A Partial Memoir," in Johnson, *Philip Johnson Tapes* (2008), 8.

5. Filler, *Makers of Modern Architecture* (2007), 125.

6. H. I. Phillips, "The Sun Dial," *New York Sun*, January 7, 1949.

7. Rodman, *Conversations with Artists* (1961), 70; and Selden Rodman Papers, Yale University.

8. Henry S. F. Cooper, "Sound and Fury," *Yale Daily News*, September 22, 1955, 2. Variant versions survive of the Yale evening of September 20, 1955, but I tend to hew to Cooper's since it was published just two days after the events. Others who have told the tale include Vincent Scully and Selden Rodman, as cited. Cooper also recounted added details for Meryle Secrest in a much later interview for her *Frank Lloyd Wright* (1992); see 544–45.

9. Scully, "Frank Lloyd Wright and Philip Johnson at Yale" (1986), 94.

10. Rodman Papers.

11. *Yale Daily News*, September 21, 1955.

12. Rodman, "Series II: Journals," Rodman Papers.

13. "Exploring Wright Sites in the East," *Frank Lloyd Wright Quarterly* 7, no. 2 (Spring 1996).

14. Tafel, *About Wright* (1993), 53.

15. Rodman, *Conversations with Artists* (1961), 47.

CHAPTER 1: *Two Conversations*

1. FLW to Lewis Mumford, ca. June 1930, in Pfeiffer and Wojtowicz, *Frank Lloyd Wright* (2001).

2. Lewis Mumford, "The Poison of Good Taste," *American Mercury* (1925), 92.

3. FLW to Lewis Mumford, August 7, 1926, in Pfeiffer and Wojtowicz, *Frank Lloyd Wright* (2001).

4. Lewis Mumford to FLW, August 23, 1926, in Pfeiffer and Wojtowicz, *Frank Lloyd Wright* (2001).

5. Mumford, *Sticks and Stones* (1924), 13, 140.

6. Wright, "In the Cause of Architecture" (1914), 406.

7. Mumford, *Sketches from Life* (1982), 432.

8. Wright, *Autobiography* (1943), 165, 167.

9. Ibid., 190.

10. Mumford, *Sketches from Life* (1982), 432–33.

11. FLW to Lewis Mumford, undated (fall 1929?), in Pfeiffer and Wojtowicz, *Frank Lloyd Wright* (2001).

12. Mumford, *Sketches from Life* (1982), 433.

13. FLW to Mumford, August 7, 1926.

14. FLW to Fiske Kimball, April 30, 1928, Fiske Kimball Papers, Philadelphia Museum of Art.

15. Mumford, *Sketches from Life* (1982), 433.

16. Thomson, *Virgil Thomson* (1966), 220.

17. Barr to Dwight Macdonald, 1953, quoted in Kantor, *Alfred H. Barr, Jr.* (2002), 91.

18. Johnson, *Philip Johnson Tapes* (2008), 24.

19. Schulze, *Philip Johnson* (1994), 43.

20. Alfred H. Barr to Katherine Gauss, December 23, 1921, Archives of American Art.

21. Macdonald, "Action on West Fifty-Third Street" (December 12, 1953), 81.

22. Interview with Philip Johnson. Tomkins Papers, MoMA Archives.

23. Hitchcock, "Architectural Work of J. J. P. Oud" (1928), 97, 98, 102.

24. Alfred H. Barr to Paul Sachs, August 3, 1925, Sachs Papers, Harvard Art Museum Archives.

25. Kantor, *Alfred H. Barr, Jr.* (2002), 92.

26. Barr to Dwight Macdonald, 1953, quoted in Kantor, *Alfred H. Barr, Jr.* (2002), 102.

27. Ibid., 105.

28. Hitchcock, "Modern Architecture" (1968), 229.

29. Hitchcock, *Modern Architecture* (1929), 106.

30. Barr, "NECCO Factory" (1928), 292–95.

31. Calvin Tomkins, "The Art World: Alfred Barr," *New Yorker*, November 16, 1981, 184.

32. Alfred H. Barr Jr., "A Modern Art Questionnaire," *Vanity Fair* 28 (August 1927): 85, 96–98.

33. Ada Louise Huxtable to Calvin Tomkins, 1977, Tomkins Papers.

34. PJ quoted in Tomkins, "Forms Under Light" (1977), 47.

CHAPTER 2: *Plotting a Comeback*

1. FLW to Alexander Woollcott, January 13, 1932, Woollcott Papers, Houghton Library, Harvard University.

2. Adams, *A. Woollcott* (1945), 23.

3. Wright, *Autobiography* (1943), 39.

4. Ibid., 25.

5. Alexander Woollcott to Frank Lloyd Wright, December 3, 1927. Woollcott Papers.

6. Woollcott, "Prodigal Father" (1930), 24, 25.

7. Wright, *Autobiography* (1943), 171.

8. Woollcott, "Prodigal Father" (1930), 25.

9. Wright, *Autobiography* (1943), 259.

10. Ibid., 260.

11. Ibid., 263.

12. Woollcott, "Prodigal Father" (1930), 25.

13. Wright also had left Silsbee's practice with a taste for Japanese prints like those displayed on the office walls, which had been selected by Ernest Francisco Fenollosa, an orientalist and Silsbee cousin.

14. *Modern Architecture: International Exhibition* (1932), 31.

15. "Surface and Mass–Again!," *Architectural Record*, July 1929, reprinted in Wright, *Frank Lloyd Wright Collected Writings* (1992), 1:325.

16. Woollcott, "Prodigal Father" (1930), 25.

17. Ibid., 22.

18. Ibid.

19. Adams, *A. Woollcott* (1945), 310.

20. Alexander Woollcott to FLW, September 15, 1937, in Woollcott, *Letters of Alexander Woollcott* (1944), 193.

21. Secrest, *Frank Lloyd Wright* (1992), 374.

22. John Howe and Herbert Fritz interviews with Meryle Secrest, in Secrest, *Frank Lloyd Wright* (1992), 397.

23. FLW to Alexander Woollcott, January 1, 1929, Woollcott Papers.

24. Woollcott, "Prodigal Father" (1930), 25.

25. Lewis Mumford to FLW, July 1, 1930, in Pfeiffer and Wojtowicz, *Frank Lloyd Wright* (2001).

26. Lewis Mumford, *Brown Decades* (Mineola, NY: Dover, 1931, 1971), 75.

27. PJ quoted in Miller, *Lewis Mumford* (1989), 487.

CHAPTER 3: *European Travels*

1. Johnson, *Philip Johnson Tapes* (2008), 142n19.

2. PJ to Mrs. Homer Johnson, July 22, 1926. This letter and Johnson's correspondence with his mother, family, and friends as cited hereafter are in the Philip Johnson Papers, Special Collections, Getty Research Institute.

3. PJ to Mrs. Homer H. Johnson, June 20, 1930.

4. PJ to Alfred H. Barr, October, 16, 1929, Barr Papers, Archives of American Art.

5. PJ to Louis Johnson, October 3, 1929.

6. PJ to "Dear family," November 18, 1929.

7. Schulze, *Philip Johnson* (1994), 54.

8. Johnson, "Whence and Whither" (1965), 168.

9. J. B. Neumann to Alfred H. Barr Jr., quoted in Roob, "Alfred H. Barr, Jr." (1987), 13.

10. Roob, "Alfred H. Barr, Jr." (1987), 12.

11. Alfred H. Barr Jr., "Modern Art in London Museums," *Arts* 14 (October 1928): 190.

12. Meyer, *What Was Contemporary Art?* (2013), 93.

13. Barr, "Dutch Letter" (1928), 48.

14. PJ to "Dear family," July 28, 1929.

15. PJ to Louise Johnson, September 22, 1929.

16. PJ to Alfred H. Barr, October 16, 1929, Barr Papers, Archives of American Art.

17. PJ to Louise Johnson, September 22, 1929.

18. Barr, "Dutch Letter" (1928), 49.

19. Walter Gropius, *Program of the Staatliche Bauhaus* (Weimar), in Kantor, *Alfred H. Barr, Jr.* (2002), 153.

20. Barr, "Preface," in Herbert Bayer et al., *Bauhaus, 1919–1928* (New York: MoMA, 1938).

21. Card postmarked October; see Schulze, *Philip Johnson* (1994), 55.

22. PJ letter to Alfred H. Barr, October 16, 1929, Barr Papers, Archives of American Art.

23. PJ to Louis Johnson, November 8, 1929.

24. Alfred H. Barr to Paul Sachs, July 1, 1929, quoted in Kantor, *Alfred H. Barr, Jr.* (2002), 189.

CHAPTER 4: *The New Museum*

1. A. Conger Goodyear, in Lynes, *Good Old Modern* (1973), 9.

2. Barely a decade later, the towering Rockefeller residence would be demolished. In its place the Abby Aldrich Rockefeller Sculpture Garden would be installed, in 1953, a Philip Johnson–designed space on the north side of what had, by then, become MoMA's permanent home.

3. Story recounted in Lynes, *Good Old Modern* (1973), 4ff.

4. Barr, *Painting and Sculpture* (1967), 620.

5. Roob, "Alfred H. Barr, Jr." (1987), 19.

6. Ibid.

7. Mrs. Alfred H. Barr to Calvin Tomkins, June 2, 1976, Tomkins Papers.

8. Riley and Sacks, "Philip Johnson: Act One, Scene One—the Museum of Modern Art?," in Petit, *Philip Johnson* (2009), 60.

9. Margaret Scolari Barr, in Tomkins, "Forms Under Light" (1977), 47.

10. Filler, "Philip Johnson: Deconstruction Worker" (1988), 105.

11. Hitchcock, "Modern Architecture" (1968), 227.

12. Searing, "Henry-Russell Hitchcock" (1990).

13. Hitchcock, "Modern Architecture" (1968), 229. The benefactor was James Thrall Soby, the year 1935.

14. Lynes, *Good Old Modern* (1973), 85–86.

15. PJ to Louise Johnson, August 6, 1930.

16. PJ to Louise Johnson, July 7, 1930.

17. Barr, "Modern Architecture" (1930), 435.

18. PJ to Louise Johnson, June 1930.

19. Miës van der Rohe, lecture at the Vienna Werkebund conference (1930), quoted in Wolf Tegethoff, "A Modern Residence in Turbulent Times," in Hammer-Tugendhat and Tegethoff, *Ludwig Miës van der Rohe* (2000), 46.

20. Philip Johnson to Louise Johnson, September 1, 1930.

21. Blake, *Master Builders* (1960), 203.

22. Grete Tugendhat, "On the Construction of the Tugendhat House," an address given in Brno, Czech Republic, on January 17, 1969, reprinted in Hammer-Tugendhat and Tegethoff, *Ludwig Miës van der Rohe* (2000), 5.

23. Hammer-Tugendhat, "Living the Tugendhat House," in Hammer-Tugendhat and Tegethoff, *Ludwig Miës van der Rohe* (2000), 12.

24. Tugendhat, "On the Construction of the Tugendhat House," 5.

25. Ibid., 6.

26. Interview with Philip Johnson, Tomkins Papers.

27. Blake, *Master Builders* (1960), 155.

28. *Modern Architecture: International Exhibition* (1932), 116.

29. Ibid., 116.

30. Schulze and Windhorst, *Miës van der Rohe* (2012), 205.

31. Johnson, "Whence and Whither" (1965), 172.

32. PJ to Henry-Russell Hitchcock, September 2, 1930, Hitchcock Papers, Archives of American Art.

CHAPTER 5: *An Invitation Issued*

1. Stern, Gilmartin, and Mellins, *New York 1930* (1987), 469.

2. Minutes of meeting of the Modern Architectural Exhibition committee, January 17, 1931, Registrar files, Exhibition 15.

3. Barr, "Our Campaigns" (1987), 25.

4. Ms. prepared by Mrs. Alfred H. Barr Jr. for Calvin Tomkins, attachment to letter of June 2, 1967, Tomkins Papers.

5. Riley, *International Style* (1992), 18.

6. *Modern Architecture: International Exhibition* (1932), 13.

7. Interview with Kantor, *Alfred H. Barr, Jr.* (2002), 291.

8. Ms. prepared by Barr for Tomkins.

9. PJ to Louise Johnson, August 6, 1930.

10. PJ to Alfred Barr, undated letter, Registrar files, Exhibition 15.

11. Registrar files, Exhibition 15.

12. Minutes of meetings of the Modern Architectural Exhibition committee, January 17 and 24, 1931, Registrar files, Exhibition 15.

13. Johnson, *Built to Live In* (1931), reprinted in Johnson, *Philip Johnson: Writings* (1979), 28–31.

14. Douglas Haskell, "The Column, the Globe, and the Box," *Arts* 17 (June 1931): 636–39.

15. *Rejected Architects* (1931), reprinted in Riley, *International Style* (1992), 215.

16. *New York Times*, April 26, 1931.

17. Helen Appleton Read, *Brooklyn Eagle*, quoted in Stern, *George Howe* (1975), 153n35.

18. *Rejected Architects* (1931), 433–35.

19. Lewis Mumford to FLW, March 29, 1931. Frank Lloyd Wright's letters, telegrams, and other correspondence were consulted on microfiche, as published by the Frank Lloyd Wright Foundation, Scottsdale, together with the accompanying index, *Frank Lloyd Wright: An Index to the Taliesin Correspondence*, ed. Anthony Alofsin (N.Y.: Garland, 1988). Unless otherwise specified, the Wright letters and other documents cited here and below are found in that collection.

20. PJ to FLW, April 1, 1931.

21. FLW to PJ, April 3, 1931.

22. PJ to Lewis Mumford, January 3, 1931, Mumford Papers, University of Pennsylvania.

23. "peut-être le plus grand Américain du premier quart du XX siècle": Hitchcock, *Frank Lloyd Wright* (1928).

24. Hitchcock, "Modern Architecture" (1968), 230.

25. Wright did hold out some hope for Hitchcock in a more temperate moment: "You know, Lewis, I am sorry I called poor Hitchcock a fool . . . He is at least sincere. What if he doesn't know? He may learn." FLW to Lewis Mumford, December 17, 1930.

26. FLW to Lewis Mumford, April 7, 1931, in Pfeiffer and Wojtowicz, *Frank Lloyd Wright* (2001).
27. Fistere, "Poets in Steel" (1931), 58.
28. FLW to Mumford, April 7, 1931.
29. PJ to FLW, April 30, 1931.
30. PJ to FLW, May 22, 1931.

CHAPTER 6: *Wright vs. Johnson*
1. Alfred H. Barr to PJ, August 19, 1931, quoted in Riley, *International Style* (1992), 52.
2. PJ to Alan Blackburn, August 15, 1931, quoted in Riley, *International Style* (1992), 56.
3. PJ to FLW, December 14, 1931.
4. FLW to PJ, telegram of January 3, 1932, and letter fragment of January 5, 1932.
5. FLW telegram to PJ, January 18, 1932.
6. FLW to PJ, January 19, 1932.

CHAPTER 7: *The Show Must Go On*
1. PJ telegram to FLW, February 4, 1932.
2. Riley, *International Style* (1992), 75; and Barr, "Our Campaigns" (1987), 23.
3. Riley, *International Style* (1992), 92.
4. *Modern Architecture: International Exhibition* (1932), 12–17.
5. Douglas Haskell, "Architecture: What the Man About Town Will Build," *Nation*, April 13, 1932, 441–43.
6. Mumford, "Sky Line: Organic Architecture" (1932), 49.
7. William Adams Delano, "Man Versus Mass," *Shelter* 2 (May 1932): 12.
8. PJ to J. J. P. Oud, March 17, 1932.
9. *New York Sun*, February 13, 1932.
10. Wright, "The House on the Mesa/The Conventional House," in Wright, *Frank Lloyd Wright Collected Writings* (1993), 3:128. Italics added.
11. FLW, "The Disappearing Cave," quoted in *Denver Post*, December 14, 1930, 2; quoted in Wojtowicz, "A Model House" (2005), 523.
12. Wright, "In the Cause of Architecture" (1925), reprinted in Wright, *Frank Lloyd Wright Collected Writings* (1992), 1:212.

13. FLW to Lewis Mumford, July 7, 1930. Full quote: "though pupil, I think I was never his disciple. (It is the disciple who is hindered by his master.) Sullivan is on the record as gratefully acknowledging this."

14. Scully, "Wright vs. the International Style" (1954), 34.

15. Hitchcock and Johnson, *International Style* (1932), 25–26.

16. "Modern Architecture Exhibition by Museum of Modern Art," undated draft in Registrar files, MoMA Archives.

17. Hitchcock and Johnson, *International Style* (1932), 38.

18. Ralph Flint, "Present Trends in Architecture in Fine Exhibit," *Art News*, February 13, 1932, 5.

19. *Modern Architecture: International Exhibition* (1932), 15.

20. FLW to PJ, February 11, 1932.

21. FLW to PJ, April 19, 1932.

22. Henry-Russell Hitchcock to FLW, April 22, 1932. The text of the letter is in the MoMA Archives, but the original does not appear in the Wright papers, which may indicate Hitchcock never mailed the letter. Regardless, Hitchcock no doubt wished to convey to Wright the scalding sentiments expressed, even if Wright never felt them.

23. PJ to FLW, April 25, 1932.

24. PJ to J. J. P. Oud, April 16, 1932.

25. FLW to PJ, May 24, 1932.

26. FLW, "In the Show Window at Macy's," *Architectural Forum*, November 1933, reprinted in Wright, *Frank Lloyd Wright Collected Writings* (1993), 3:146.

27. Quoted in Tomkins, "Forms Under Light" (1977).

28. Interview with George Goodwin, July 27, 1992, Archives of American Art.

29. *Early Modern Architecture: Chicago, 1870–1910* (1933), 27.

30. Mumford to FLW, January 10, 1932, in Pfeiffer and Wojtowicz, *Frank Lloyd Wright* (2001).

31. FLW to Henry-Russell Hitchcock, February 26, 1932.

32. Johnson, *Philip Johnson Tapes* (2008), 41.

33. Schulze, *Philip Johnson* (1994), 61.

34. William Wesley Peters, *Taliesin Times*, quoted in headnote to William Wesley Peters interview in Tafel, *About Wright* (1993), 156.

35. PJ interview with George Goodwin, July 27, 1992, Archives of American Art.

36. PJ to Louise Johnson, July 7, 1930.

37. Filler, "Philip Johnson: Deconstruction Worker" (1988) 105.

38. FLW to Fiske Kimball, April 30, 1928, in Pfeiffer and Wojtowicz, *Frank Lloyd Wright* (2001), 51.

39. *New York Sun*, March 10, 1934.

CHAPTER 8: *The Banks of Bear Run*

1. PJ to his family, August 13, 1929. Johnson would later recollect the painting as Manet's *Execution of Maximilian* in Mannheim. See Johnson, *Philip Johnson Tapes* (2008), 49.

2. McAndrew quoted in Lynes, *Good Old Modern* (1973), 178.

3. PJ to Louise Johnson, September 22, 1929.

4. http://150.vassar.edu/histories/art/.

5. MoMA press release, http://www.moma.org/momaorg/shared/pdfs/docs/press_archives/395/releases/MOMA_1937_0035.pdf?2010.

6. McAndrew to Donald Hoffmann, December 5, 1975, quoted in Hoffmann, *Frank Lloyd Wright's Fallingwater* (1978), 91.

7. McAndrew quoted in Lynes, *Good Old Modern* (1973), 180.

8. Toker, *Fallingwater Rising* (2003), 31.

9. Ibid., 30.

10. *Taliesin Fellowship Prospectus* (1932, 1933), in Wright, *Frank Lloyd Wright Collected Writings* (1993), 3:159–66.

11. David G. De Long, "Kaufmann Family Letters: Edgar Kaufmann jr., Frank Lloyd Wright, and Fallingwater," in Waggoner, *Fallingwater* (2011), 174.

12. Caroline Wagner interview, cited in Toker, *Fallingwater Rising* (2003), 364.

13. Kaufmann, *Fallingwater* (1986), 36.

14. Wright, *Letters to Apprentices* (1982), 204.

15. Kaufmann, *Fallingwater* (1986), 36.

16. Wright, *An Autobiography* (1943), 151.

17. Henning, *"At Taliesin"* (1992), 16.

18. E. J. Kaufmann to FLW, August 16, 1934.

19. FLW to E. J. Kaufmann, September 18, 1934.

20. Toker, *Fallingwater Rising* (2003), 118–19.

21. FLW to E. J. Kaufmann, September 28, 1934.

22. Henning, *"At Taliesin,"* (1992), November 22, 1934.

23. Kaufmann, *Fallingwater* (1986), 36.

24. E. J. Kaufmann to FLW, December 4, 1934.

25. E. J. Kaufmann, "To Meet—to Know—to Battle—to Love—Frank Lloyd Wright," in Reed and Kaizen, *Show to End All Shows* (2004), 171.

26. Wright, *Letters to Clients* (1986), 83.

27. Max Putzel, "A House That Straddles a Waterfall," *St. Louis Post-Dispatch Magazine*, March 21, 1937, 1, 7. It seems likely that Wright was his source, though Putzel does not cite him.

28. Lewis Mumford, "The Sky Line," *New Yorker*, April 27, 1935, 79–80.

29. FLW to E. J. Kaufmann, March 8, 1935, quoted in Hoffmann, *Frank Lloyd Wright's Fallingwater* (1978), 14.

30. E. J. Kaufmann to FLW, May 4, 1935, quoted in Hoffmann, *Frank Lloyd Wright's Fallingwater* (1978), 15.

31. Ibid.

32. FLW to E. J. Kaufmann, June 15, 1935.

33. FLW, "In the Cause of Architecture I: The Logic of the Plan," *Architectural Record*, January 1928, reprinted in *Frank Lloyd Wright Collected Writings* (1992), 1:249.

34. Samuel Taylor Coleridge, *Biographia Literaria* (1817).

35. Edgar Kaufmann jr., "La Casa sulla Cascata di F. Lloyd Wright" (1962), reprinted in Brooks, *Writings on Wright* (1981), 69.

36. Hoppen, *Seven Ages of Frank Lloyd Wright* (1993), 97.

37. The story of Fallingwater's paperwork conception has been told often, based upon a number of recollections written by the men who were there, including Edgar Tafel, Bob Mosher, and Cary Caraway (see the notes that follow). The recollections of these witnesses were subject to the vagaries of human memory; written years after the events, the versions, unsurprisingly, don't agree on every particular. In reconstructing events three quarters of a century later in these pages, it doesn't help that, at the time, Wright's dramatic display of designing prowess didn't so much as merit a mention in the Fellowship's weekly paper, *At Taliesin*. But the composite view, as presented, is likely close to the truth.

38. Cary Caraway, interview with Meryle Secrest, in Secrest, *Frank Lloyd Wright* (1992), 419.

39. Ibid.

40. Wright, *An Autobiography* (1943), 239.

41. Tafel, *Years with Frank Lloyd Wright* (1979), 3.

42. Ibid., 7.

43. Bob Mosher letter to Donald Hoffman, January 20, 1974, quoted in Hoffman, *Frank Lloyd Wright's Fallingwater* (1978), 17.

44. FLW during talk to Taliesin Fellowship, May 1955, quoted in *Frank Lloyd Wright Quarterly* 10, no. 3 (Summer 1999): 11.

45. Interview with Hugh Downs, NBC Television, taped on May 8, 1953.

46. Morris Knowles to E. J. Kaufmann, April 18, 1936, in Hoffman, *Frank Lloyd Wright's Fallingwater* (1978), 30. Italics added.

47. Hoffman, *Frank Lloyd Wright's Fallingwater* (1978), 37.

48. FLW letter and telegram of August 27, 1936.

49. FLW to E. J. Kaufmann, August 31, 1936.

50. The cumulative effect of design flaws, decades of weathering, and natural settlement required a major reconstruction of the cantilevered house (to the tune of almost $12 million) in 2001–2.

51. Neil Levine has written insightfully on this point in relation to Taliesin; see Levine, *Architecture of Frank Lloyd Wright* (1996), 99.

52. John H. Howe, quoted in Hoffman, *Frank Lloyd Wright's Fallingwater* (1978), 26.

53. Putzel, "House That Straddles," 1, 7.

54. Edgar J. Kaufmann jr. and Liliane Kaufmann to FLW, quoted in Hoffmann, *Frank Lloyd Wright's Fallingwater* (1978), 87.

55. Hedrich, Oral history (1992), 82.

56. Ibid., 83.

57. Ibid., 61.

58. Ibid.

59. Ibid., 62.

60. Minutes of Committee Meeting, MoMA Archives.

61. FLW telegram to John McAndrew, January 5, 1938.

62. *Time*, January 17, 1938.

63. *Life*, January 17, 1938.

64. Hoffmann, *Frank Lloyd Wright's Fallingwater* (1978), 92.

65. McAndrew, *Guide to Modern Architecture* (1940), 12.

66. Mumford, "The Sky Line: At Home, Indoors and Out" (1938), 59.

67. Ibid., 58.

68. Wright, *Architectural Forum*, January 1938, 36.

69. Architectural historian Vincent Scully, among others, has written persuasively of Wright's melding of Internationalism with his own organic architecture;

see especially Scully, "Wright vs. the International Style" (1954), 32–35, 64–66. See also the ensuing discussion in the September 1954 issue of *Art News*, 48–49.

70. Brierly, *Tales of Taliesin* (1999), 5.

71. Sources conflict on when Wright uttered these words, but since Brierly told Franklin Toker directly that it was on July 3, 1935, I have used their chronology. See Toker, *Fallingwater Rising* (2003), 140–41; and "Exploring Wright Sites in the East," *Frank Lloyd Wright Quarterly* 7, no. 2 (Spring 1996).

72. PJ, "Retreat from the International Style to the Present Scene" (lecture, Yale University, May 9, 1958), reprinted in Johnson, *Philip Johnson* (1979), 93.

73. Kaufmann, *Fallingwater* (1986), 56.

74. Johnson, *Philip Johnson* (1979), 269.

CHAPTER 9: *Politics and Art*

1. Warburg interview with Calvin Tomkins, Tomkins Papers.

2. Schulze, *Philip Johnson* (1994), 106.

3. Barr, "Our Campaigns" (1987), 34.

4. Johnson, "Architecture in the Third Reich" (1933), 137–39.

5. Dennis, *Is Capitalism Doomed?* (1932), 85–86.

6. *New York Times*, December 18, 1934.

7. Johnson, *Philip Johnson Tapes* (2008), 19.

8. Blodgett, "Philip Johnson's Great Depression" (1987), 9.

9. Ibid., 6.

10. Philip Johnson to Frau Bodenschatz, December 1939, FBI dossier, in Schulze, *Philip Johnson* (1994), 139.

11. Shirer, *Berlin Diary* (1941), 213.

12. Lynes, *Good Old Modern* (1973), 93.

13. *Herald Tribune*, December 18, 1934.

14. Sorkin, "Where Was Philip?" (1988), 138, 140.

15. Utley, *Odyssey of a Liberal* (1970), 265.

16. PJ to Frank D. Welch, January 1993, in Welch, *Philip Johnson & Texas* (2000), 18.

17. Alfred Barr to Miës van der Rohe, February 11, 1937, Barr Papers, MoMA.

18. Helen Resor to Alfred Barr, July 12, 1937, Barr Papers.

19. Miës van der Rohe to FLW, September 8, 1937.

20. Goldberg interview, quoted in Lambert, *Miës in America* (2001), 61.

21. "Freiheit. Es Ist ein Reich!" Interview of William Wesley Peters by Franz Schulze, October 12, 1982, in Schulze and Windhorst, *Miës van der Rohe* (2012), 183.

22. Blake, *Master Builders* (1960), 215.

23. Miës van der Rohe, "A Tribute to Frank Lloyd Wright," was written for an unpublished catalog for the 1940 MoMA exhibition *Frank Lloyd Wright: American Architect*, MoMA Archives.

24. Gropius, *Apollo in the Democracy* (1968), 167.

25. Ibid., 168.

26. The origin of the designation *Usonian* continues to be debated; what is clear is that Wright in his Usonian frame of mind sought to create designs of high quality at middle-class prices. He succeeded to a considerable degree—many of the five dozen or so Usonian homes are very expressive examples of Wright's work—although many cost more than their owners were led to expect.

27. FLW telegram to John McAndrew, September 10, 1940.

28. FLW telegram to John McAndrew, September 16, 1940.

29. John McAndrew to FLW, September 18, 1940.

30. Invitation to *Frank Lloyd Wright: American Architect*, November 12, 1940–January 5, 1941, Registrar Exhibition Files, Exhibition 114, MoMA archives.

31. *New York Times*, November 24, 1940.

32. Brown, "Frank Lloyd Wright's First Fifty Years" (1940), 37.

33. Ludwig Miës van der Rohe, "1940: Frank Lloyd Wright," in Reed and Kaizen, *Show to End All Shows* (2004), 169–70.

34. PJ to Louise Johnson, June 20, 1930.

35. Johnson, *Philip Johnson Tapes* (2008), 77.

36. Lewis and O'Connor, *Philip Johnson* (1994), 19.

37. Carter H. Manny Jr. letter to his family, October 10, 1940, Manny Papers, Art Institute of Chicago.

38. John Johansen interview with Frank D. Welch, January 1992, in Welch, *Philip Johnson & Texas* (2000), 19.

39. "Oral History of Carter Manny," quoted in Schulze, *Philip Johnson* (1994), 31.

40. Barr, "Foreword," *Modern Architecture: International Exhibition* (1932), 12.

41. *Cambridge Chronicle-Sun*, April 23, 1942, http://www2.cambridgema.gov /historic/L94_evaluation.pdf.

42. Johnson, *Miës Van der Rohe* (1947), 96.

43. Tomkins, "Forms Under Light" (1977), 50.

44. *Architects Journal*, cited in Cambridge Historical Commission report, May 28, 2010, http://www2.cambridgema.gov/historic/L94_evaluation.pdf.

45. Tomkins, "Forms Under Light" (1977), 50.

46. Ibid.

47. Welch, *Philip Johnson & Texas* (2000), 21.

48. Mrs. Alfred H. Barr to Calvin Tomkins, June 2, 1976, Tomkins Papers.

CHAPTER 10: *Wright's Manhattan Project*

1. Hilla Rebay to FLW, June 1, 1943. Here and after, unless otherwise specified, the Guggenheim Museum correspondence is found in Wright, *Frank Lloyd Wright: The Guggenheim Correspondence* (1986).

2. Gill, *Many Masks* (1987), 416.

3. Rebay to FLW, June 1, 1943.

4. Letter agreement of June 29, 1943, between the Frank Lloyd Wright Foundation and the Solomon R. Guggenheim Foundation in Wright, *Frank Lloyd Wright: The Guggenheim Correspondence* (1986), 8–9.

5. Hilla Rebay, quoted in Brigitte Salmen, "The Path to Non-Objective Art," in *Art of Tomorrow* (2005), 62.

6. Lukach, *Hilla Rebay* (1983), 45.

7. Hilla Rebay to Rudolf Bauer, October 7, 1918, quoted in *Art of Tomorrow* (2005), 68.

8. Rudolf Bauer quoted in *Art of Tomorrow* (2005), 71.

9. Hilla Rebay, "The Power of Spiritual Rhythm," in *Art of Tomorrow* (1939), 8.

10. Ise Gropius to Joan M. Lukach, October 19, 1977, in Lukach, *Hilla Rebay* (1983), 75.

11. Hilla Rebay to Rudolf Bauer, April 16, 1930, quoted in Lukach, *Hilla Rebay* (1983), 63.

12. Ibid.

13. Rebay's assertion that she thought Wright deceased in the early 1930s was made in 1967; given Wright's visibility in the Depression era, there is reason to doubt the accuracy of Rebay's much later recollection. See Vail, *Museum of Non-Objective Painting* (2009), 219n134.

14. Robert Delaunay to Hilla Rebay, June 1930, quoted in Lukach, *Hilla Rebay* (1983), 69.

15. Hilla Rebay to Rudolf Bauer, March 30, 1931, quoted in Lukach, *Hilla Rebay* (1983), 135.

16. Rudolf Bauer to Hilla Rebay, February 19, 1937, quoted in Vail, *Museum of Non-Objective Painting* (2009), 187.

17. Rudolf Bauer to Hilla Rebay, February 19, 1937, quoted in Vail, *Museum of Non-Objective Painting* (2009), 181.

18. *Modern European Art* (1933) and *Modern Works of Art* (1934).

19. *New York Times*, June 4, 1939.

20. FLW to Harry Guggenheim, January 20, 1956, http://www.guggenheim.org /new-york/collections/library-and-archives/archive-collections/A0006/.

21. Hilla Rebay to FLW, June 23, 1943, quoted in Vail, *Museum of Non-Objective Painting* (2009), 204.

22. Solomon R. Guggenheim, quoted in FLW letter to Harry Guggenheim, May 14, 1952.

23. FLW to Solomon Guggenheim, July 23, 1943.

24. Hoppen, *Seven Ages of Frank Lloyd Wright* (1993), 117.

25. Iovanna Wright, *My Life*, n.p., quoted in Vail, *Museum of Non-Objective Painting* (2009), 219n134.

26. Wright, *Frank Lloyd Wright: The Guggenheim Correspondence* (1986), 30.

27. FLW to Hilla Rebay, December 18, 1943.

28. Ibid.

29. FLW to Hilla Rebay, December 30, 1943.

30. FLW to Solomon Guggenheim, December 31, 1943.

31. FLW lecture to the Taliesin Fellowship, September 12, 1952, quoted in Bruce Brooks Pfeiffer, "A Temple of the Spirit," in Pfeiffer, *The Solomon R. Guggenheim Museum* (1994), 6.

32. FLW to Russell Sturgis, 1909, in Quinan, "Frank Lloyd Wright's Reply to Russell Sturgis" (1989), 238–44.

33. Taliesin senior apprentice Curtis Besinger recalled Rebay laying claim to the idea on a visit to Spring Green in 1951; see Besinger, *Working with Mr. Wright* (1995), 229, 295n88.

34. FLW to Hilla Rebay, January 20, 1944.

35. Few of the surviving early drawings for the Museum of Non-Objective Art were dated by Wright or his apprentices. I have relied upon the sequence worked out by Bruce Brooks Pfeiffer and Neil Levine in recounting this story; see Pfeiffer, "A Temple of the Spirit" (1994), and Neil Levine, "The

Guggenheim Museum's Logic of Inversion," in Levine, *Architecture of Frank Lloyd Wright* (1996).

36. FLW to Hilla Rebay, January 26, 1944.
37. Jacobs and Jacobs, *Building with Frank Lloyd Wright* (1978), 83.
38. Hilla Rebay to FLW, April 5, 1943.
39. FLW to Hilla Rebay, July 6, 1944.
40. FLW to Hilla Rebay, February 6, 1944.
41. FLW recounted the story in a May 14, 1952, letter to Harry Guggenheim.
42. S. R. Guggenheim to FLW, July 27, 1944.
43. *Life*, October 8, 1945.
44. Pfeiffer, "A Temple of the Spirit" (1994), 21.
45. FLW to Hilla Rebay, March 3, 1944; and FLW to S. R. Guggenheim, October 1, 1945.
46. *Life*, October 8, 1945.
47. *Architectural Forum*, January 1946, 82.
48. "Optimistic Ziggurat," *Time*, October 1, 1945, 74.
49. *Architectural Forum*, January 1946, 82.
50. "Optimistic Ziggurat" (1945), 74.
51. *Architectural Forum*, January 1948, 54.
52. Ibid.
53. Ibid., 138.
54. FLW to Hilla Rebay, June 23, 1949.
55. FLW to Albert E. Thiele, October 4, 1951.

CHAPTER 11: *Philip Comes Out Classical*

1. Manny oral history, http://digital-libraries.saic.edu/cdm/fullbrowser/collection /caohp/id/7663/rv/compoundobject/cpd/8196, 41.
2. PH to Carter H. Manny Jr., January 2, 1945, quoted in Schulze, *Philip Johnson* (1994), 167.
3. Interview with George Goodwin, July 27, 1992, Archives of American Art.
4. PJ to FLW, September 25, 1945.
5. Philip Johnson to Gerald M. Loeb, August 8, 1946, Exhibition Records, MoMA.
6. Story recounted by Johnson in Johnson, *Philip Johnson Tapes* (2008), 109; and FLW to PJ telegram, September 25, 1946.

7.   FLW to Charles Duell, June 1, 1941.

8.   Back ad of Wright, *Autobiography* (1943).

9.   Johnson, "Frontiersman" (1949), 105.

10. Schulze, *Philip Johnson* (1994), 223.

11. Not all versions of the story agree on all the particulars. See PJ interview with George Goodwin, July 27, 1992, Archives of American Art.

12. Rodman, *Conversations with Artists* (1961), 54.

13. Jon Stroup, interview with Franz Schulze, quoted in Schulze, *Philip Johnson* (1994), 187. Landis Gores offered a detailed description of the site in his memory piece "Philip Johnson Comes to New Canaan" (1986), 4.

14. Earls, *Harvard Five* (2006), 44.

15. Whitney and Kipnis, *Philip Johnson* (1993), vii.

16. Gores, "Philip Johnson Comes to New Canaan" (1986), 3.

17. Ibid., 4.

18. Welch, *Philip Johnson & Texas* (2000), 24.

19. Ely, "New Canaan Modern" (1967), 16.

20. Ibid., 15.

21. Marcel Breuer quoted in Earls, *Harvard Five* (2006), 38.

22. PJ to Henry-Russell Hitchcock, May 16, 1945, Henry-Russell Hitchcock Papers, Archives of American Art.

23. PJ to Henry-Russell Hitchcock, Henry-Russell Hitchcock Papers. Italics added. The letter is undated, but from various contemporary cultural references, the likely date appears to be mid-1946.

24. Gores, "Philip Johnson Comes to New Canaan" (1986), 5.

25. PJ to J. J. P. Oud, January 1, 1946.

26. Robert A. M. Stern makes the case for the Wright link in "The Evolution of Philip Johnson's Glass House, 1947–1948" (1977).

27. Gores, "Philip Johnson Comes to New Canaan" (1986), 3.

28. Trial transcript of *van der Rohe v. Farnsworth*, No. 9352, Illinois Circuit Court, Kendall County, 320, cited in Schulze and Windhorst, *Mies van der Rohe* (2012), 250.

29. Lambert, *Mies in America* (2001), 338.

30. Calvin Tomkins interview with Ulrich Franzen, May 27, 1976, Tomkins Papers.

31. Interview with Eugene George, July 1998, in Welch, *Philip Johnson & Texas* (2000), 28.

32. Ms. prepared by Mrs. Alfred H. Barr Jr. for Calvin Tomkins, attachment to letter June 2, 1967, Tomkins Papers.

33. *New York Times*, December 1948, quoted in Earls, *Harvard Five* (2006), 43.

34. Mary Roche, "Living in a Glass House," *New York Times Magazine*, August 14, 1949.

35. "A Glass House in Connecticut," *House & Garden*, October 1949, 168.

36. H. I. Phillips, "The Sun Dial," *New York Sun*, January 7, 1949.

37. Johnson, "House at New Canaan" (1950), 152, editor's headnote.

38. Ibid., 156.

39. Johnson, *Miës van der Rohe* (1947), 162.

40. Johnson, "House at New Canaan" (1950), 153.

41. Johnson, "Whence and Whither" (1965), 32.

42. Johnson, "House at New Canaan" (1950), 157.

43. Drexler, "Architecture Opaque" (1949), 4.

44. Ibid., 6.

45. Ogden Gnash-Teeth, "Cantilever Heaven or Wearing Out Your Welcome," *New Canaan Advertiser*, March 13, 1952, 1; reprinted in Earls, *Harvard Five* (2006), 164.

46. Though recounted elsewhere, the quotes here are drawn from Paul Goldberger's speech to the National Trust for Historic Preservation Board of Trustees meeting, held at the Glass House on May 24, 2006.

47. Philip Johnson interview in Lewis and O'Connor, *Philip Johnson* (1994), 33.

48. Johnson, "100 Years, Frank Lloyd Wright and Us" (1957), 193, 194.

49. Welch, *Philip Johnson & Texas* (2000), 18.

50. Johnson told and retold the tale. Two slightly different versions appear in Tafel, *About Wright* (1993), 53; and Johnson, *Philip Johnson Tapes* (2008), 123.

51. Blake, *No Place Like Utopia* (1993), 151.

52. The story of Wright and Johnson's Nadelman sculpture comes down in variant versions. The most detailed recounting appears in Gwen North Reiss, "Pedro Guerrero and Friend (Frank Lloyd Wright) and Their 1958 Visit to the Glass House," Pedro Guerrero, *Glass House Blog*, posted July 26, 2010, https://philipjohnsonglasshouse.wordpress.com/?s=wright.

53. Johnson, "House at New Canaan" (1950), 159.

54. Johnson partisan Robert A. M. Stern supplied a different punch line: "[Wright] had to admit that it looked absurd there and should be restored to its original place." Editor's note in Johnson, *Philip Johnson: Writings* (1979), 192.

CHAPTER 12: *The Whiskey Bottle and the Teapot*

1. FLW to Alan [*sic*] Bronfman, March 17 and April 19, 1952, in Lambert, *Building Seagram* (2013), 28.
2. Ellis D. Slater, interoffice memo, quoted in Lambert, *Building Seagram* (2013), 28.
3. Ludvigsen, "Baron of Park Avenue" (1972), 165.
4. "Frank Lloyd Wright Designs a Commercial Installation" (1955), 133.
5. Calvin Tomkins interview with Philip Johnson, April 5, 1976, Tomkins Papers.
6. Peter Reed, "The Space and the Frame: Philip Johnson as the Museum's Architect," in *Philip Johnson and the Museum of Modern Art* (1998), 75.
7. Johnson, *Philip Johnson Tapes* (2008), 112.
8. Ely, "New Canaan Modern" (1967), 16.
9. *Architectural Forum*, quoted in Stern, Mellins, and Fishman, *New York 1960* (1995), 342.
10. Phyllis Lambert to Samuel Bronfman, June 28, 1954. A facsimile of Lambert's letter appears in appendix 1 in Lambert, *Building Seagram* (2013), 240–47.
11. Johnson, *Philip Johnson Tapes* (2008), 137.
12. Phyllis Lambert to Eve Borsook, October 30, 1954, quoted in Lambert, "How a Building Gets Built" (1959), 16.
13. Lambert, "How a Building Gets Built" (1959), 14.
14. Ibid., 36.
15. Ibid., 122.
16. The story has been told multiple times. Sources include Lambert, *Building Seagram* (2013), 9; Scully, "Philip Johnson: The Glass House Revisited" (1986), 154; and Bjone, *Philip Johnson and His Mischief* (2014), 23.
17. PJ quoted in Joseph Giovannini, "Johnson and His Glass House: Reflections, *New York Times*, July 16, 1987.
18. PJ quoted in Robert A. M. Stern, "Encounters with Philip Johnson: A Partial Memoir," in Johnson, *Philip Johnson Tapes* (2008), 150.
19. Calvin Tomkins interview with Philip Johnson, ca. 1976, Tomkins Papers.
20. Lambert to Borsook, October 30, 1954, quoted in Lambert, "How a Building Gets Built" (1959), 17.
21. Seagram notes, Tomkins Papers, MoMA Archives.
22. "Monument in Bronze," *Time* 71 (March 3, 1958): 55.
23. Lambert, *Building Seagram* (2013), 50.
24. Lambert to Borsook, October 30, 1954, 17.

25. Lambert, *Building Seagram* (2013), 50.

26. Phyllis Lambert to Anthony and Caroline Benn, March 18, 1955, quoted in Lambert, *Building Seagram* (2013), 262n39.

27. FLW to Albert E. Thiele, February 9, 1950.

28. Olgivanna Wright, *Shining Brow* (1960), 185–86.

29. FLW to Harry F. Guggenheim, August 6, 1951.

30. Aline Louchheim, "Museum in Query," *New York Times*, April 22, 1952.

31. Arthur Cort Holden to FLW, February 26, 1952, Arthur Cort Holden Papers, Rare Books and Special Collections, Harvey S. Firestone Library, Princeton University.

32. "House of Wright Is Previewed Here," *New York Times*, October 21, 1953.

33. *Usonian House: Souvenir of the Exhibition* (1953).

34. Bruce Brooks Pfeiffer, "Frank Lloyd Wright in Manhattan," *Frank Lloyd Wright Quarterly* 7, no. 2 (1996): 8.

35. Mumford, *Sketches from Life* (1982), 437.

36. Quoted in Pfeiffer, "Frank Lloyd Wright in Manhattan," 5.

37. Arthur C. Holden interview, January 20, 1971, 12, Arthur Cort Holden Papers.

38. Elizabeth Gordon, "Threat to the Next America," *House Beautiful*, April 1953.

39. Kay Schneider, quoted in Pfeiffer, *Frank Lloyd Wright: The Crowning Decade* (1989), 188.

40. *Conversations with Elder Wise Men*, May 17, 1953.

41. Harry Guggenheim to Frank Lloyd Wright, July 2, 1956, quoted in Lomask, *Seed Money* (1964), 184.

42. Bruce Brooks Pfeiffer, "A Temple of the Spirit" (1994), 21. Other sources specify seven sets.

43. Saarinen, "Tour with Mr. Wright" (1957), 22.

44. Ibid., 69.

45. "An Open Letter," undated, in Wright, *Frank Lloyd Wright: The Guggenheim Correspondence* (1986), 242. Though accounts conflict, the letter probably arrived on or about May 1, 1957.

46. Curtis Besinger to William Short, December 23, 1958, William H. Short Papers, Special Collections, Firestone Library, Princeton University.

47. Pfeiffer, "Frank Lloyd Wright in Manhattan," 9.

48. Johnson, *Philip Johnson Tapes* (2008), 144.

49. "Monument in Bronze," 55.

50. The stage curtain remained in situ at the Four Seasons for fifty-five years until its removal, in 2014, after a dispute between new owners of the Seagram Building and the New York Landmarks Conservancy. Today the conserved canvas is on view in a new home, the New-York Historical Society.

51. Seagram notes, Tomkins Papers. See also Mariani and von Bidder, *Four Seasons* (1994), 32–33.

52. Johnson, "100 Years, Frank Lloyd Wright and Us" (1957), 196–98.

53. PJ lecture at Yale, May 2, 1958, 14, Philip Johnson Papers, MoMA Archives.

54. *Yale Daily News*, March 3, 1950.

55. Johnson, "Whence and Whither" (1965), 151.

56. Rodman, *Conversations with Artists* (1961), 58.

57. Mariani and von Bidder, *Four Seasons* (1994), 39.

58. "The Four Seasons," *Interiors*, December 1959, 80.

59. Mariani and von Bidder, *Four Seasons* (1994), 150.

60. Curtis Besinger to William Short, November 17, 1958, William H. Short Papers.

61. Cranston Jones, "Pride and Prejudices of the Master," *Life*, April 27, 1959, 54.

62. Mumford, "The Sky Line: What Wright Hath Wrought" (1959), 110.

63. Johnson, *Philip Johnson Tapes* (2008), 147.

64. Saarinen, *Proud Possessors* (1958), 282.

65. Robert Alden, "Art Experts Laud Wright's Design," *New York Times*, October 22, 1959.

66. Johnson, "Letter to the Museum Director," in *Museum News*, January 1960, 25.

67. Rodman, *Conversations with Artists* (1961), 70.

68. Johnson, "Whence and Whither" (1965), 151.

69. Ada Louise Huxtable, "That Museum Wright or Wrong?," *New York Times*, October 25, 1959.

70. Alden, "Art Experts Laud Wright's Design."

71. Lomask, *Seed Money* (1964), 185.

72. Mumford, "The Sky Line: The Lesson of the Master" (1958), 142, 145, 151.

73. Olgivanna Wright, *Shining Brow* (1960), 22.

EPILOGUE: *A Friendly Wrangle*

1. Colloquially known for some years as Idlewild—the name was borrowed from an adjacent resort development on New York's Jamaica Bay—the airport

would became John F. Kennedy International in late 1963 after the president's assassination.

2. William H. Short, note to file, February 5, 1958, William H. Short Papers.

3. Henry-Russell Hitchcock to FLW, March 2, 1958, Archives of American Art.

4. *Yale Daily News*, May 7, 1957.

5. PJ lecture at Yale, May 2, 1958, 11–12, Philip Johnson Papers.

6. PJ interview in Tafel, *About Wright* (1993), 48–49, 54.

7. Interview with George Goodwin, July 27, 1992, Archives of American Art.

8. Neil Levine, "Afterword," in Jenkins and Moheny, *Houses of Philip Johnson* (2001), 270.

9. *Yale Daily News*, February 16, 1959.

10. "The International Style—Death or Metamorphosis," reprinted in Johnson, *Philip Johnson: Writings* (1979), 122.

11. Johnson, *Architecture of Philip Johnson* (2002), 21.

12. PJ, "Full Scale False Scale," *Show* (June 1963), reprinted in Whitney and Kipnis, *Philip Johnson* (1993), 24.

13. "David Whitney, 66, Renowned Art Collector, Dies," *New York Times*, June 14, 2005.

14. See Levine, *Architecture of Frank Lloyd Wright* (1996), 426.

15. Scully, "Philip Johnson: The Glass House Revisited" (1986), in Whitney and Kipnis, *Philip Johnson* (1993), 156.

16. Johnson, *Architecture of Philip Johnson* (2002), 4.

17. PJ, quoted in *MOMA*, summer 1975, unpaginated.

18. Whitney and Kipnis, *Philip Johnson* (1993), vii.

19. Johnson, *Philip Johnson Tapes* (2008), 133.

20. Louis Sullivan, "The Tall Office Building Artistically Considered," *Lippincott's Magazine*, 1896.

21. Johnson, *Philip Johnson Tapes* (2008), 64.

22. Vincent Scully, *Modern Architecture: The Architecture of Democracy* (1961), 118.

23. Andersen, "Philip the Great" (1993), 137.

24. "What Makes Me Tick" (1975), reprinted in Whitney and Kipnis, *Philip Johnson* (1993), 49.

25. Johnson, *Philip Johnson Tapes* (2008), 172.

26. Calvin Tomkins interview with Philip Johnson, Tomkins Papers.

27. Tafel, *About Wright* (1993), 47–48.

28. Filler, "Philip Johnson: Deconstruction Worker" (1988), 105.

29. Tafel, *About Wright* (1993), 55.

30. Lewis and O'Connor, *Philip Johnson* (1994), 28.

31. Interview with George Goodwin, July 27, 1992, Archives of American Art.

32. Lewis and O'Connor, *Philip Johnson* (1994), 30–33.

33. Johnson, *Philip Johnson Tapes* (2008), 107.

34. Tomkins, "Forms Under Light" (1977), 66.

35. Ibid., 60.

36. "Behind the Glass Wall," *New York Times*, June 7, 2007.

37. *Charlottesville Tapes* (1985), 15, 19.

38. FLW, "Architecture, Architecture, and the Client" (1896), in Wright, *Frank Lloyd Wright Collected Writings* (1992), 1:31.

39. In developing this line of thinking, I am indebted to William Cronon and his essay "Inconstant Unity: The Passion of Frank Lloyd Wright," in Riley, *Frank Lloyd Wright* (1994), 8–31.

40. Mumford, "The Sky Line: What Wright Hath Wrought" (1959), 105.

41. Johnson, "Responsibility of the Architect" (1954), 46.

42. Yes, yes, I will stipulate that either of Wright's Taliesins—to cite just two of his most personal projects—could equally well be seen as the best embodiment of his essential nature. But here we are looking with the eyes of the world—so please accept the premise that the world most closely identifies Wright (wrong or right) with the more widely known and recognized Kaufmann house.

43. *A Handbook for Travelers in North Wales*, 3rd ed. (London: John Murray, 1868), v.

44. Jeffrey Kipnis, "Introduction," in Whitney and Kipnis, *Philip Johnson* (1993), xi.

45. See John M. Jacobus Jr.'s text to his monograph *Philip Johnson* (1962), 18. It brings to mind Vincent Scully's notion of Johnson's "stored mind," cited above.

46. PJ to Stern, in Johnson, *Philip Johnson Tapes* (2008), 178.

SOURCES

WRITING A BOOK of this sort means consulting the papers. For Frank Lloyd Wright, the most essential source of correspondence is the Getty Research Institute, Los Angeles, California, where in excess of one hundred thousand original documents are archived. Other storehouses I consulted for Wright materials include Manhattan's Museum of Modern Art and Columbia University; the latter's Avery Library has become the repository for the bulk of his drawings. I found valuable materials at the Victoria and Albert Museum, London. I've also drawn upon related research done for a previous book on Wright, which involved many hours spent at the Frank Lloyd Wright Home and Studio in Oak Park, Illinois, and the Frank Lloyd Wright Foundation Archives, then located at Taliesin West in Scottsdale, Arizona, prior to their recent relocation east to Columbia and MoMA. For Philip Johnson, the two principal repositories for his correspondence and papers are the Getty and MoMA.

Other papers consulted include those of Alfred H. Barr, found in the Archives of American Art in Washington, D.C.; Peter Blake, Avery Library, Columbia University; Henry-Russell Hitchcock, Archives of American Art; Arthur Cort Holden, Rare Books and Special Collections, Harvey S. Firestone Library, Princeton University; Fiske Kimball, Philadelphia Museum of Art; Carter H. Manny Jr., Art Institute of

Chicago; Lewis Mumford, University of Pennsylvania; Hilla von Rebay, Solomon R. Guggenheim Museum, New York; Selden Rodman, Yale University; Paul J. Sachs, Harvard Art Museums Archives; William H. Short, Harvey S. Firestone Library, Princeton University; Calvin Tomkins, MoMA; Alexander Woollcott, Houghton Library, Harvard University.

What follows is a selected bibliography of the published material consulted.

Adams, Samuel Hopkins. *A. Woollcott: His Life and His World.* New York: Reynal & Hitchcock, 1945.

Andersen, Kurt. "Philip the Great." *Vanity Fair,* June 1993, 130–38, 151–57.

"Architectural Student Jonathan Barnett Interviews Architect Philip Johnson." *Architectural Record* 128, no. 6 (December 1960): 16.

Art of Tomorrow: Fifth Catalogue of the Solomon R. Guggenheim Collection of Non-Objective Paintings. New York: Guggenheim Foundation, 1939.

Art of Tomorrow: Hilla Rebay and Solomon R. Guggenheim. New York: Guggenheim Museum, 2005.

"Art Museum Designed as Continuous Ramp, New York City." *Architectural Forum* 88, no. 1 (January 1948): 136–38.

Barr, Alfred H., Jr. "Dutch Letter." *Arts,* January 1928, 48–49.

——. "Modern Architecture." *Hound and Horn,* June 1930, 431–35.

——. "The NECCO Factory." *Arts,* May 1928, 292–95.

——. *Painting and Sculpture in the Museum of Modern Art, 1929–1967.* New York: MoMA, 1967.

Barr, Margaret Scolari. "'Our Campaigns': Alfred H. Barr, Jr., and the Museum of Modern Art: A Biographical Chronicle of the Years 1930–1944." *New Criterion* (New York: Foundation for Cultural Review), special issue, Summer 1987, 23–74.

Besinger, Curtis. *Working with Mr. Wright.* New York: Cambridge University Press, 1995.

Bjone, Christian. *Philip Johnson and His Mischief: Appropriation in Art and Architecture.* Victoria, Australia: Images Publishing, 2014.

Blake, Peter. "The Guggenheim: Museum or Monument?" *Architectural Forum,* December 1959, 86–92.

——. *The Master Builders.* New York: Alfred A. Knopf, 1960.

———. *No Place Like Utopia.* New York: Alfred A. Knopf, 1993.

———. *Philip Johnson.* Basel: Birkhäuser Verlag, 1996.

———. "Philip Johnson Knows Too Much." *New York* 11 (May 15, 1978): 58–61.

Blodgett, Geoffrey. "Philip Johnson's Great Depression." *Timeline*, June–July 1987, 2–17.

Brierly, Cornelia. *Tales of Taliesin: A Memoir of Fellowship.* Tempe, AZ: Arizona State University, 1999.

Brooks, H. Allen. *Writings on Wright: Selected Comment on Frank Lloyd Wright.* Cambridge, MA: MIT Press, 1981.

Brown, Milton. "Frank Lloyd Wright's First Fifty Years." *Parnassus* 12, no. 8 (December 1940): 37–38.

Campbell, Robert. "The Joker: Philip Johnson, the Corporate Architect as Clown." *Lear's*, September 1989, 108–114, 178.

The Charlottesville Tapes. New York: Rizzoli, 1985.

Cleary, Richard L. *Merchant Prince and Master Builder: Edgar J. Kaufman and Frank Lloyd Wright.* Pittsburgh, PA: Heinz Architectural Center, 1999.

Cooke, Alistair. "Memories of Frank Lloyd Wright." *AIA Journal* 32 (October 1959): 42–44.

Corbusier, Le. *Towards a New Architecture.* Essex, UK: Butterworth Architecture, 1989.

Dennis, Lawrence. *Is Capitalism Doomed?* New York: Harper & Brothers, 1932.

Drexler, Arthur. "Architecture Opaque and Transparent." *Interiors & Industrial Design*, October 1949, 99–101. Reprinted in Whitney and Kipnis, *Philip Johnson* (1993).

———. *The Drawings of Frank Lloyd Wright.* New York: Horizon, 1962.

Earls, William D. *The Harvard Five in New Canaan: Midcentury Modern Houses by Marcel Breuer, Landis Gores, John Johansen, Philip Johnson, Eliot Noyes and Others.* New York: W. W. Norton, 2006.

Einbinder, Harvey. *An American Genius: Frank Lloyd Wright.* New York: Philosophical Library, 1986.

Ely, Jean. "New Canaan Modern: The Beginning, 1947–1952." *New Canaan Historical Society Annual*, 1967, 3–12.

Filler, Martin. *Makers of Modern Architecture.* New York: New York Review of Books, 2007.

———. "Philip Johnson: Deconstruction Worker." *Interview* 18 (May 1988): 102–6, 109.

———. "Philip Johnson: The Architect as Theorist." *Art in America* 67, no. 8 (December 1979): 16–19.

Fistere, John Cushman. "Poets in Steel." *Vanity Fair* 36 (December 1931): 58–59, 98.

Four Great Makers of Modern Architecture: Gropius, Le Corbusier, Miës van der Rohe, Wright. A Verbatim Record of a Symposium Held at the School of Architecture from March to May 1961. New York: Columbia University, 1961.

"The Four Seasons." *Interiors*, December 1959, 80–85.

"Frank Lloyd Wright: A Special Portfolio." *Architectural Forum* 110, no. 6 (June 1959): 117–46.

"Frank Lloyd Wright Designs a Commercial Installation: A Showroom in New York for Sports Cars." *Architectural Forum*, July 1955, 132–33.

Frank Lloyd Wright: From Within Outward. New York: Guggenheim Museum, 2009.

"Frank Lloyd Wright's Masterwork." *Architectural Forum* 96, no. 4 (April 1952): 141–44.

Friedman, Alice T. *Women and the Making of the Modern House.* New York: Harry N. Abrams, 1998.

Gill, Brendan. *Many Masks: A Life of Frank Lloyd Wright.* New York: G. P. Putnam's Sons, 1987.

"A Glass House in Connecticut." *House & Garden*, October 1949, 158–73.

Goldberger, Paul, ed. *Philip Johnson/Alan Ritchie Architects.* New York: Monacelli Press, 2002.

Goodyear, A. Conger. *The Museum of Modern Art: The First Ten Years.* New York: MoMA, 1943.

Gores, Landis. "Philip Johnson Comes to New Canaan." *New Canaan Historical Society Annual* 10, no. 2 (1986): 3–12.

Gropius, Walter. *Apollo in the Democracy: The Cultural Obligation of the Architect.* New York: McGraw-Hill, 1968.

The Guggenheim: Frank Lloyd Wright and the Making of the Modern Museum. New York: Guggenheim Museum, 2009.

Hammer-Tugendhat, Daniela, and Wolf Tegthoff, eds. *Ludwig Miës van der Rohe: The Tugendhat House.* Vienna: Springer-Verlag, 2000.

Heckscher, Morrison K. "Outstanding Recent Accessions. 19th-Century Architecture for the American Wing: Sullivan and Wright." *Metropolitan Museum of Art Bulletin* 30, no. 6 (June–July, 1972): 300–304.

Hedrich, William C. Oral history, Betty J. Blum, interviewer. Chicago Architects Oral History Project, Art Institute of Chicago, 1992. http://www.artic.edu/research/archival-collections/oral-histories/william-c-hedrich-1912-2001.

Henken, Priscilla J. *Taliesin Diary: A Year with Frank Lloyd Wright.* New York: W. W. Norton, 2012.

Henning, Randolph C. *"At Taliesin": Newspaper Columns by Frank Lloyd Wright and the Taliesin Fellowship, 1934–1937.* Carbondale: Southern Illinois University Press, 1992.

Hession, Jane King, and Debra Pickrel. *Frank Lloyd Wright in New York: The Plaza Years, 1954–1959.* Layton, UT: Gibbs Smith, 2007.

Hitchcock, Henry-Russell, Jr. "The Architectural Work of J. J. P. Oud." *Arts* 13, no. 2 (February 1928): 97–103.

———. *The Architecture of H. H. Richardson and His Times.* Hamden, CT: Archon Books, 1961.

———. *Frank Lloyd Wright.* Paris: Cahiers d'Arts, 1928.

———. *In the Nature of Materials: The Buildings of Frank Lloyd Wright.* New York: Duell, Sloan and Pearce, 1942.

———. "Modern Architecture: A Memoir." *Journal of the Society of Architectural Historians* 27, no. 4 (December 1968): 227–33.

———. *Modern Architecture: Romanticism and Reintegration.* New York: Payson and Clarke, 1929.

Hitchcock, Henry-Russell, Jr., and Arthur Drexler. *Built in U.S.A.: Post-War Architecture.* New York: MoMA/Simon and Schuster, 1953.

Hitchcock, Henry-Russell, Jr., and Philip Johnson. *The International Style: Architecture Since 1922.* New York: W. W. Norton, 1932.

———. *Modern Architecture: International Exhibition.* New York: MoMA, 1932.

Hoffman, Donald. *Frank Lloyd Wright's Fallingwater.* New York: Dover Publications, 1978.

Hoppen, Donald W. *The Seven Ages of Frank Lloyd Wright.* Santa Barbara, CA: Capra Press, 1993.

Hoyt, Edwin P. *Alexander Woollcott: The Man Who Came to Dinner.* London: Abelard-Schuman, 1968.

Jacobs, Herbert, and Katherine Jacobs. *Building with Frank Lloyd Wright: An Illustrated Memoir.* San Francisco, CA: Chronicle Books, 1978.

Jacobus, John M., Jr. *Philip Johnson.* New York: George Braziller, 1962.

Jenkins, Stover, and David Mohney. *The Houses of Philip Johnson.* New York: Abbeville, 2001.

Johnson, Philip. "Architecture in the Third Reich." *Hound and Horn* 5 (October–December 1933): 137–39.

——. "The Architecture of the New School." *Arts* 17, no. 6 (March 1931): 393–98.

——. *The Architecture of Philip Johnson.* Boston: Bulfinch Press, 2002.

——. "Beyond Monuments." *Architectural Forum* 138 (January–February 1973): 54–68.

——. "The Frontiersman." *Architectural Review* 106 (August 1949). Reprinted in Johnson, *Philip Johnson* (1979).

——. "Full Scale False Scale." *Show* 3 (June 1963).

——. "The German Building Exposition of 1931." *T-Square* 2, no. 1 (1932): 17–19, 26–27.

——. "House at New Canaan, Connecticut." *Architectural Review* 107, no. 645 (September 1950): 152–59. Reprinted in Johnson, *Philip Johnson* (1979).

——. Interview with George Goodwin, July 27, 1992. Archives of American Art.

——. "Letter to the Museum Director." *Museum News*, January 1960, 22–25.

——. *Miës van der Rohe.* New York: MoMA, 1947. Revised 1978.

——. "The Next Fifty Years." *Architectural Forum* 94 (June 1951): 167–70.

——. "100 Years, Frank Lloyd Wright and Us." *Pacific Architect and Builder* 13 (March 1957): 35–36.

——. *The Philip Johnson Tapes: Interviews by Robert A. M. Stern.* Edited by Kazys Varnelis. New York: Monacelli Press, 2008.

——. *Philip Johnson: Writings.* New York: Oxford University Press, 1979.

——. "The Responsibility of the Architect." *Perspecta* 2 (1954): 45–57.

——. "The Seven Crutches of Modern Architecture." *Perspecta* 3 (1955): 40–44.

——. "The Skyscraper School of Modern Architecture." *Arts* 17, no. 8 (May 1931): 569–75.

——. "Whence and Whither: The Processional Element in Architecture." *Perspecta* 9/10 (1965): 167–78.

Johnson, Philip, and Edgar Kaufmann, Jr. "American Architect: Four New Buildings." *Horizon* 93–94 (October 1947): 62–65.

Jordy, William H. *The Impact of European Modernism in the Mid-Twentieth Century.* Vol. 5, *American Buildings and Their Architects.* New York: Oxford, 1972.

Kantor, Sybil Gordon. *Alfred H. Barr, Jr., and the Intellectual Origins of the Museum of Modern Art.* Cambridge, MA: MIT Press, 2002.

Kaufmann, Edgar, Jr. *Fallingwater: A Frank Lloyd Wright Country House.* New York: Abbeville, 1986.

——. "Frank Lloyd Wright's Architecture Exhibited: A Commentary by Edgar Kaufmann, Jr." *Metropolitan Museum of Art Bulletin* 40, no. 2 (Autumn 1982): 4–47.

——. "Frank Lloyd Wright's Years of Modernism, 1925–1935." *Journal of the Society of Architectural Historians* 24, no 1 (March 1965): 31–33.

——. *9 Commentaries on Frank Lloyd Wright.* Cambridge, MA: MIT Press, 1989.

——. "Precedent and Progress in the Work of Frank Lloyd Wright." *Journal of the Society of Architectural Historians* 39 (May 1980): 145–49.

Ketcham, Diana. "'I Am a Whore': Philip Johnson at Eighty." *New Criterion* 5, no. 4 (December 1986): 57–64.

Lambert, Phyllis. *Building Seagram.* New Haven, CT: Yale University Press, 2013.

——. "How a Building Gets Built." *Vassar Alumnae Magazine* 44, no. 3 (February 1959): 13–19.

——, ed. *Mies in America.* New York: Harry N. Abrams, 2001.

Levine, Neil. *The Architecture of Frank Lloyd Wright.* Princeton, NJ: Princeton University Press, 1996.

Lewis, Hilary, and John O'Connor. *Philip Johnson: The Architect in His Own Words.* New York: Rizzoli, 1994.

Lomask, Milton. *Seed Money: The Guggenheim Story.* New York: Farrar, Straus, 1964.

Ludvigsen, Karl E. "The Baron of Park Avenue." *Automobile Quarterly* 10, no. 2 (Second Quarter 1972): 152–67.

Lukach, Joan M. *Hilla Rebay: In Search of the Spirit in Art.* New York: George Braziller, 1983.

Lynes, Russell. *Good Old Modern: An Intimate Portrait of the Museum of Modern Art.* New York: Atheneum, 1973.

Macdonald, Dwight. "Action on West Fifty-Third Street." *New Yorker*, 2 parts, December 12, 1953, 49–82, and December 19, 1953, 35–72.

Manny, Carter H. "Oral History of Carter Manny." Franz Schulze, interviewer. Chicago: Art Institute of Chicago, 1994. http://digital-libraries.saic.edu/cdm/fullbrowser/collection/caohp/id/7663/rv/compoundobject/cpd/8196.

Manson, Grant Carpenter. *Frank Lloyd Wright to 1910: The First Golden Age.* New York: Reinhold Publishing, 1958.

Mariani, John, and Alex von Bidder. *The Four Seasons: A History of America's Premier Restaurant.* New York: Crown Publishers, 1994.

Marquis, Alice Goldfarb. *Alfred H. Barr, Jr.: Missionary for the Modern.* Chicago: Contemporary, 1989.

McAndrew, John. "Architecture in the United States." *Bulletin of the Museum of Modern Art* 6, no. 102 (February 1939): 9–10.

——, ed. *Guide to Modern Architecture: Northeast States.* New York: MoMA, 1940.

Mendelsohn, Eric. *Eric Mendelsohn: Letters of an Architect.* Edited by Oscar Beyer. New York: Abelard-Schuman, 1967.

Menocal, Narciso G., ed. *Fallingwater and Pittsburgh.* Carbondale: Southern Illinois University Press, 2000.

Meyer, Richard. *What Was Contemporary Art?* Cambridge, MA: MIT Press, 2013.

Miller, Donald. *Lewis Mumford: A Life.* New York: Weidenfeld and Nicolson, 1989.

Modern Architecture: International Exhibition, New York, February 10 to March 23, 1932. New York: MoMA, 1932.

"The Modern Gallery: The World's Greatest Architect, at 74, Designs the Boldest Building of his Career." *Architectural Forum* 84, no. 1 (1946): 81–88.

Mumford, Lewis. "Frank Lloyd Wright and the New Pioneers." *Architectural Record* 65 (April 1929): 414–16.

——. "New York *vs.* Chicago in Architecture." *Architecture* 56, no. 5 (November 1927): 241–44.

——. "The Poison of Good Taste." *American Mercury* 6 (September 1925): 92–94.

——. *Sketches from Life: The Autobiography of Lewis Mumford, the Early Years.* New York: Dial Press, 1982.

——. "The Sky Line: A Phoenix Too Infrequent." *New Yorker*, 2 parts, November 28, 1953, 133–39, and December 12, 1953, 116–27.

——. "The Sky Line: At Home, Indoors and Out." *New Yorker*, February 12, 1938, 58–59.

——. "The Sky Line: Organic Architecture." *New Yorker*, February 27, 1932, 49–50.

——. "The Sky Line: The Lesson of the Master." *New Yorker*, September 13, 1958, 141–48, 151–52.

——. "The Sky Line: What Wright Hath Wrought." *New Yorker*, December 5, 1959, 105–30.

——. "The Sky Line: Windows and Gardens." *New Yorker*, October 2, 1932, 121–24, 127–29.

——. *Sticks and Stones: A Study of American Architecture and Civilization.* New York: Boni and Liveright, 1924.

Nelson, James, ed. *Wisdom: Conversations with the Elder Wise Men of Our Day.* New York: W. W. Norton, 1958.

Petit, Emmanuel, ed. *Philip Johnson: The Constancy of Change.* New Haven, CT: Yale University Press, 2009.

Pfeiffer, Bruce Brooks. *Frank Lloyd Wright: The Crowning Decade.* Fresno: Press at California State University, 1989.

——. *Frank Lloyd Wright: The Heroic Years, 1920–1932.* New York: Rizzoli, 2009.

Pfeiffer, Bruce Brooks, and Robert Wojtowicz, eds. *Frank Lloyd Wright & Lewis Mumford: Thirty Years of Correspondence.* Princeton, NJ: Princeton Architectural Press, 2001.

Philip Johnson. Charles Noble, introduction. Yukio Futagawa, photographs. New York: Simon and Schuster, 1972.

Philip Johnson and the Museum of Modern Art. New York: MoMA/Harry N. Abrams, 1998.

Philip Johnson: Architecture, 1949–1965. Henry-Russell Hitchcock, introduction. New York: Holt, Rinehart and Winston, 1966.

Philip Johnson: Processes. The Glass House, 1949, and the AT&T Corporate Headquarters, 1978. New York: Institute for Architecture and Urban Studies, 1978.

Quinan, Jack. "Frank Lloyd Wright's Guggenheim Museum: A Historian's Report." *Journal of the Society of Architectural Historians* 52, no. 4 (December 1993): 466–82.

——. "Frank Lloyd Wright's Reply to Russell Sturgis." *Journal of the Society of Architectural Historians* 41 (1989): 238–44.

Rebay, Hilla. Oral history interview, 1966. Archives of American Art. http://www .aaa.si.edu/collections/interviews/oral-history-interview-hilla-rebay-11723.

Reed, Peter, and William Kaizen, eds. *The Show to End All Shows: Studies in Modern Art 8.* New York: MoMA, 2004.

Riley, Terence, ed. *Frank Lloyd Wright: Architect.* New York: MoMA, 1994.

——. *The International Style: Exhibition 15 and the Museum of Modern Art.* New York: Rizzoli, 1992.

Rodman, Selden. *Conversations with Artists.* New York: Capricorn Books, 1961.

Roob, Rona. "Alfred H. Barr, Jr.: A Chronicle of the Years 1902–1929." *New Criterion* (New York: Foundation for Cultural Review), special issue, Summer 1987, 1–19.

Saarinen, Aline B. *The Proud Possessors: The Lives, Times and Tastes of Some Adventurous American Art Collectors.* New York: Random House, 1958.

——. "Tour with Mr. Wright." *New York Times Magazine*, September 22, 1957, 22–23, 69–70.

Scarlett, Rolph. *The Baroness, the Mogul, and the Forgotten History of the First Guggenheim Museum.* New York: Midmarch Arts Press, 2003.

Schulze, Franz. *Philip Johnson: Life and Work.* Chicago: University of Chicago Press, 1994.

Schulze, Franz, and Edward Windhorst. *Mies van der Rohe.* Rev. ed. Chicago: University of Chicago Press, 2012.

Scully, Vincent. *Frank Lloyd Wright.* New York: George Braziller, 1960.

——. "Frank Lloyd Wright and Philip Johnson at Yale." *Architectural Digest,* March 1986, 90, 94.

——. "Philip Johnson: The Glass House Revisited." *Architectural Digest,* November 1986. Reprinted in Whitney and Kipnis, *Philip Johnson* (1993).

——. *The Shingle Style: Architectural Theory and Design from Richardson to the Origins of Wright.* New Haven, CT: Yale University Press, 1955.

——. "Wright vs. the International Style." *Art News* 53 (March 1954), 32–35, 64–66.

Searing, Helen. "Henry-Russell Hitchcock: The Architectural Historian as Critic and Connoisseur." In *The Architectural Historian in America,* edited by Elisabeth Blair MacDougall. Washington, DC: National Gallery of Art, 1990.

——, ed. *In Search of Modern Architecture: Tribute to Henry-Russell Hitchcock.* Cambridge, MA: MIT Press, 1982.

——. "International Style: The Crimson Connections." *Progressive Architecture* 63 (February 1982): 88–91.

Secrest, Meryle. *Frank Lloyd Wright.* New York: Alfred A. Knopf, 1992.

Shirer, William L. *Berlin Diary: The Journal of a Foreign Correspondent, 1934–1941.* New York: Alfred A. Knopf, 1941.

The Solomon R. Guggenheim Museum. Architect: Frank Lloyd Wright. New York: Horizon, 1960.

The Solomon R. Guggenheim Museum. New York: Solomon R. Guggenheim Foundation, 1994.

Sorkin, Michael. "Where Was Philip?" *Spy,* October 1988, 138, 140.

"Speaking of Pictures . . . New Art Museum Will Be New York's Strangest." *Life,* October 8, 1945, 12–14.

Staniszewski, Mary Anne. *The Power of Display: A History of Exhibition Installations at the Museum of Modern Art.* Cambridge, MA: MIT Press, 1998.

Stern, Robert A. M. "The Evolution of Philip Johnson's Glass House, 1947–1948." *Oppositions,* Fall 1977, 56–67.

——. *George Howe: Toward a Modern Architecture.* New Haven, CT: Yale University Press, 1975.

Stern, Robert A. M., Gregory Gilmartin, and Thomas Mellins. *New York 1930: Architecture and Urbanism Between the Two World Wars.* New York: Rizzoli, 1987.

Stern, Robert A. M., Thomas Mellins, and David Fishman. *New York 1960: Architecture and Urbanism Between the Second World War and the Bicentennial.* New York: Monacelli Press, 1995.

Tafel, Edgar. *About Wright: An Album of Recollections by Those Who Knew Frank Lloyd Wright.* New York: John Wiley and Sons, 1993.

——. *Years with Frank Lloyd Wright: Apprentice to Genius.* New York: Dover, 1979.

Teichmann, Howard. *Smart Aleck: The Wit, World, and Life of Alexander Woollcott.* New York: Morrow, 1976.

Tell, Darcy. "An Atmosphere Instead of a Frame." *Archives of American Art Journal* 51, nos. 1–2 (2012): 70–73.

Thomson, Virgil. *Virgil Thomson: An Autobiography.* New York: Alfred A. Knopf, 1966.

Toker, Franklin. *Fallingwater Rising: Frank Lloyd Wright, E. J. Kaufmann, and America's Most Extraordinary House.* New York: Alfred A. Knopf, 2003.

Tomkins, Calvin. "Forms Under Light." *New Yorker,* May 23, 1977, 43–80.

The Usonian House: Souvenir of the Exhibition: 60 Years of Living Architecture, the Work of Frank Lloyd Wright. New York: Guggenheim Museum, 1953.

Utley, Freda. *Odyssey of a Liberal.* Washington, D.C.: Washington National Press, 1970.

Vail, Karole, ed. *The Museum of Non-Objective Painting: Hilla Rebay and the Origins of the Solomon R. Guggenheim Museum.* New York: Guggenheim Museum, 2009.

Waggoner, Lynda, ed. *Fallingwater.* New York: Rizzoli, 2011.

——. *Fallingwater: Frank Lloyd Wright's Romance with Nature.* New York: Universe Books, 1996.

Watkin, David. "Frank Lloyd Wright & the Guggenheim Museum." *AAA Files* 21 (Spring 1991): 40–48.

Welch, Frank D. *Philip Johnson & Texas.* Austin: University of Texas Press, 2000.

What Is Happening to Modern Architecture? A Symposium at the Museum of Modern Art, February 11, 1948. Reprinted in *Museum of Modern Art Bulletin* 15, no. 3 (Spring 1948): 1–21.

Whitney, David, and Jeffrey Kipnis, eds. *Philip Johnson: The Glass House.* New York: Pantheon Books, 1993.

Wiseman, Carter. *Shaping a Nation.* New York: W. W. Norton, 1998.

Wojtowicz, Robert. "Lewis Mumford: The Architectural Critic as Historian." In *The Architectural Historian in America,* edited by Elisabeth Blair MacDougall. Washington, D.C.: National Gallery of Art, 1990.

——. "A Model House and a House's Model: Reexamining Frank Lloyd Wright's House on the Mesa Project." *Journal of the Society of Architectural Historians* 64, no. 4 (December 2005): 522–51.

Woollcott, Alexander. *The Letters of Alexander Woollcott.* Edited by Beatrice Kaufman and Joseph Hennessey. New York: Viking Press, 1944.

——. "The Prodigal Father." *New Yorker*, July 19, 1930, 22–25.

Wright, Frank Lloyd. *An Autobiography.* New York: Duell, Sloan and Pearce, 1943.

——. *Frank Lloyd Wright Collected Writings.* 5 vols. New York: Rizzoli, 1992–95.

——. *Frank Lloyd Wright: The Guggenheim Correspondence.* Edited by Bruce Brooks Pfeiffer. Fresno: Press at California State University, 1986.

——. "In the Cause of Architecture: Second Paper." *Architectural Record* 35 (May 1914): 405–13.

——. *Letters to Apprentices.* Edited by Bruce Brooks Pfeiffer. Fresno: Press at California State University, 1982.

——. *Letters to Architects.* Edited by Bruce Brooks Pfeiffer. Fresno: Press at California State University, 1984.

——. *Letters to Clients.* Edited by Bruce Brooks Pfeiffer. Fresno: Press at California State University, 1986.

——. "Sullivan Against the World." *Architectural Record* 105, no. 630 (June 1949): 295–98.

Wright, Olgivanna Lloyd. *The Shining Brow: Frank Lloyd Wright.* New York: Horizon, 1960.

INDEX

Note: Page numbers in italics refer to images. *Figures* refer to images found in the insert.

Abby Aldrich Rockefeller Sculpture
    Garden (MoMA), 268,
    289n2
abstract art, 35, 46–47, 66–67, 138, 214,
    256. *See also* non-objective art
Adler, Dankmar (Adler and Sullivan),
    34, 35
Alsop, Joseph, 147
Aluminum Company of America
    (Alcoa), 42–43, 73
American Mercury, 15
Architectural Forum, 134, 136, 137–138,
    189–190, 228, 243
Architectural League, 74–76
Architectural Record, 119, 121
Architectural Review, 198, 212–215
Arp, Hans (Jean), 170
Art Deco, 49, 74, 78, 112, 176
Art News, 95
Arts, 24–25, 72

Ash Street house (Thesis House
    [Cambridge, MA]), 159–166,
    204, 229, 269
AT&T Building (now Sony Plaza
    [NYC]), 270–271
Autobiography, An (Wright), 32, 36,
    111, 126
Automobile Objective and Planetarium
    (Frederick, MD), 183–184

Barr, Alfred H.
    education, 22, 23–24
    European travels, 45–46
    on Hitchcock's *Modern
        Architecture*, 61
    and the *International Exhibition*, 70,
        71–73, 88
    marriage, 60
    on Modernism, 24, 25–27, 46, 47–48,
        71, 90

at Museum of Modern Art (MoMA), 23, 51, 56–58

and *Rejected Artists* show (MoMA), 75–76

relationship with Johnson, 22, 24–25, 27–28, 58–59

at Wellesley College, 25–27

on Wright, 95–96

Barr, Marga (née Margaret "Daisy" Scolari Fitzmaurice), 58, 60, 69, 70, 71, 143, 166, 209

Bauer, Rudolf, 171, 172, 175, 176, 182

Bauhaus, 48–50, 50, 57, 74, 81, 89, 107, 142, 148, 151, 153, *154*, 174, 175

Bauhaus Stairway (Schlemmer), 142–143, 217–218

Bear Run house. *See* Fallingwater

Beaux Arts, 2, 34, 35, 47, 91, 132

Berlin Diary (Shirer), 147

Bernstein, Aline. *See* Saarinen, Aline (née Bernstein)

Blackburn, Alan, 70, 142, 143, 144–146

Bliss, Lillie P., 55, 56

Breuer, Marcel, 4, 48, 158, 166, 202–203, 212

Brierly, Cornelia, 138–139

Broadacre City, 114, 119, 120, 168

Bronfman, Allan, 225

Bronfman, Samuel, 225, 230–231, 232, 236, 237, 251

Brooklyn Eagle, 76

Brown Decades, The (Mumford), 39–40

Built to Live In (Johnson), 73–74, 76, 82

Burgee, John, 257, 271, 277

Burial of Phocion (Poussin), 218

Cahiers d'Arts, 78–79

Cambridge Chronicle-Sun, 161–162

Castle Stewart, Eleanor, 239

Castle Stewart, Lord, 238–239

Chandler, Alexander, 108, 119, 196

Cheney, Mamah, 18, 19

Clark, Stephen, 70, 76

Classicism, 17–18, 203, 215–218, 276, 277

Conversations with Elder Wise Men (NBC), 244

Coughlin, Charles, 145–146, 147

Crandall, Lou R., 231, 232, 236

Cranmer, George, 92

Creative Art, 76

Crowninshield, Frank, 56

Crystal Palace (London, England), 73, 214

Delano, William Adams, 91

Dennis, Lawrence, 143–144, 146

Downs, Hugh, 244

Drexler, Arthur, 218

European Modernism, 43–45, 46–51, 96, 98, 138, 148, 150–154

Fallingwater (Bear Run, PA), 105–139, *figures IX, X, XI, XII*

construction, 128–131

description of, 131–132

vs. Glass House, 212–214, 278

Hedrich's photograph of, 133–135, *135, figure XI*

and International Style, 138–139, 275

Johnson on, 139

living spaces, 133

Museum of Modern Art exhibition on, 105, 135–137

as organic construction, 128

plans, 120–128, 295n37

publicity, 136–137

site, 115–118

Wright's perspective drawing of, 132–133

Farnsworth, Edith, 206–207, *figure XIX*

Farnsworth house (Plano, Illinois), 206–207, 214, 215, *figures XVIII, XIX*

Fascism, 142–144, 146–148

Feininger, Lyonel, 48

Foster, Richard, 256–257

Four Seasons Restaurant (Seagram Building, NYC), 251–252, 254–255, 306n50

Frank Lloyd Wright: American Architect (MoMA), 154–157

Franzen, Ulrich, 159, 164, 166, 207

Fuller, R. Buckminster, 4–5

George A. Fuller Company, 231

Glass House (New Canaan, CT), 199–224, *217, figures XVI, XVII, XIX*

buildings added to the property, 264–268, 269–270

and Classicism, 215–216

construction, 208–209

design process, 203–205

experience of living in, 209–210

vs. Fallingwater, 212–214, 278

furnishings, 218–219, 223–224

Johnson's article in *Architectural Review*, 212–215

landscaping, 209

Miës's visits to, 233

Newman's photograph of, 214–215

as part of Yale architectural curriculum, 5–6

plan and drawings, 207–208

property and site, 199–200

public curiosity and press coverage, 210–212, 218–219

Saarinen's visit to, 222–223

Wright's criticism of, and Johnson's reply, 221–222

Wright's visits to, 6–7, 223–224

Goethe, Johann Wolfgang, 128

Goodyear, A. Conger, 56, 72–73, 106

Gordon, Elizabeth, 242

Gores, Landis, 201–203, 204, 207, 208, 229, 257

Graves, Michael, 271–272

Gropius, Ise, 153, *154,* 174

Gropius, Walter, 4, 48–50, 81, 152–154, 174, 201

GSD. *See* Harvard Graduate School of Design

Guggenheim, Harry, 238, 244

Guggenheim, Irene, 171

Guggenheim, Solomon R., 167, 172–174, 173, 174–175, 176–177, *188*

Guggenheim Museum (NYC), 167–191, *figures XIII, XIIIa, XIV, XV*

architect selection, 175–176

art installation debate, 247–249

building permits, 240

commentary about, 258–259

construction, 244–247

drawings and plans, 185–187

Guggenheim's death and, 238–239

Johnson on, 258

model, *188*

New York Times interview of Wright, 245–247

preconstruction press coverage, 187–191

Rebay as director, 239–240

Rebay's invitation to Wright, 167–169

Rebay's vision for, 178–179

site, 179–180, 181, 239

Sixty Years of Living Architecture: The Work of Frank Lloyd Wright, 241

the spiral design of, 181–184

Wright's last visit to, 255

Hardwick Hall (Derbyshire, England), 214

Harvard Five, 201–203

Harvard Graduate School of Design (GSD), 4, 158–160, 201–202

Heckscher Building, 57, 89, 90

Hedrich, William "Bill," 134–135, *135,* 136, 214

Hillside Home School of the Allied Arts, 109–110

Hitchcock, Henry-Russell
  Arts articles, 24–25, 78–79
  early life, 59–60
  European travels with Johnson, 60–61
  and *International Exhibition* (MoMA), 71–72
  lecture at Wellesley College, 25–26
  Modern Architecture, 61, 71, 79
  visit to Taliesin, 98–100

and Wright, 78–79, 94, 96–97, 99–100, 196, 291n25

Hitler, Adolf, 142–143, 147, 149

Hoffman Motor Car Company showroom (NYC), 227–228

Holden, Arthur Cort, 240, 242

Holiday, 3

"House at New Canaan, Connecticut" (*Architectural Review*), 211–212

House Beautiful, 242

House & Garden, 141, 211

Howe, George, 5, 89, 165, 231

Howe, John "Jack," 132, 190, 277

Huxtable, Ada Louise, 28, 258

Illinois Institute of Technology (IIT), 205–206

Imperial Hotel (Tokyo, Japan), 19, 38, 126

In the Nature of Materials (Hitchcock), 156, 196

Interiors, 255

Interiors & Industrial Design, 218

International Exhibition. See *Modern Architecture: International Exhibition* (MoMA)

International Style. See also *Modern Architecture: International Exhibition* (MoMA)
  principles of, 90, 242
  use of term, 76
  Wright and, 85, 94–95, 138–139, 275

International Style Since 1922, The (Hitchcock and Johnson), 95, 96

Is Capitalism Doomed? (Dennis), 144

Johansen, John, 4, 5, 159, 166, 202–203
Johnson, Herbert "Hib," 273
Johnson, Homer (Philip's father), 41, 42,
    77, 81, 145
Johnson, Louise (Mrs. Homer Johnson,
    Philip's mother), 24, 41, 42,
    50–51, 69, 77, 81, 163, 274
Johnson, Philip, *9, 143, 233, 264, figures
    II, XXIV. See also* Wright *vs.*
    Johnson, differences, similarities
    and influence
AT&T Building (now Sony Plaza
    [NYC]), 270–271, *figure II*
as "Dean of American Architecture,"
    271–272
death of, 275
desire to be influential, 72, 100, 102,
    148, 258, 277
early design efforts, 141–142
education, 4, 22–23, 158–160, 201–202
European travels, 41–42, 43–51,
    60–67, 81–82, 106–107, 146–147
exhibition at Yale Art Gallery, 5
homes
    childhood family home, 62–63
    father's house (New London,
        Ohio), 146
    first Manhattan apartment,
        69–70, *70*
    Forty-Ninth Street apartments,
        141–142
    Glass House (*see* Glass House [New
        Canaan, CT])
    Thesis House (Cambridge, MA),
        159–166, 204, 229, 269
    military service, 193

as museum architect, 265, 266, 268
at Museum of Modern Art, 60, 101,
    142, 157, 194–196, 205 (see also
    *Modern Architecture: International
    Exhibition* [MoMA])
on photographs of architecture, 44–45
and politics, 142–149
Pritzker Architecture Prize, 271
reinvention as architect, 157–160
Rockefeller guest house (NYC),
    228–229
Seagram Building (*see* Seagram
    Building)
sexuality and relationships, 22, 44,
    85–86, 148, 199–200, 266
and skyscrapers, 270–272
wealth of, 4, 42–43
writings
    Built to Live In, 73–74, 76, 82
    "House at New Canaan,
        Connecticut" (*Architectural
        Review*), 211–212
    The International Style Since 1922, 95
at Yale, 3–5, 262
Johnson, Theodate (Philip's sister),
    21–22, 141, 208
Johnson Home (proposed, Pinehurst,
    North Carolina), 81
Johnson Wax Building (Racine, WI),
    134, 155, 180, 194, 273, *figure XX*

Kaufmann, Edgar, jr., 110–112, 113,
    117–118, 119, 120, 122, 139, 155,
    194–195
Kaufmann, Edgar and Liliane, 107–108,
    112–115, 119, 127, 129–133, 155,

246, *figure IX. See also*
Fallingwater
Kiesler, Frederick, 176
Kirstein, Lincoln, 269–270
Kirstein Tower (New Canaan, CT),
269–270, *figure XXIII*

Lambert, Phyllis, 229–233, *233*, 235–236,
237, 249, 250, 251, 263
Le Corbusier
Barr on, 27
and the Guggenheim, 175, 176, 182,
213
Hitchcock on, 24–25, 25–26
Johnson and, 61, 142
Miës and, 64
Villa Savoye, 81–82, 90, 242
Wright and, 150, 151, 242
Ledoux, Claude Nicolas, 205, 214,
271
"Less is More," 66
Life, 136, 188, *189*, 258
Ling Po, 248, *figure XV*
Lloyd Jones family, 31, 36–37,
109–110, 273
Loeb, Gerald M., 195
Long, Huey, 144–145
Loos, Adolf, 78
Luce, Henry, 136, 190

Machine Art, 101
Mahony, Marion, 35, 277
Malevich, Kazimir, 205, 207–208,
214
Manny, Carter H., Jr., 159, 160, 193
Martin, Darwin, 112

Mary Fiske Stoughton house, 161
McAndrew, John
European travels with Johnson, 45,
106–107
and Fallingwater, 108, 133, 135–137
Frank Lloyd Wright: American Architect
(MoMA), 154–157
at Museum of Modern Art (MoMA),
105–106, 107
trip to Mexico, 107
war years, 194
at Yale, 262
Meeks, Carroll L. V., 8
Metzger-Richardson Company, 129–130
Miës van der Rohe, Ludwig, *233*
early life, 64
Farnsworth house, 206–207, 214, 215,
figures XVIII, XIX
furniture designs, 70, 73
Illinois Institute of Technology (IIT),
205–206
influence on and relationship with
Johnson, 62, 64, 67, 162, 164,
205–207, 233, 257, 263–264
and International Exhibition
(MoMA), 82
"Less is More," 66
relationship with Wright, 150–152
Resor house, 150–151
Seagram Building, 231–233, 235–237,
249–250, 256–258
Tugendhat House, 62–67, 82, 91–92,
131–132
visit to Taliesin, 151–152
on Wright, 157
Mike Wallace Interview, 244

Modern Architecture (Hitchcock), 61,
71, 79
*Modern Architecture: International
Exhibition* (MoMA), 69–101
additional venues, 76, 91, 98
contributors, 72–73, 76–77, 81–82
critical reception, 91–92
dress rehearsal for, 74–76
initial meeting to discuss, 69–72
installation, 88–90
Johnson as Exhibition Director, 81, 88
proposal for, 72–73
prospectus and funding for, 73–74
as rite of passage for Johnson, 100–101
Wright's role in, 77–79, 82-88,
92–98, 101
Modernism. *See also* European
Modernism; International Style;
Museum of Modern Art
(MoMA)
Barr and, 24, 25–27, 46, 47–48, 71, 90
and the *International Exhibition*
(MoMA), 71–73
Johnson's conversion to, 24, 43–44, 45,
46–47, 276
Johnson's movement away from, 215,
263–265, *266*
in New Canaan, 4, 201–203
New Style, 74, 75, 78
social aspects of, 148
Moses, Robert, 179, 180, 259
Mosher, Bob, 122, 123, *124,* 125, 127,
129, 130
Mumford, Lewis
on Broadacre City, 119
The Brown Decades, 39–40

and *International Exhibition* (MoMA),
77, 78, 79, 87–88, 91
lunch with Wright, 15–21
on the Seagram Building, 231, 259
Sticks and Stones, 17–18, 152
on Wright, 100, 110, 119, 137, 155,
241, 256, 277
and Wright's resurgent career, 39–40,
167, 175, 256
Museum of Modern Art (MoMA)
Abby Aldrich Rockefeller Sculpture
Garden, 268, 289n2
Barr as director of, 51, 56–58
board members, 55–57
first home of, 89
Frank Lloyd Wright: American Architect,
154–157
initial exhibition, 57
International Exhibition (see *Modern
Architecture: International
Exhibition* [MoMA])
Johnson and, 60, 101–102, 142,
194–196, 205
McAndrew and, 105–108, 135–137
*A New Country House by Frank Lloyd
Wright,* 195
*A New House by Frank Lloyd Wright on
Bear Run, Pennsylvania,* 105–108,
135–137
Rejected Architects, 74–76
Museum of Non-Objective Art,
177–178, 239–240, 300n35.
See also Guggenheim Museum

Nadelman, Elie, 223–224
Nation, 91

NECCO factory (Cambridge, MA), 26

New Canaan (CT), 3, 201–203. *See also* Glass House (New Canaan, CT)

New Canaan Advertiser, 219

New Country House by Frank Lloyd Wright, 195

New London (Ohio) politics, 145–146

New Style, 74, 75, 78

New York Herald Tribune, 147

New York Mirror, 259

New York Sun, 5, 91, 101, 211

New York Times, 76, 108, 119, 144, 156, 210–211, 239, 258, 266, 272

New Yorker, 5, 37, 91, 119, 137, 256

Newman, Arnold, 214–215

Newsweek, 258

Noel, Miriam, 19–20

non-objective art, 170, 172–173, 177–178

Noyes, Eliot, 201–203

"Of Thee I Sing" (*Shelter*, Wright), 96

organic architecture, 10, 18, 128, 268, 276

"Ornament und Verbrechen" (Ornament and Crime, Loos), 78

ornamentation, 25, 47, 75, 78, 90, 94

Oud, J.J.P., 24–25, 47, 61, 72, 77, 81, 82, 106

Palladio, Andrea, 212, 215–217

Parnassus, 156

Paxton, Joseph, 73, 214

Peters, Wes, *124*, 190

Phillips, H. I., 211–212

Picasso stage curtain, 251

Plaza Hotel (NYC), 2, 242–244

Post-Modernism, 10, 270–272, 276

Poussin, Nicolas, 218

Prairie Style, 10, 33, 35–36, 66, 74, 110, 131

Pritzker Architecture Prize, 271

Read, Helen, 142

Rebay, Hilla, *188. See also* Guggenheim Museum

early life, 170–172

and the Guggenheims, 172–174

health problems, 180–181

invitation to Wright, 167–168, 169, 244

and Museum of Non-Objective Painting, 175–187, 191, 238, 240, 246

Reich, Lilly, 69–70

Rejected Artists (MoMA), 74–76

Resor house (Wyoming), 150–151

Richardson, H. H., 26, 40, 161, 205

Roche, Mary, 210–211

Rockefeller, Abby, 55, 147

Rockefeller guest house (NYC), 228–229

Romanticism, 11, 79, 95, 121, 220

Romeo and Juliet Windmill (Spring Green, WI), 268–269, *figure XXII*

Ross, Harold, 37

Ruhtenberg, Jan, 45, 70

Russell, Bertrand, 148–149

Saarinen, Aline (née Bernstein), 107, 244–247, 257

Saarinen, Eero, 222–223, 231

Sachs, Paul J., 56

Schlemmer, Oskar, 142, 217–218

Schulze, Franz, 42, 142, 272, 276

Scully, Vincent, 4, 8, 268, 271
Seagram Building (NYC), *figure XXI*
    effect on Johnson's reputation, 256–258
    fountain, *234*
    Four Seasons Restaurant, 251–252,
        254–255, 306n50
    interiors, 250
    Johnson and Miës as architects,
        229–233, 249–250
    site and design, 234–238
    Wright on, 259
    Wright's pitch to the Bronfman
        brothers, 225–226
Shelter, 96
Shingle Style, 34, 35, 161
Shirer, William, 147
Short, William, 255, 262
Show, 265
Silsbee, Joseph Lyman, 33, 34, 256
*Sixty Years of Living Architecture: The Work
    of Frank Lloyd Wright*, 241
skyscrapers, 34, 49, 89, 98, 99, 181, 235,
        246, 270–272
Social Justice, 145–146, 147, 148
spirals, in science, art and literature, 182
St. Louis Post-Dispatch, 133
Stern, Robert A. M., 4, 271–272, 275
Sticks and Stones (Mumford), 17–18, 152
Stoughton House (Cambridge, MA),
        161
Stroup, Jon, 199–200, 209
Sullivan, Louis (Adler and Sullivan),
        33–35, 94, 99, 102, 161, 220–221,
        259, 271
Sullivan, Mary Quinn, 55, 56
Sweeney, James Johnson, 247–248, 256

Tafel, Edgar, 122, 123, *124,* 125, 126, 127
Taliesin (Spring Green, WI),
        figures III, IV
    design and construction of, 36–37
    fires at, 19, 32–33
    Johnson and Hitchcock's visit to, 97,
        98–100
    Kaufmanns at, 112–115
    Miës van der Rohe's visit to, 151–152
    Romeo and Juliet Windmill, 268–269
    Woollcott's visit to, 29–31, 32–33
Taliesin East (Plaza Hotel, NYC), 2,
        242–244
Taliesin Fellowship and fellows, 109–110,
        111, 112–113, 124, 168, 190
Taliesin West (Scottsdale, Arizona), 2,
        196–197, 196–198, 253–254, 273
Thesis House (Ash Street house
        [Cambridge, MA]), 159–166
Time, 136, 190, 255, 258, 270
Tugendhat House (Grete and Fritz
        Tugendhat), 62–67, 82, 91–92,
        131–132, *figure V*
Two Circus Women (Nadelman), 223–224

Usonian houses, 155, 156, 205, 241,
        298n26

Vanity Fair, 26–27, 79, 272
Villa Almerico (Villa Rotonda [Vicenza,
        Italy]), 216–217
Villa Savoye (Poissy-sur-Seine, France),
        81–82, 90, 242

Warburg, Edward, 141
Wasmuth portfolio, 19, 66, 94, 150, 152

Wellesley College, 21–22, 25–27

Whitehead, Alfred North, 22–23

Whitney, David, 266

Winslow House (River Forest, IL), 99

Woollcott, Alexander, "Aleck," 29–31,
32–33, 37–39

Wright, Frank Lloyd, 9, *16*, *124*, *figure I*.
See also Wright *vs.* Johnson,
differences, similarities and
influence

Broadacre City, 114, 119, 168

career decline and resurrection, 15,
20–21, 37–40, 78–79, 84–85,
95–96, 101, 108, 119–120,
137–138 (*see also* Fallingwater)

children, 20

death of, 255–256, 261–262

early jobs, 33–36

family and early life, 31–32

Frank Lloyd Wright: American Architect
(MoMA), 154–157

Guggenheim Museum (*see*
Guggenheim Museum)

Hillside Home School of the Allied
Arts, 100, 109–110

Hoffman Motor Car Company
showroom, 227–228

House on the Mesa, 83, 88, 90, 92–95,
96, 108, 119, 132, *figure VI*

Imperial Hotel (Tokyo, Japan), 38, 126

International Exhibition (see *Modern
Architecture: International
Exhibition* [MoMA])

Johnson Wax Building (Racine,
Wisconsin), 134, 152, 155, 180,
196, 198, 232, 262, 273, 274

marriages and affairs, 18–20

*A New Country House by Frank Lloyd
Wright* (MoMA), 195

*A New House by Frank Lloyd Wright on
Bear Run, Pennsylvania* (MoMA),
105, 108, 135–137

organic architecture, 10, 18, 128,
268, 276

Plaza Hotel (NYC), 2, 16, 19, 20,
172, 176, 188, 189, 234,
242–244, 263

Seagram Building, 225–226

*Sixty Years of Living Architecture: The
Work of Frank Lloyd Wright*
(Guggenheim Museum), 241

Taliesin (*see* Taliesin (Spring
Green, WI))

Taliesin Fellowship and fellows,
109–110, 111, 112–113, 124, 168,
190

Taliesin West (Scottsdale, Arizona), 2,
196–197, 196–198, 253–254, 273,
figures VII, VIII

television appearances, 1, 128, 244

Usonian houses, 155, 156, 205, 241,
298n26

Wasmuth portfolio, 19, 66, 94, 150,
152

Winslow House, 99

writings

An Autobiography, 32, 36, 111, 126

in *Architectural Forum*, 137–138

in *Architectural Record*, 121

"Of Thee I Sing" (*Shelter*), 96

Wright, Henry, 190–191

Wright, Catherine "Kitty," 18, 34, 36

Wright, Olgivanna, 20, 92, 108, 109, 114, 180–181, 243, 259
Wright *vs.* Johnson, differences, similarities and influence
artist *vs.* aesthete, 220–221, 276–277
aspirations, 277–278
evolving camaraderie, 139, 195–196, 198–199, 262–263, 274
Fallingwater *vs.* Glass House, 212–214, 278
influence on each other, 12, 268, 273–275
Johnson's changing opinion of Wright, 97, 101, 139, 220, 252–254
legacies, 279–280

penchant for control, 222–224
personal reinvention, 275–276
pushing technological boundaries, 273
shared characteristics, 10–12
their homes as testing grounds, 268–270
Wright on Johnson, 254

Yale University
architecture program at, 4–5
Johnson at, 3–5, 222, 231, 262, 263
"Perspectives" series, Wright and Johnson at, 1–3, 7–10, 273

ziggurat, 185–186, 190

A NOTE ON THE AUTHOR

Hugh Howard's numerous books include *The Painter's Chair, Dr. Kimball and Mr. Jefferson, Mr. and Mrs. Madison's War,* and the memoir *House-Dreams.* He is also the author of *Houses of the Founding Fathers, Wright for Wright, Houses of the Presidents, Houses of Civil War America,* and *Thomas Jefferson, Architect,* all of which are collaborations with photographer Roger Straus III.